PAST LIVES THAT MATTER

HOW TO REMEMBER, HEAL AND TRANSFORM THEM

ISISI ALLTHINGS

BALBOA.PRESS
A DIVISION OF HAY HOUSE

Balboa Press books may be ordered through booksellers or by contacting:

Balboa Press
A Division of Hay House
1663 Liberty Drive
Bloomington, IN 47403
www.balboapress.com
844-682-1282

Because of the dynamic nature of the Internet, any web addresses or links contained in this book may have changed since publication and may no longer be valid. The views expressed in this work are solely those of the author and do not necessarily reflect the views of the publisher, and the publisher hereby disclaims any responsibility for them.

The author of this book does not dispense medical advice or prescribe the use of any technique as a form of treatment for physical, emotional, or medical problems without the advice of a physician, either directly or indirectly. The intent of the author is only to offer information of a general nature to help you in your quest for emotional and spiritual well-being. In the event you use any of the information in this book for yourself, which is your constitutional right, the author and the publisher assume no responsibility for your actions.

Any people depicted in stock imagery provided by Getty Images are models, and such images are being used for illustrative purposes only.
Certain stock imagery © Getty Images.

Print information available on the last page.

ISBN: 979-8-7652-3612-3 (sc)
ISBN: 979-8-7652-3613-0 (e)

Balboa Press rev. date: 03/29/2023

CONTENTS

PREFACE

In this unusual collection of past life stories, Isisi aspires to inspire others on their own journey of discovery. Her observations are spun into threads of mythical tales, with a need and a reason to be told. In this work she has developed metaphysical ideas about the true nature of reality and the cycles of life. These discoveries lead us along a pathway to a more unusual, but wholly authentic, perception of life's mysteries and purpose. As she follows the breadcrumb trail of clues using sacred keys, she unlocks secrets leading to healing from painful patterns and trauma, rippling down through the centuries.

This tapestry of tales describes lead character, Rose's, spiritual awakening. It is narrated by her chosen muse, the famous medieval anchorite and nun, Julian of Norwich. St. Julian wrote the first religious book by a woman in England, in the Middle Ages. Based on the wisdom garnered from Julian's near-death experience during the Black Death and subsequent mystical visions and insights, Rose begins her discovery of three of her reincarnations, during the Dark Ages. Gradually it dawns on her that some of her loved ones and friends in her current life, are involved in repeating scenarios from their distant past, some of whom she had seemingly left behind her, forever. Strangely, they seemed to play an important role in what she discovered about their past lives as a soul group and how they were healing together.

INTRODUCTION

I happened to be thinking about the correlation between our tempestuous times and other tumultuous periods in history. Especially since 2020, with the worldwide viral pandemic, lockdowns, medical mandates, Black Lives Matter debacle in the US, and Freedom Truckers protests, which sprang up initially in Canada. Then, in early 2022 came further chaos and worldwide political unrest with a new war and the looming energy and supply chain threats due to international sanctions exacerbating the already looming international inflation and forecast financial collapse.

I had been writing for some years about medieval times in England in connection with my past lives. One cannot help comparing events hundreds of years ago, such as the Black Death, or Bubonic Plagues, civil unrest including uprisings such as the Peasants' Revolts in England, with today. In those days, there were huge injustices around unfair taxes and poaching of the common land by the gentry. There was also the Hundred Years' War between France and England, to name another example of why this period of history was named The Dark Ages.

It struck me that these grinding human problems have always been with us, but somehow, we as a human race seem to suffer amnesia when it comes to learning from our mistakes. These existential threats would always primarily affect the little man and small businesses first, who were struggling to keep afloat. It would condemn those already in poverty and living on the breadline, grappling to survive... along with those in the service, travel, and entertainment industries. I thought about how fragile our systems still are, despite the huge advances in technology and AI (Artificial Intelligence), that had been made in the last couple of decades.

I felt lucky to have lived in England in veritably queenly style all my life in comparison to three-quarters of the world who didn't have clean water, good sanitation, or enough nutritious food to eat. Maybe this would change for the Western world now and we would face similar or worse circumstances I pondered. I'm not the type of person to live in fear as I know how destructive that energy is, but I also felt I needed to be realistic and make some preparations. There are many examples we could look at in history, but one famous civilizational collapse is indelibly marked in the calendar on the 15th of March. The assassination of Julius Caesar in 44 BC. This is an event very much kept alive in our memories today, through William Shakespeare's play "Julius Caesar" about the collapse of the Roman Empire. I knew that this was again today, a pivotal time in history and I wanted to feel at least somewhat prepared for what was to come.

I had learned in my own personal dealings, to take baby steps forward in faith and trust and then to leave the workings and outcome to the Universe. Just as a toddler would learn how to walk. I knew that it would be a spiritual partnership, with humans rising up in a gradual awakening on their enlightenment journey, but supported by the benign, unseen spirit world. That is what appealed so much to me about Julian of Norwich and her wise words, when under similar circumstances all those centuries ago. You will come to know how her profound realisations will help you, as we trace the history and learn lessons of resilience, from her.

In light of the stark realisations above, we may feel that we are unable to affect the course of history, facing these seemingly inevitable repeating patterns of world history. There is a strong sense amongst a small but rapidly growing minority of spiritually sensitive people, that would disagree. They feel that their current life is a greatly significant timeline on this planet and an opportunity to end these cycles of pain and suffering, bringing all beings back into harmony with themselves and the earth. It's talked about in many circles as a Golden Age or a transition from 3D physical reality to a 5th-dimensional state of spiritual being. Translated, this means a raising of one's energetic vibration, which can be sensed and even seen by some in the aura, by energy healers, and those who have developed their psychic abilities. This knowledge brings with it the hope, that just as things look their darkest on the world scene, this is the ripening time for the old system to come crashing down and to facilitate growth and a new way of being on the earth.

For this to happen, there is some preparation to be undertaken by each individual that becomes aware of what is transpiring, behind the scenes. The purpose of this book is to unfold the steps to waking up, to this inter-dimensional reality.

These tales are inspired by the guidance I had been given, by a shamanic healer and also a psychic friend. This was some years previous to writing this account. It was also before the worldwide viral pandemic even heralded the onslaught of the so-called Great Reset. I will explain what I learnt from these mysterious messages I received and how I learnt to trust my own inner knowing and intuition along the way. This will pave the way for understanding our individual and collective responsibility, to heal. We hear often that we need to go within and lick our deepest wounds clean lest they fester, both those in our present and from our past lives.

We must learn to truly and deeply love ourselves. Only then, can we move forward and outwards again in strength, forgiveness, compassion, vulnerability, authenticity, gratitude, and most important of all, unconditional love. This type of love is known in Greek as Agape and it will bring a ripple of healing to our personal pond, which then trickles into the streams and rivers of those whose lives we touch. As we flow towards our ultimate destination, we can personally contribute to the healing of the very oceans of mankind. Each of our own efforts supports the human collective and of course, all other creatures, who share this space with us, on earth.

In the following chapters, you will be shown how this process unfolded for me and how crucial it is for all of us to follow suit, if we wish to preserve the society that we have become accustomed to. To improve our own inner dialogue, building our trust and hope that "all will be well," just as Julian of Norwich famously wrote. We will now learn about this key medieval character, who will serve not only as an example in these turbulent times but also as the narrator for the fascinating tales, about to unfold.

Since the beginning of time and before written records, we humans have related stories which we can tell and read back to our conscious mind at bedtime. These tales then follow us into the Dreamtime in the form of bold creatures of the night and unfathomable scenarios. These unconscious scenes, in turn, attempt to drop themselves like a pebble, into our waking consciousness in the morning. They appear now in the form of dreams, that we know were fantastical but don't fully comprehend. We remember them only partially and then they ripple away, leaving the mind as a smooth pond, once again. Perhaps part of "waking up" is to learn the language of dreams and stories and grasp the coded messages they have for us, so that we may be empowered to heal from them. Some call this the soul's calling or alchemy, the process of becoming 'enlightened', or an 'ascension pathway.' The aim is, to rise up from living only an unconscious hum drum existence, to an understanding of our powerful holographic state. With this knowledge, we can learn how to flit between the worlds, like a dragonfly.

Although this tale of various reincarnations and my conclusions about them are subjective and anchored to my Western cultural background, I feel there will be many parallels in other cultures and timelines. These experiences may be very different from mine but can share a similar longing to truly know our soul, where it came from, and where it is calling us to go. I feel that one of the main reasons for listening to the mystics—is because they awaken the mysterious in us. Carl Jung wrote, "It is to the mystics that we owe what is best in humanity."

Having explained this aspiration of mine, I commence my book as a collection of personal realisations narrated through the eyes of a medieval nun and Anchorite, Julian of Norwich, who I think you will find a rather fascinating character. I will divulge what a religious Anchor is, as we progress through her story. I invite you to join me on a quirky experiential journey leading me to the hope that these famous words written by the first woman in England to write a religious book in 1373 are true, that;

> All shall be well, and all shall be well, and all manner of thing shall be exceeding well. - Revelations of Divine Love' scribed by Lady Julian.

Please visit the website dedicated to her works. Here, another of her famous sayings follows:

> He (God) said not: Thou shalt not be tempested, thou shalt not be travailed, thou shalt not be dis-eased; but he said, Thou shalt not be overcome.

There is good reason to have quoted St. Julian's words and chosen her as a muse, which you will discover later on. Please find further information about her in the footnote.[1] I became very interested in the relationship between Margery Kempe and Julian of Norwich because I had already intuited that I may have been Julian in a past life or that she may be a guide or an archetype for me, in this life. I had lived near her shrine when I was first in Norwich, Norfolk and I was given the name 'Julian' in the spiritual circle I sat with. I related well to her, as she had written a book about her understandings when she was in her cell, which had taken her twenty years to complete.

It began when she had the initial mystical visions during her near-death experience and she captured these experiences in a short version. This then ripened into the full-length version of her 'shewings' and now famous book, with many editions. She completed this in 1395 at the age of fifty-three. I left the religion of my parents, Jehovah's Witnesses, some twenty-eight years ago and finally published my account about this cult and how I escaped it, in 2019. As with Julian, the writing process of "Rising from the Ashes of Jehovah's Witnesses," had taken me a couple of decades to complete and I was a similar age when I finished it. Please avail yourself of more information on my Isisi Allthings Author Page on Amazon linked in the footnote[2] and purchase at Amazon.[3]

A parallel mystic from Norfolk, Margery Kempe, is also famous for writing about her life, travels, and pilgrimages at that time and may have also discussed her writings, with Lady Julian. Both of them were the first women in England to write a theological book and an autobiography, respectively. Margery had employed some scribes, the last one who completed the writings for her, was a religious cleric. The original scribe had written in an unintelligible language and died before it was finished, so she had employed another scholar to re-write the whole book. This was the reason it had taken her so long to complete. Margery's book was not finalised until just four years before she died, when in her sixties.

When I was discussing my possible connection to Julian and her

---

[1] https://julianofnorwich.org/collections/popular-resources
[2] https://www.amazon.co.uk/-/e/B0BGLNBC73
[3] https://www.amazon.co.uk/gp/product/B0BGJP3PNJ/ref=dbs_a_def_rwt_hsch_vapi_tkin_p1_i0

compatriot Margery with my friend Teal in the summer of 2016, we both felt 'truth shivers' or 'angel tingles' as we like to call them and all the hairs went up on our bodies. This was strange, considering it was a hot sunny day in August, on a campsite. As I will reveal in more detail in the following chapters, we would simultaneously feel these experiential body signs when discussing matters relating to our past lives and lessons. That is when I first felt that we had a past life connection as these two women, Julian and Margery. It did not end there and as I determined to explore further, I began to realise that Teal and I had passed over in death and were reincarnated concurrently into two more medieval lives back-to-back. I then further discovered other soul family connections linking our characters with other actors in the play of life. As Shakespeare said, "we are the actors and the world is the stage". You may ask how this is relevant, but as you accompany me on this curious journey, it will begin to unfold secrets hidden from us all, that are essential for us to grasp now.

'Julian of Norwich Shrine, Norwich'

I love to sit in the garden behind the shrine where Julian of Norwich was encased as an anchorite over six hundred years ago and enjoy the tranquil setting, with the shrubs and beautiful trees there. I prayed to her whilst sitting on a bench facing the delightful little garden and asked if she would show me a feather to prove her presence. As I opened my eyes, a fluttering caught my attention, and not surprisingly, a tall grey feather was gently lifting from the path a couple of feet away, caught by a light breeze. I knew then that Dame Julian had drawn close to help me write and compile these stories and so I decided that she would be the perfect narrator for them.

The author, Isisi Allthings

CHAPTER 1

Julian of Norwich, Mystic Muse

I, Julian of Norwich, am an ancient storyteller but not only as this particularly interesting English medieval character. As an eternal soul, I have had many previous lives. One such was as a scribe where I served as assistant to the high priest, carving hieroglyphics onto stone in ancient Egypt. My writing skills came to the fore again when I was a Catholic Sackite monk, penning and reading aloud Bible texts. Then I was a female code breaker, during the Second World War in England. My present incarnation living in 2022 was a woman, Rose, also born in Norfolk, England. She was raised as a full-time minister for Jehovah's Witnesses. In this role, she had been a prolific note-taker at their religious meetings and after leaving, she became a personal assistant in her work career, taking copious notes at board meetings finally, she became an author, this being the second of her books.

Rose had eventually come to understand that writing and coding was her gift, but what was the subject and learning thread that wove the tapestry of all these lifetimes together, for her to remember? That is one of the main topics of this book and the reason that she picked up the pen again in this lifetime, becoming an author. As you observe her understanding open up, I will develop these subjects as her chosen muse, so that you may feel it relevant to you also, on your unique journey of personal discovery and illumination.

As Lady Julian, I became one of the thousands of examples of dear ones that sacrificed a normal life for the love and devotion to their God, over the centuries. In this particular Christian Catholic past life of mine,

I would have been a fairly extreme example, as an Anchorite nun. I was born and lived in Norwich from the year 1343 to approximately 1416 AD, or thereafter. It was in the days before the English monarch King Henry VIII disbanded the numerous monks' cells across England and Norfolk, creating the Church of England of which he, by his wily design, became the head. What is an Anchorite you may ask? These were Catholic individuals of a particularly pious nature who could volunteer to become an Anchor (male) or an Anchoress (female). This would normally be seen as an act of utter dedication to the Lord and the Catholic Church, requiring nuns, priests, and others to give up all worldly goods, homes, and family to live in a tiny cell, usually built onto the side of a church.

We anchors swore on the bible, never to leave this small room again for the rest of our earthly lives and the Bishop blessed us and then sealed the door shut, for good. There were normally three little built-in windows for us. One facing the exterior world so that we could share counsel and solace with passers-by. We could exchange knowledge of the Bible with them and give comfort to those enquiring of us. The second window was a service hatch, where our food and water could be passed through and any excrement taken away. The third small window opened into the church itself, in order that we could listen to the sermons and ceremonies that took place within. We were naturally dedicated to prayer and scribing copies of holy writings and various scriptures, for the church. I also helped with sewing clothes for the poor children and with stitching and needlework for the kneelers and altar. How could these humble individuals be of any relevance to you today, you might ask?

You may call me a multi-life old crone, with too many incarnations for her own good and say that I am surely getting everything muddled up after all these existences, but I assure you, there is nothing wrong with my memory here in spirit! It is sharper than William the Conqueror's sword and certainly a lot clearer now, than it was towards the end of my life, as Julian of Norwich. I became a little forgetful in my seventies, it's true. Of all my past life roles on earth, I am one of Rose's favourites! She chose me to narrate to you the unfolding of this mysterious story. She realised strangely, that you are experiencing many of the things that I did over six hundred years before your time.

In 1349 when still a child, I experienced the Bubonic plague, which swept through Norwich for two years, as I mentioned earlier. Along with this was the long 'Hundred Years' War' between England and France and then to add to our woes, there were plenty of uprisings and protests, the Peasants' Revolt being one of the more famous. This will be relevant to the following tales, of which the story of the rebellion leaders The Kett Brothers culminating in 1549, reached up as far up as Norfolk. This was my home county, more than a century after my death. The first major uprising was when King Richard II met and confronted the rebels on 14 June 1381 as they were ransacking the Tower of London. As we traverse these various dramatic events, I would like you to keep their importance in your mind, as these act as golden keys Rose discovered. I helped her to unlock clues to other past lives in medieval and Tudor times and will show you how these repeating events are still affecting us today.

To give you a little historical background as Julian of Norwich, here lies a summary of the underlying tensions during the forty years after the first ravages of the Bubonic plague, which have been described in Wikipedia and I quote:

> The revolt had various causes, including the socio-economic and political tensions generated by the Black Death pandemic in the 1340s, the high taxes resulting from the conflict with France during the Hundred Years' War, and instability within the local leadership of London. The final trigger for the revolt was the intervention of a royal official, John Bampton, in Essex on 30 May 1381. His attempts to collect unpaid poll taxes in Brentwood ended in a violent confrontation, which rapidly spread across the south-east of the country. A wide spectrum of rural society, including many local artisans and village officials, rose up in protest, burning court records and opening the local gaols. The rebels sought a reduction in taxation, an end to the system of unfree labour known as serfdom, and the removal of the King's senior officials and law courts. - The Peasants' Revolt, Wikipedia[4]

The Peasants' Revolt was eventually quashed in November of that same year, 1381. As you may have begun to realise, these issues are known to

---

[4] https://en.wikipedia.org/wiki/Peasants'_Revolt

you also in the 21ˢᵗ Century and in particular from 2020 onwards. Things had previously started to bubble on **25 May 2020** with a **'Black Death'** of sorts, when an American man named George Floyd, died pinned down on the street with his neck under the knee of a white American police officer in Minnesota, sparking a huge riot. Worldwide protests quickly sprang up in major cities on 26 May and continued for weeks despite the health quarantines for the virus, that were put in place by the governments internationally. This was the perfect storm when centuries of perceived racial inequalities bubbled over and groups such as 'Black Lives Matter' found their voice against injustice.

It was in fact around the same few days at the end of May that the **Peasants' Revolt** had started 639 years earlier –on **30 May 1381!** Here we find our first key to a date synchronicity and another cyclical event in history, as quoted from the same article in Wikipedia:

> Interpretations of the revolt have shifted over the years. It was once seen as a defining moment in English history, but modern academics are less certain of its impact on subsequent social and economic history. The revolt heavily influenced the course of the Hundred Years' War, by deterring later Parliaments from raising additional taxes to pay for military campaigns in France. The revolt has been widely used in socialist literature, including by the author William Morris and remains a potent political symbol for the political left, informing the arguments surrounding the introduction of the Community Charge in the United Kingdom during the **1980s.**

Did you notice, beloveds, a further date parallel with the Peasant's Revolt in 1381 and the uprising against the Community Charge in the 1980s some six hundred years later? I will be discussing date synchronicities and numerology further along in these tales. Although the issues that caused the rebellions all across England were different, they were precipitated by the Black Death pandemics. Something interesting but predictable happened as a result of losing fifty percent of the population to the Bubonic Plague in the middle ages, as quoted below:

The death rate among the peasantry meant that suddenly land was relatively plentiful and labourers in much shorter supply. Labourers could charge more for their work and, in the consequent competition for labour, wages were driven sharply upwards. In turn, the profits of landowners were eroded. The trading, commercial and financial networks in the towns disintegrated.

It seemed at first, that there would be a more even distribution of wealth and indeed the labourers did find themselves in an advantageous situation. As is normally the case over thousands of years of human history, the wealthy soon put paid to the working classes becoming more powerful and having more freedom of choice, as Wikipedia continues:

> The authorities responded to the chaos with emergency legislation; the Ordinance of Labourers was passed in 1349, and the Statute of Labourers in 1351. These attempted to fix wages at pre-plague levels, making it a crime to refuse work or to break an existing contract, imposing fines on those who transgressed. The system was initially enforced through special Justices of Labourers and then, from the 1360s onwards, through the normal Justices of the Peace, typically members of the local gentry. Although in theory these laws applied to both labourers seeking higher wages and to employers tempted to outbid their competitors for workers, they were in practice applied only to labourers, and then in a rather arbitrary fashion. The legislation was strengthened in 1361, with the penalties increased to include branding and imprisonment. The royal government had not intervened in this way before, nor allied itself with the local landowners in quite such an obvious or unpopular way.

The use of emergency legislation finds its comparison in 2022 with the Canadian Prime Minister having called for unparalleled interference from the Government. This was to deal with the peaceful protests against mandated medical passports to cross the border to the US. The uprising was nick-named the Freedom Truckers or Freedom Convoys. With his new powers, he brutally shut down access to protesters' bank accounts.

Anyone assisting them was warned they would suffer the same fate. Interestingly the people responded by initiating an Inquiry into this uncalled-for authoritarian 'Emergency Act', which at the time of writing, is still ongoing. Rose also thought about the impending microchip that was rumoured to be coming, the insertion of which would take away more of the peoples' freedoms, controlling their finances and even their medication. It seemed like a more sophisticated version of the branding used all those centuries earlier!

Returning again to the medieval equivalent, I continue to quote from the above article in Wikipedia as follows;

> Over the next few decades, economic opportunities increased for the English peasantry. Some labourers took up specialist jobs that would have previously been barred to them, and others moved from employer to employer, or became servants in richer households. These changes were keenly felt across the south-east of England, where the London market created a wide range of opportunities for farmers and artisans. Local lords had the right to prevent serfs from leaving their manors, but when serfs found themselves blocked in the manorial courts, many simply left to work illegally on manors elsewhere. Wages continued to rise, and between the 1340s and the 1380s the purchasing power of rural labourers increased by around 40 percent. As the wealth of the lower classes increased, Parliament brought in fresh laws in 1363 to prevent them from consuming expensive goods formerly only affordable by the elite. These sumptuary laws proved unenforceable, but the wider labour laws continued to be firmly applied.

The commoners were not allowed unbridled access to good quality items, perhaps also better food so that they grew healthier and could lift themselves out of poverty and sickness! This sounds so similar to life now, in the 21st century, where the underprivileged can only afford junk food. In fact, some poor souls are having to choose between bodily sustenance or heating their homes due to a horrendous tenfold price rise in their energy bills. This is only set to rise even further in the autumn of 2022. It seems that mankind has still not learned the lessons of unity and equality, at all! Even more sinister is the emergence of a rumoured Global Reset bearing the slogan "Own Nothing, Be Happy" - will the end goal of the elites behind the scenes, be to force everyone onto a social credit system? This would mean not owning any personal property with all private and business monetary transactions funnelling through a central digital banking system owned by the nations' governments. The implications of this can already be seen with the freezing of bank accounts and blocking of donations through charities such as GoFundMe, during the Trucker Convoy protests in Ottawa, Canada. These government actions could become more oppressive if the alleged One World Order or Great Reset proposed by the German businessman, Klaus Schwab, at Davos annual meeting of key billionaires in Switzerland, proceeds any further.

I expect you are wondering how on earth, looking back deep into our own past can help with these repeating societal issues. This book aims to clarify the importance of taking personal responsibility for healing our individual pain patterns and therefore contributing to a ripple effect of healing energy, not only in this lifetime but those on other timelines. These occur simultaneously and all interlink, affecting each other in a mysterious way that science and physics are as yet unable to grasp. There is an answer to this, we do have the power to change timelines for the better if enough of us wake up!

There is now an urgent need to assist in raising the collective lighter energy vibration, or greater consciousness. This in turn leads one further into feeling love and connection to yourself and those around you and will therefore penetrate out ever further to Gaia and the Universe itself. Ancient mystics such as myself, came to learn and understand these principles and that is the offering I have to give you, dear reader. Hope and trust that you can bring yourself into a space of alignment, despite all that appears wrong with the world around you. To ascend gracefully in your inner being, knowing that you truly make a difference, as each drop makes up the ocean and each wave ripples and moves within the sea.

Now that I have set the scene of events occurring before, during, and after my birth, as Julian of Norwich, I will regale you with my extraordinary life experiences in these difficult times. In my current incarnation as Rose, I chose the pen as my instrument, as I thought it mightier than the sword. I chose a life of heartfelt love above hate, that I might lead by example.

Eventually, after so many incarnations, Rose started to awaken in her fifties to remembering what she had come to earth to do, even though she had done this so many times before in other lifetimes.

Rose followed the trail of breadcrumbs I gave her, through the sacred lands and forests, up and down mountains, in and out of holy temples. The pieces of the jigsaw puzzle she picked up along the way, grew slowly into a beautiful picture of life and the meaning it held uniquely for her. She came to understand it was not only her journey, it was a beautiful golden key that she could bequeath to other initiates. That these in turn may walk their own adventures and unlock their individual mysteries, entering secret walled gardens and collecting their ingredients therein, for their personal Holy Grail. Such elements once gathered and smelted in their cauldron of inspirations, could be taken into the chalice of their heart, in purification. Once Rose had become a master alchemist she was able to instruct her pupils in the secrets of their spiritual alchemy, so that they may also find the gold within and come home to their indestructible nature, their own soul's luminescence.

Well, this is enough rambling for now, suffice it to say my memory has never been better in spirit, but my ability to make a long story short has not improved! If I say so myself, I am become as sharp as a thousand reflecting mirrors, drawing me into the infinite vortex, that has no time limits.

My birth name is unknown in your times, but I have been named after the Church of Julian, off Rouen Road, Norwich in the county of Norfolk, England, as mentioned previously. I had been a survivor of what historians say may have been three rounds of the plague. I came very close to death, and in my seemingly last moments of life, was delirious with fever. I had what you would now call an NDE or a near-death experience. When I was younger than thirty I asked to bear witness to the passion of Christ and to fall gravely ill so that I may understand what Jesus suffered on our behalf. It seemed that my wish came true. Be careful what you pray and ask for! The visions I had on my near-deathbed were of Christ's crucifixion, which I experienced as my own.

During this time, the curate, a member of the Catholic church, had been called to my sick bed in order to offer me the Last Rites. As was tradition, he held the crucifix up for me to gaze upon, at the end of the bed. A practice that would enable my safe passing to the heavenly realms.

Whilst preparing myself for my last moments on this earth, gazing upon my Lord on the cross, I began to have visions, sixteen in total, as the body on the crucifix swam in and out of focus. These were intense and mystical in nature. I felt his suffering and pain, but nothing else, outside of his radiating warmth, sweetness, and ineffable joy towards the human race. There was not an iota of condemnation from him.

Eventually, I closed my eyes in exhaustion expecting never to open them in this world again. But I was wrong; slowly the fever abated and I started to recover until I eventually regained full health. It was a miracle and one I attributed to the power of faith and the love of my God. Not much is known of my personal or familial circumstances leading up to this time, but it can be assumed that many of my family may have already died of the bubonic plague. What historians do know, because I left them some clues, is that I had previously received an education to the degree that I could read and write.

I had a working knowledge of Hebrew, so my parents would have been seen as fairly wealthy. Women very rarely received this type of education in these past centuries, unless they were aristocracy or became nuns. In any event, I felt that I now owed my life to my Saviour. I gladly applied to be an anchoress in St. Julian's church, serving faithfully to the end, which in my case was till my death at around seventy-four and certainly a ripe old age for those times of plague and unrest.

Initially, after my near-death experience, I wrote a secret synopsis of my visions of Christ. The things I had been shown in these dreams contrasted with the current patriarchal teachings of the Catholic Church. It rankled me, and I quote from my own book 'Revelations of Divine Love,'[5]

> Nowhere in all that was revealed to me, did I see a trace of sin and yet "sinners" is what we were branded as, day in and day out. I now saw that 'sin has no substance, not a particle of being, and can only be detected by the pain it causes.'

In other words, when we make mistakes and suffer the results of them, we humble ourselves and God loves us all the more. We are not doing anything 'wrong' but simply hurting ourselves. For non-Christians, one

---

[5] https://en.wikipedia.org/wiki/Revelations_of_Divine_Love

could swap the word sin for shame, or blame. We make mistakes, but that opens a portal in our internal universe, where we can find soul-searching answers to our questions and return with a more awakened attitude. Suffering leads to growth, not condemnation.

One of my primary goals in the theology of my writings was to teach a view of the feminine divine. This would have been really 'out there' in my day. My version of the Holy Trinity, rather than God the Father, Son, and Holy Spirit, was that the second person in the Trinity, Jesus, is actually like the maternal aspect (not the masculine Son).

> As truly as God is our father," I wrote, "just as truly is God our mother… Who else but a mother, I asked, would break herself open and pour herself out for her children? Only God could ever perform such duty. - Revelations of Divine Love, by Julian of Norwich

My concept of mother God portrayed a loving presence in our darkest hours, as a mother would tend to her sick child in the middle of the night. This idea was a combination of the unconditional love of Mother Mary for the Catholics, along with other Goddesses such as the Chinese Kuan Yin, Goddess of Mercy, and in ancient Egypt for example with the Goddess Isis, depicted as the nurturer and often pictured with babe in arms. When we fall down or transgress, we want to hide in shame. But,

> Our courteous Mother doesn't want us to flee," I had mused, "Nothing would distress her more. She wants us to behave as a child would when he is upset or afraid: rush with all our might into the arms of the mother. - Revelations of Divine Love, by Julian of Norwich

In my understanding at that time, the good news was not merely the reward we will receive one day when we die, or when the paradise earth comes. Every second of our lives is a chance to realise that we are perfectly loved and perfectly lovable, just as we are. Unconditional love, in its truest form. This was an amazing opportunity for me, to realise that even within the staunch Christian dogma of the Middle Ages, there was hope and light, being brought gently into view through mine own self, a woman. As I relate this story to you, it shakes me to the core to think of the enormity of the stance I undertook at that time!

Women have so much to contribute, to contrast the active, militarist, and macho view of the male Godhead, The Protector. This is why women are needed as equals in the cloth and your corporate-run world today. The sacred feminine seeks to enhance and balance our perceptions of what is 'in here' and what is 'out there,' teaching us that we don't always have to pick up a bow and arrow and destroy the perceived enemy. In your terms today it may be described as being like the angels, "a-sexual" with the meaning of becoming neither a man, nor a woman, in a spiritual sense. It is a form of emancipation from the traditional roles of male and female, becoming as described of angels in the bible, as non-sexual beings.

One of my absolute favourites, Saint Jerome of the 1st Century, spoke of this and I quote him:

> While a woman serves for birth and children, she is different from man as body is from soul. But when she wants to serve Christ more than the world, then she shall cease to be called a woman and shall be called man. - Writings of Julian of Norwich, JSTOR.org[6]

In my neutral position as an anchorite and woman of God with a direct connection to the Lord, I braved the subject of why he allowed things to be less than perfect here on earth. Subsequently I was inspired to write the following:

> And so, when the final judgment comes, we shall clearly see in God all the secrets that are hidden from us now. Then none of us will be moved in any way to say, 'Lord, if only things had been different, all would have been well.' Instead, we shall all proclaim in one voice, 'Beloved One, may you be blessed, because it is so: ALL IS WELL. - Revelations of Divine Love, by Julian of Norwich

Occasionally I like to eavesdrop on your current day culture and I

---

[6] https://www.jstor.org/stable/2445287

noticed a film named 'The Best Exotic Marigold Hotel' which stated: "Everything will be alright in the end...if it's not right, then it's not the end." Beyond its context in that film, these words convey a profound theological truth, which seed I like to think, I had originally planted and that Oscar Wilde the Irish poet and playwright penned. I see he was influenced by my words when he said in the 1980s;

> Everything is going to be fine in the end. If it's not fine it's not the end.

In later centuries people have remarked that these words expressed were deep and meaningful and beautifully written. Remember, it would have been dangerous for me to reveal these mystical visions to anyone in the church during the Dark Ages, as I may have been branded a heretic or a Lollard which could bring me to my early death by torture or even burning! How my writings contrasted with the established church at that time, was that I taught a unique way of looking at God and his love for his creation and his presence in our suffering. I simply could not paint him as the vengeful, warmonger of the Old Testament, but had come to understand that all his ways were love. My tone was one of hope and trust in God, overflowing with love for mankind. Hence the full sentence from mine quote above, being my favourite;

> All shall be well: and you shall see, yourself, that all manner of thing shall be well.

I noticed with some little pride, if a spirit creature such as I am can have such a thing, that an amazing documentary about my life was created in 2016. It aired on a UK TV channel called BBC4 and was entitled 'The search for the lost manuscript: Julian of Norwich.' Presented by medieval art historian Dr. Jamina Ramirez, it tells the incredible story of a book hidden for centuries in the shadows of history. It was the first religious book ever written in England by a woman, Julian of Norwich, in 1373. I thoroughly recommend watching this show. It was very well received and has been repeated on TV.[7]

---

[7] https://www.bbc.co.uk/programmes/b0716bd0

Dr. Ramirez explores all avenues in her quest to bring to light the exciting passageway of my hidden writings. She explains how they almost disappeared for many centuries until they were discovered hundreds of years later and brought to light. They had luckily been copied and preserved, initially by the Benedictine nuns who I handed them over to, for safe-keeping. Today, I see that I have become world famous, not that I will let that go to my head. Many people from the USA, Canada, and other international visitors make the pilgrimage here to come and read about me, at the shrine in Norwich.

My last incarnation, Rose, finally awakened to the messages I was planting in her psyche over the years and moved from London to Trowse Newton. I ensured that she found a suitable abode a few miles from this church, in King Street, but was a little frustrated that it took her three years to visit inside the chapel, and that, only when she had already moved away! Eventually, I had to inspire one of her friends to mention my shrine, to garner her curiosity. Once she had taken an interest, I gave her some further messages through other folk to confirm what she had started to think, that she was possibly a future incarnation of myself.

We got there in the end. She became very curious when walking into my cell, imaging what I must have seen and experienced whilst living there hundreds of years previously. It dawned on her through her studies and research thereafter, what a vindication my life had been for a woman in those dark medieval times. My writings seemed a real testimony to my perseverance and purpose. Once she was on the breadcrumb trail following the clues I had given her, she wrote copiously about me, deciding to use me as a muse for her book. She was then inspired to record some short stories about me and a special visit from my colleague, also now in spirit, Margery Kempe. This you can watch on her @isisiallthings3940 YouTube channel,[8] if you so wish. I find these short tales quite amusing myself, for Rose was trying to imagine conversations that had taken place hundreds of years ago and recreate our characters, but I will say that she managed fairly well under the circumstances.

On one of Rose's visits, she determined to buy a new version of my book 'Revelations of Divine Love by Julian of Norwich', which has an

---

[8] https://www.youtube.com/channel/UCTbuMxfjpOHKCZQFtJSdaPg

introduction by A.N. Wilson[9]. This she read and quoted from when compiling this novel, I am pleased to say, as it had taken some considerable work to bring her to this point. I knew that she would be a vessel for truth, once she grasped the meaning of it from her modern point of view. To show her that she was on the right track with her writing, in the August of 2019 she had not been feeling very well and had made an appointment with the herbalist Cherie for some medicines. As she had walked into the alternative healing section of the Complimentary Clinic in Exchange Street, Norwich, Cherie had appeared in the doorway looking like the archetypal white witch. She had long grey hair falling loosely to her waist, was petite and mature, but with large friendly blue eyes and an affable smile.

Rose got into conversation with this very wise and spiritual lady and was talking about her second book and how she had been researching medieval past lives in Norwich. Suddenly and unprompted, Cherie had said "I am getting the name Julian around you". Rose looked at her in surprise and said "yes, actually that is one of the characters I am writing about, I think I may have been Julian in a past life, or she is, at any rate, a mystical muse. "Cherie looked at her and smiled and said, "yes, I can see her materialising over your face." That was nice confirmation for her and quite satisfying to me too up here in spirit, as I was observing Rose's awakening progress, with great interest.

Now I knew that she was very keen and hot on the trail. Not long after this incident, she booked a psychic reading with her friend and was again explaining to her that she had been writing about her medieval past lives. Ruth said, "I am being shown the shrine of Julian for some reason." Rose looked very pleased with this further unprompted confirmation and explained to Ruth that she believed Julian was possibly a guide for her at this time. Ruth's spirit team then passed on a message, "they are telling me that it is one of the greatest reasons that St. Julian incarnated in this lifetime, Rose, to tell the truth!"

Towards the end of a later reading for Rose, in February 2022, Ruth suddenly remembered that she had been watching a TV series about midwives in the forties through to the sixties. She had meant to mention it to Rose before because In one of the later series there was a character

[9] https://www.waterstones.com/book/revelations-of-divine-love/a-n-wilson/julian-of-norwich/9780281077076

named Mother Julian. She was an experienced midwife who had a sudden heart attack. When the younger nurses were comforting her at her bedside, fearing she would pass away, one of them remarked how unfair it was for her to fall gravely ill. It seemed unjust, when this experienced midwife still had so much of her life ahead of her and had helped so many into this world, through her good work. Ruth remembered that Mother Julian had replied to the nurses, paraphrasing the words of Julian of Norwich, also known as Mother Julian. She described the medieval mystic's radical acceptance of what suffering was, and her being at peace with it. Having observed the devastating pain and loss that the Black Death had wrought all around her from the age of seven, she had made sense of it all in her mind. St. Julian had described it thus: "that our wounds are not ours, but the world's and Mother Earth's."

I, Julian of Norwich, became famous for resisting all temptations to victimhood. Quoting from the Daily Meditations with Matthew Fox website about my writings, David Paladin describes how we should view our pains and ills:

> Take our trials and dis-eases as lightly as we can. For the more lightly we take them and the less price we set on them, for love, the less pain we will have in feeling them and the more thanks and refreshment we will have for them.[10]

Rose became aware of yet another non coincidence as she was completing this book. She was invited to an art exhibition by one of her soul tribe, Matthew. She made the trip to Aldeburgh on 20 July 2022 with another of her soul family, James. The musician and the artist had not met each other, but as expected, the energy felt electric and serene concomitantly, when the three of them came together. They wandered around the spacious loft space and admired the stunning images and paintings. Whilst chatting over a glass of Prosecco, one of the other artists present, Delia, joined the conversation. When she found out that Rose came from Norwich, she said she had visited there recently to see the shrine of Julian of Norwich. Rose could feel an energy connection to

---

[10] https://dailymeditationswithmatthewfox.org/2021/04/30/david-paladin-and-julian-of-norwich-on-suffering-and-initiation/

this woman and allowed the subject to unfurl. As she described how she enjoyed visiting the little church of St. Julian, Rose mentioned that she was writing a book about her and in fact, she had chosen her as a muse to narrate her medieval tales. Out of the blue, the artist exclaimed that Julian is very strongly present at the moment, in the world. Rose was struck by her comment and agreed that Julian had discovered the secret of thriving in crises, due to the development of a rich inner world of trust and hope.

Synchronicities seemed to be coming thick and fast now as Rose dove deeper into the flow of her conscious timeline travel. It was a bit like the movie 'Back to the Future', except she was now in the driving seat, rather than being the confused passenger. This artist, Delia, just happened to mention she had been meaning to go again and purchase her book. I, of course, had written the short and long versions of 'Revelations of Divine Love' in secret over the forty years I had lived confined in the anchorite cell. I had carefully entrusted the nuns to securely keep and make copies of it, for them to share amongst themselves. I knew very well, from their writings or hearsay, of those saints who had lost their lives when scribing a different narrative from the Catholic Church, about The Lord and his unconditional agape love. Firstly these dear brave ones' writings would have been destroyed as a stark warning to all that dissented from the Papal teachings of the bible and then they could have been burned at the stake. One such example preceding Julian of Norwich was Marguerite Porete. Wikipedia describes her such:

> Margeuerite Porete, born in the 13th century – died 1 June 1310. She was a French-speaking mystic and the author of Mirror of Simple Souls, a work of Christian mysticism dealing with the workings of agape (divine love). She was burnt at the stake for heresy in Paris in 1310 after a lengthy trial, refusing to remove her book from circulation or recant her views. - Marguerite Porete, Wikipedia[11]

Regarding her teachings, I would now like to quote an excerpt from

---

[11] https://en.wikipedia.org/wiki/Marguerite_Porete

Meggan Watterson's book 'The Divine Feminine Oracle' [12] regarding this brave mystic:

> Marguerite Porete is the essence of divine love and the truth that all we are is love. Marguerite was a French Beguine born in the mid-13th century. The Beguine movement was a spiritual revival among women in the late Middle Ages that emphasized an imitation of Christ's life. These beguines, or holy women, lived together in semi-monastic communities. They were not nuns, they didn't take formal vows and could leave at any point, but they lived with shared spiritual intention.
>
> Marguerite wrote a spiritual masterpiece titled 'The Mirror of Simple Souls.' It reveals the spiritual process she went through to be transformed by divine love; "I am God, says Love, for Love is God and God is Love, and this Soul is God by the condition of Love." (Mirror, p.104). By 1306, the Bishop of Cambrai deemed her work heretical and condemned it to be burned at the stake in Porete's presence. Even so, it continued to be circulated widely throughout the Middle Ages and in some ecclesiastical centres it was embraced as an almost canonical piece of theology. Porete was ordered to stop circulating her book and to recant her ideas of God as love. But she refused. Marguerite was arrested as a relapsed heretic and a Free Spirit.

The Catholic Church conducted an unprecedented trial to decide her fate. Like Joan of Arc, much of her life is recorded because of the transcripts of her lengthy trial. She maintained her truth that the soul has no other will but God's, and that when the soul is united with God's love this state of union causes the soul to transcend the contradictions of this world. She suggests that we can be transformed by divine love into love itself, which isn't separate from God. And that ultimately no outside source is needed in this transformation. It's between the soul and God alone.

---

[12] https://www.megganwatterson.com/the-divine-feminine-oracle

Marguerite was burned at the stake in 1310 along with her book 'The Mirror of Simple Souls.' It continued to gain in popularity but was distributed as an anonymous text, until 1946, when Romana Guarnieri identified Latin manuscripts of 'The Mirror' in the Vatican. Marguerite's name was returned to the text when it was published for the first time in 1965. There's nothing more powerful than remembering that we are love. And there's nothing and no one outside of us that is needed in order to realize this. It's between our experience of the divine and our own soul. We can let go of what we think we need to prove, or who we think we need to be in order to receive love because we remember that we are love. Then we can stand in that truth, even through flames.

Marguerite is a courageous truth teller. And the truth of her experience is that love alone can free us. Not the love another might give us, not the love of family, or of friends. All of this is powerful, and significant. But, the true source of love for us is in the fact that we are a soul, and that the soul is in union with the divine. She reminds us when we've forgotten, that love is the essence of who we are. And that true love is found within. Marguerite says, "Love has no beginning, no end, and no limit, and I am nothing except Love." This is a time to own and to know this truth more fully. It is the most profound and radical act we can ever take: knowing the love we already are.

These were dangerous times for independent-minded souls such as us. I, Julian, had written similarly heartfelt words about the unconditional mother love of Christ, as an important aspect of God. In some ways, your days seem to be becoming as dangerous as the Dark Ages. As the tide slowly turns from democracy to autocracy, sweeping the globe once again in its inimitable pattern, it reflects this recurring theme of power and control, besmirching agape love, throughout history. In your day social media has been hijacked by the super-rich, the hidden elite, and huge corporations with much more power and money than the world governments, which they have manipulated behind the scenes.

Freedom of mind, body, and soul was gradually becoming a dangerous thing to possess! Mine own ideas conceived of in person during my near-death experience and the visions I had of the true nature of Jesus Christ, contained heretical ideas. One such was my conviction, as mentioned before, that The Trinity was formed not only of male energy, our God Almighty, The Father but that it also held an equal third of the Divine Feminine or mother love. These deeply felt qualities, Jesus had dearly impressed upon me when I gazed upon him, during my delirious state. I was always aware that I would have been burned at the stake just as Margeurite had been. Not too far from my church was the terrifying Lollard's Pit where poor wretched ones could be heard to scream and wail, awaiting their gruesome death by burning. There stands in its place only a public house now known by the same name, Lollard's Pit. Many folk claim to have heard screams of the ghosts of these pitiful ones, even to this day. If I had dared to teach these heretical thoughts or publish this work I had written, the same fate may have befallen me.

After all these heavy thoughts, as a form of light entertainment for you, dear ones, I will now narrate some small stories within this greater tale. Rose created these as a little video series, whilst she was finishing her book, in order that you may experience a few days as if in the life of an anchorite and experience the blessed visitation of her friend Margery Kempe, whom she found to be the most amusing mystic in the land.

To set the scene, when I was around thirty-two years of age, I became a Catholic anchorite. Records survive in your day showing that I had a maid named Alice and then later, another named Sarah. Four known wills mention me, and the earliest of these was 1393/4 as recorded by Roger Reed, in Norwich, who made a bequest that twelve shillings be paid to Julian anakorite. Other wills mention bequests to my maids also. Rose begins with a preamble to set the scene you are becoming familiar with, in the next chapter.

CHAPTER 2

A Day in the Life of Julian of Norwich

A nine-part short-story series

As was typical of an Anchor or an Anchorite, there was a proper ceremony to signify our willing internment and then the door was sealed behind us by the Bishop and a vow was taken to remain in this room for the rest of our life. Shocking as it may seem that I willingly chose this self-isolation, there were many benefits to this life in medieval times for me, which we will understand, as I narrate some light-hearted yarns of my daily life. I shall begin with my morning rituals so that you can peek into how my day began.

Part I. Morning Rituals

Dear Children of God, my eyes flutter open with the first rays of dawn, piercing like a golden sword through one of my three tiny windows. This one faces the East and is my small opening to the beloved ones living outside of this church of St Julian in Norwich, England in the 14th Century. As I lie on my unforgiving horse-hair mattress in contemplation, I stretch to make myself more comfortable and bring my hands together over my heart in readiness for my first morning prayers of thanks, to the Lord God, the source of all that is. My hands are icy cold on my rosary, as I live in a stone room attached to this Catholic place of worship and there are few luxuries in these medieval times. My assistant will light a fire in the hearth once I am risen.

Having recited The Lord's Prayer I consider the many things that I have to be grateful for in these perilous times. The bubonic plague swept through Norwich for two whole years in 1349 when I was just seven years old, but I survived. I myself very nearly died of the plague when I was thirty and this I consider a miracle from which many blessings have sprung. When I was thirty-nine, during the times of The Hundred Years' War, I also heard many accounts of the Peasant's Revolt from those who came to my window for words of comfort. Those were times of great injustice, fear, anxiety, and lack of security for many. This is similar to that which you dear ones are experiencing today with the Corona Virus, self-isolation, and worries about finances. In return for my counsel, I would be given small portions of food or water, whatever could be spared by the folk.

If it were not for this kindness and my dowry, I would not be alive at fifty-eight and writing the longer version of my book 'Revelations of Divine Love.' It is about the shewings and visions I had of Christ's Passion, during my near-death experience twenty-six years ago. I am grateful to be alive and in good health when all around me outside is disease, filth, and stench from the streets. I reach for my pomander of sweet herbs and take a deep breath to clear my head and uplift my spirits. It contains lavender which I find so calming.

As I lie in this reverie I feel a slight pull on my linen gown and a sudden pounce brings my dear feline companion to light on my lap. This delightful cat is named Amelia which means "work" and she is my protector. If it were not for her, my holy cell would no doubt be overrun by mice and rats looking for any sparse crumbs of dry bread I may drop. I stroke her soft fur and am thankful for her purring warmth, kneading comfort into my soul.

I hear a rustling coming from the second little opening in my room, which I know to be my church assistant bringing me a bowl of water for my toilette and the second assistant to light the fire. Amelia plops off my bed as I throw back the roughly woven woolen blankets and cotton covers and fetch my covered bowl of excrements to hand the attendant in return. This provision is given in grace of my promise to Christ that I will remain sealed in this chamber in his service, till the end of my days and I am called an Anchorite for this reason. I am also referred to as a Mystic due to the nature of my visions, which are considered direct communication from God. It seems there had been no shewings recorded for the last couple of hundred years, so a rare thing indeed it was.

Once my physical routine is attended to by a brief wash in icy cold water from a tin bowl with a roughly woven cloth, and my hair is brushed and tied back behind my white headdress, I am fresh to start the new day of contemplation and devotion. I am in a world betwixt and between, fully in the present moment between life and death, each day. Although I was blessed into this position by the Bishop, I needed my family fortune to bequeath to the church, which was left to me when all had passed away with the plague. This now acts as a pledge for my keep, that I may not be a burden on the church or the people, for the rest of my time here.

This small private space that only I inhabit is similar to that of a Hermit or recluse and is just as many of you are now experiencing if you are alone in your home due to the government restrictions of what you call Lock-down, to stem the flow of the Corona Virus. This may be the first and last time you will ever experience the self-isolation that I live with for so many years till my death. It is all the more difficult for you dear ones as it was not something you chose as I did, but it is now an opportunity for you to turn inwards and connect to the divine, in your meditations of mindfulness and prayers.

This state of living that I surrender to became known as "liminality" and allows spiritual experience to occur as it can for you if approached in the right manner. You can choose to complain about your lot, unable to visit your friends or enjoy a meal in a restaurant or you can use this time wisely for your personal growth. It is a marginal existence, one of poverty that I live, neither in the past, nor in the future, but is a state of pure potential each day. You will understand it in your now time by the terms of a time of personal transition, transcendence, and transformation, although I simply understand it as a state of grace.

I am curiously outside of social everyday experience but strangely still a part of it too, as you are with your technology and social media. It can be a blessed time without the normal concerns the people would speak to me of. I am protected from vile diseases and without the worries of finding a roof over my head or clothing and sustenance. I surrender the experience of joining with another in physical love and begetting children but in place of this, I have become as without sexual gender, respected by clergymen of the cloth just as much as by the women who look to me, as a mystic with a direct connection of divine spiritual experience, for which I am honoured.

I have the advantage of coming from a family who had the funds to teach me how to read and write, even in Hebrew, which I now put to higher use in my copying of sacred texts onto parchment for the church and speaking of the wisdom gained through my insights, to those who clamour at my window each day in times of duress. You would call me a mentor or counsellor perhaps. Yes, I weave, sew and embroider as a woman would in these days, and my offerings are for the altars and kneeling hassocks here and for the poor ones who have no clothes.

In your terms today you may describe me as "a-sexual" with the meaning of becoming neither a man nor a woman, in a spiritual sense. It is a form of emancipation from the traditional roles of male and female, becoming as the angels are described in the bible, as non-sexual beings.

Saint Jerome of the 1st Century AD spoke of this and I quote him:

> While a woman serves for birth and children, she is different from man as body is from soul. But when she wants to serve Christ more than the world, then she shall cease to be called a woman and shall be called man.[13]

> Saint Jerome from Emona in Italy was "The protégé of Pope Damascus I, who died in December of 384, Jerome was known for his teachings on Christian moral life, especially to those living in cosmopolitan centres such as Rome. In many cases, he focused his attention on the lives of women and identified how a woman devoted to Jesus should live her life. This focus stemmed from his close patron relationships with several prominent female ascetics who were members of affluent senatorial families.

In the footnote, you will find a fuller description of Anchorites and their rites. I quote from this article:

---

[13] https://en.wikipedia.org/wiki/Jerome

For the most part, these are terms that have also been associated with anchoritism. Anchorites are the living dead, their cell functions as both womb and tomb, and they dwell in literal darkness (though in spiritual brightness). The profession can be traced back to the Egyptian desert, represented in Europe by the wilderness, fens, and forests. While bisexuality, as we think of it today, is not directly reflected in anchoritism, female anchorites assumed masculine characteristics after the fashion of Saint Jerome. In essence, then, once a potential anchorite crossed the threshold of the cell, he or she entered the state of liminality, which allows spiritual experience to occur.

Turner labels the threshold as a margin or limen, "when the past is momentarily negated, suspended, or abrogated, and the future has not yet begun, an instant of pure potentiality when everything, as it were, trembles in the balance." The liminal stage, "betwixt and between," is a state of transition and often one of transcendence and/or transformation. In referring to liminality, Turner also uses the term anti-structure, meaning time and space outside the structure or organization of society but nonetheless an experience of community among all participants. Again, this closely fits the anchoritic experience. Anchorites were outside normal social and religious structure but also firmly within it. - Michelle M. Sauer,"Anchoritism, Liminality, and the Boundaries of Vocational Withdrawal"[14]

So that is the conclusion of my first day and now I am weary from all these tales I tell you. Please join me on the morrow, as I take you through how I kept my sanity cooped up in this small room for so many years, in the following chapter. I bid you a good evening as my maid prepares my cot and bedclothes along with a hot tea of herbs and I bid you keep healthy and be safe my beloveds.

---

[14] https://muse.jhu.edu/article/608444

Part 2. The Power of Gratitude

Good day beautiful souls, I would like to introduce you to my little garden today. I am able to take the air through a tiny door to the outside. I love to plant my feet on the grass now it is spring, lean against my favourite oak tree and feel the warmth of the sun on my face, as she graces me with her presence this day. I feel grateful for this small but pretty high-walled space, where I may commune with nature and marvel at God's creations. The birds know me very well and, if I seat myself still enough on the stone and wooden bench, they will hop closer and closer for their morsel of dried bread. My favourite is Robin Redbreast because he sings such joyfully persistent pinking sounds as if he is willing me to join in with his chorus. Today he cocks his eye at me in curiosity, waiting for his treat. I enjoy these stolen moments before Amelia the cat arrives in a flurry and frightens them all away.

I expect now that you are more confined to your homes because of the Corona Virus lock-down from spring of 2020, some without work, or working from home and now with all your chores done, you will be spending more time in nature on your single permitted walk a day, for exercise. Many of you will be slowing down to make the most of your bid for freedom, observing the six-foot distancing rule between you and another who is not of your household, in order not to be contagious of the virus. During the bubonic plague, quarantine was a lot harsher, if it seemed as if there was no recovery in sight, the dying one was battened up in the home and left to die. So count your blessings dear ones, that you have hospitals and intensive care units.

In these isolated weeks and months, maybe you are now taking the time to really see the marvellous workings of mother earth. At a snail's pace, there are many fascinating things to be observed and appreciated, that you may have missed, in your constant work and striving for material things. For example, I have learned how the bees look after an injured one, when I watched mesmerised whilst a honey bee, which had become trapped in a case of hardened honey around its body, struggled to walk - let-alone fly. All of a sudden a rescue team of his kind appears and together chip it off his torso for a fair length of time, swapping shifts until he is clean again. I marvel that such sentient beings would abandon their busyness, to come to the aid of another and know that there are many mysteries that we do not understand about the harmony of nature. I feel that you are learning these acts of kindness also, in these unusual circumstances. Perhaps you are coming to someone's rescue, who can no longer look after themselves without your kind assistance in these difficult times. Older folk who cannot get food for themselves or sick ones that need tending and medicine.

It is during contemplation of the loving nature of the God that created these bees, that my heart swells with gratitude, as I gaze up at the sky. I feel a rush of appreciation and see golden letters suspended in the sun as if spelling out a code of sparking light language. I cannot understand it, but it is a beautiful vision and I wonder what it means. When I am busy with my tasks I do not notice such things, but when I sink into a relaxed and lucid state, all cares and thoughts melt away and I am no longer aware of the everyday sounds of daily life, coming from the nearby streets. Suddenly I am brought back from this dream time into what you call third-dimensional reality, by a splattering of raindrops on my face and hair and I hastily pick up my skirts and my throw and hurry inside.

Today I have put aside my needlework, a pair of rough breeches I am sewing for a poor young lad, in order to continue writing my secret book, which will come to be called 'Revelations of Divine Love.' It is not about these everyday thoughts but is a collection of precious shewings or visions that came upon me whilst I was fighting for my life many years ago, in 1373. At the age of thirty, I had piously begged, implored, and prayed to God that I may fall sick to the point of death, in order to more deeply understand his compassion and to know how it felt to be the Lord Jesus during his last passionate agony and prayers on the cross. He heard my prayers and struck me down with an illness from which it seemed I may not recover, so severe, was it.

After some days of agonising fever and chills I began to lose the feeling in my lower body and then I requested that I might be propped up with cushions so that I could gaze upon the cross. In the next two days, the feeling was lost in the upper half of my body also and the curate began to read me my last rites, as he held the crucifix aloft for me to look upon. I could see nothing except the dear face of my Lord, as all else became black around me and I felt shadowy entities trying to draw close, which I hoped were not demons.

Suddenly, I began to see visions and Jesus spoke with me about the nature of his unconditional love for us all. He showed me many things that I had heretofore not grasped and I began to regret that I might die before I received the full extent of these wondrous insights from him. After the sixteenth vision, I no longer had the strength to keep my eyes fixed upon him and I fell away deliriously, into what I expected to be my last waking moments on this earth.

It is at times such as these that many of you dear ones have known what you call a "Near Death Experience" (NDE). It is that world betwixt and between, which I described earlier, the void between life and death itself, where the veil is thin and miracles can happen. I have heard you tell similar stories about the light that you saw at the end of a long tunnel, where you walked into a beautiful garden or spoke with a shining Angel. I know that just as I, you may have wished to relinquish your spirit and desired to go to heaven. Here is where all is light, joy, and peace, but the Holy Spirit guided you back to earth with the words "it is not yet your time, you have not completed, that which you came here to do."

It took a long time for me to prise my eyelids open, they were as if made of lead, but I had to know if I was still in that glorious garden of God. It seemed I was not, for out of the shadows I could make out the face of my nurse, deathly pale with concern. As I turned my head and took a breath she cried out "Dear Julian, you are not taken away from us" and began to weep for joy. I smiled inside as I did not yet have the strength to move a single muscle. I knew in an instant that God had answered my prayer and that I had survived, in order to devote myself more fully to him in service. My heart swelled with love and gratitude for his mercy. In the following days, I became stronger and the will came back into me, to live again.

Here I also draw a comparison with you beautiful ones who are grateful to have experienced a similar miracle as I. Many of you have had what you call a "paradigm shift", changed your perception of what is possible, and have changed your life accordingly. Not all will have dedicated their lives to the Lord as I chose, but you will have appreciated the chance to learn a new skill, throw yourself into a new challenge or even write a book about your experience. Those of you who witnessed what comes after death as I did, will no longer fear it and maybe you are able to bring much comfort to those who have lost a loved one. I am now a woman with a mission, the fire in my soul is for Jesus only and I know that he is my only husband.

This is not for everyone, but it was my earnest heart's desire. Perhaps now you can understand why I sold the property I had been left when my family died of the plague and requested that the Bishop bless me into the role of Anchorite within this Catholic Church. I can imagine this is not the normal choice, we strive for pleasure and comfort in human form and I chose devotion and austerity instead, but each day was treasured thenceforth as a gift of service, as a reflection of his great love for me, for all.

So I pray that you will take at least this lesson in appreciation for what you have, from your enforced solitude during this global pandemic, and be grateful for the chance to slow your pace of life if you can. Be thankful in your prayers and meditations for all that is good, knowing that each moment is a precious opportunity to show your patience and resilience in the face of death, whether real or imagined. Come into your true heart centre beloved ones and know that the Kingdom of God is within you and is where you will find the centre of consciousness, or as I know it, your one true and divine soul, an everlasting part of all that is.

Part 3. God works in mysterious ways

I can hear the shuffle and falling footsteps of many who enter the church for Sunday service this day. The hushed whispers, the rustling of skirts, and the squeaking of leather breeches as the congregation settles itself onto the creaking wooden benches for morning worship. A few coughs and sneezes and then silence falls, as just one pair of heavy footsteps accompanied by the sweeping sound of heavily embroidered gown, indicate the arrival of the priest at the head of the church. I position myself at my third tiny window which gives me a bird's eye view of the pulpit, where the clergyman has now positioned himself for the opening hymn.

This is the extent of my interaction with the church as I am not able to enter, now that the interconnecting door has been permanently sealed by the Bishop of Norwich, upon my blessed vows. I take comfort in the rising beauty of the hymns which lift my spirits and the prayers of devotion that bring me close to my heart again. Sometimes so much time spent alone alienates me from the companionship of others in my worship, so these services are very precious to me. The priest has cleared his throat to deliver his weekly sermon about contrition and fasting as an act of humility in the face of our imperfect sinful nature. His voice rises and falls with the changing emotions of his subject, imagining the wrath of God when we stumble and fall. After his chiding, he reminds each and everyone that they are not lost in their sins but beholden to Jesus' sacrifice on behalf of them all. The conclusion of his speech drives the fear of God into them, commanding them to bare their souls and beg for his forgiveness, lest they suffer the fires of hell on their departure from this mortal coil.

As I walk back to my wooden stool in my cell to rest, I smile to myself whenever I hear such talk of God's punishing nature, from these men of God. As a mystic, I am granted direct communion with God and am not considered to be under their jurisdiction. They control and hold the people in fear and guilt, that they may be manipulated in their worship of him. The Lord that I know and love is like a gentle mother. One who nurtures and loves each creation utterly for what it is, to the end of time. I felt it to be a love without condition, as just the very existence of my soul was enough to receive this highest of all loves. I had experienced during my visions of Christ, that there is nothing that any soul can do that would move him to withdraw his love, as I had the profound privilege to come to know first-hand.

These are the words of comfort that I write in my secret book, for should these thoughts come to light, they would most certainly be branded as heretical. I knew that my words would never be publicly spoken in these days of the patriarchy and had resolved to keep them hidden until such time as I prepared to leave this earthly plane when I planned to hand them over to my attendants for safe carriage to the Nuns of the Bridgettine and Benedictine orders in nearby Catton. I prayed that one day these visions given to me by Jesus Christ would find a hearing ear and an open heart. I was sure it would not be for many eons of time to come or as many of you would understand it today, in Divine Timing.

Well now that I have hindsight from my vantage point in heaven, I know that you will be shocked to realise that these musings of mine, many years in the writing, were hidden and almost lost for over a hundred years.

There was no freedom of speech without the pain of a Lollard's death on the stake especially in the 1640s when the witch hunts began in earnest. The first publishing of my long text was in 1670 and then only modernised in 1843 some two hundred years later. Finally, these mystic texts emerged from obscurity in 1901, some five hundred years after my penning them and I smile wryly when I see that I am now finally considered to be an important Christian mystic and theologian in your times.

Patience is a virtue, but then there is no such thing as 'time' in the dimension where I now reside, where all things happen at the perfect time for them or simultaneously in the fabric of space. One of my own sayings has become famous as quoted by the poet that you will know as T. S. Elliot. That is "All shall be well: and you shall see, yourself, that all manner of thing shall be well" – I am glad if you can take some comfort in these words during these distressing times of global fear and anxiety about the great sickness sweeping the globe and its terrible consequences in terms of the economy. Remember that everything in God's eyes is in perfect alignment and all shall indeed be well, in the end, and if not, then it is not the end. Faith and trust in these words will bring you back to your centre of grace. Acceptance of all that is, will be the alchemy that changes your inner landscape to one of peace amongst chaos. Blessings to you all, children of God and beloved ones.

This will not do, I have sat for long enough in reverie on this creaky chair, and now my back aches, and my stomach rumbles. I will call through my interior window and see what simple fare will be brought to me today and how it will nourish my body and soul back to life. No doubt Amelia my feline companion, will come purring and rubbing herself up against my legs for her share of the meal and I am happy she is here, for otherwise, I would be as those of you in isolation now, without human touch or an arm of comfort around me. Ah here she is, slinking out of the corner as I thought, welcome back my dear furry one, did you know that I was talking about you? I think you did. Now tomorrow is a very special day Amelia, you will not believe whom we are to expect a visit from, but Margery Kempe herself! Yes, it is very exciting as she is always so wild and funny and has many a colourful tale to tell about her chaotic life and travels. I wonder what she will have to say to us, I cannot wait to see her.

Part 4. The first meeting of mystic & pilgrim, Margery Kempe

Today I am tempted to rush through my waking prayers and contemplations because I am excited to get dressed and ready to receive my special visitor, Margery Kempe. The breakfast brought by my attendant seemed as if a chore, although I normally love my food dearly. These days I am long in tooth and the rustic bread seems so heavy and chewy and difficult to swallow today. More haste, less speed I thought wryly, being careful not to crack my tooth on a hard kernel of wheat that escaped the mill. When would she arrive I thought, I do hope before the crowds start to congregate there, those who wished to seek solace from me from my little window to the street. It is still drawn though, as I am an early riser.

You may already know of Margery Kempe from Kings Lynn, North Norfolk in England, as I mention her in my book 'Revelations of Divine Love' but also because she became famous, as did I, for writing a book, the first autobiography written by a woman in England, simply called "The Book of Margery Kempe" which she completed just before her death in the two years between 1436-38. It's strange that both of our writings nearly vanished and were as if remaining hidden, for hundreds of years. Margery's book was lost from the early sixteenth century until it was mysteriously discovered amongst a pile of old manuscripts, in a cupboard in a country house in the 1930s! I wonder which Angel arranged that! I digress, the year is only 1413 and we have not even met each other yet. In your timeline, this would be around six hundred years ago, not that time really matters, but today it does, as I am unusually impatient for her arrival.

As I pace around my tiny cell, I cannot settle to my tapestry or write a single sentence in the church scrolls I am copying. My rosary twists and turns in my hands, more like worry beads than Hail Marys today. Suddenly, Amelia, the cat pricks up her ears and I know someone is approaching outside, as her sense of hearing is far more finely tuned than mine. She jumps up on the rickety wooden chair and meows. I expect she is more interested in the food she may beget from the unknown visitor, than who they are! Cupboard love, I think, smiling to myself and rushing towards the window myself.

I peek out and there is indeed a woman, she is dressed all in white and I gasp with excitement! Is that you Margery Kempe? It must be I thought as no one else has the audacity to wear white as she does and call out to the Lord on the streets in great lamenting and tears as she has become infamous for. In fact, she has been dragged in front of the courts twenty times or so, if the gossip is to be believed, for preaching as a woman about the passions of Christ and begging his forgiveness, all of which is highly unusual and considered heresy by the priests. Till now she has managed to talk her way out of being imprisoned or worse, burnt at the stake as a heretic! I cannot wait to hear how she reasoned with them, in order to be set free. She sounds a courageous and brave woman indeed. What an amazing oracle she must be!

'Margery visiting Julian of Norwich' by Norwich artist, Frances Martin[15]

[15] www.francesmartin.co.uk / Instagram: @frances.martin.norwich

A younger voice than mine, calls out loudly my name, "Mother Julian, are you arisen?" I jumped out of my skin, as I was right next to the window like an excited child, unbeknown to her! "Yes, dear one, it is I. Whom do I have the privilege of greeting so bright and early in the morn beloved child?" I ask politely, although tingling inside. "It is I, Margery Kempe from the Lynn, North Norfolk. I am your humble servant and have traveled far to speak with you if that is acceptable to your holy self. I hope and beg that you have time to hear me as I am deeply troubled and doubting of my position with our Lord Jesus. I have so many things to speak of and ask you that I know not where to start and pray that you will listen to me for my full reassurance regarding my passionate desire to travel as a pilgrim to holy places I have been shewn in visions and portents through the Christ. Oh do say you will consider me in my humble position and hear me out."

Well, that was quite an introduction and considering what I had heard of her pious and religious wretchedness, seemed to be typical of the out-bursts she is so well known for. "Dear one, I begin, please calm yourself and take a seat in the garden, we can discuss all things in a patient manner so that you are come to peace inside and are shewn the deepest unconditional love for which our Lord is the most known. I will ask my attendant to let you in and shall shortly join you myself, beloved one."

This was going to be intense but fascinating. I was to use my discernment as an honoured Anchorite to decipher her delirious but pious rantings and make a clear judgement of her senses and whether she possessed them or if she were possessed of other spirits, as so many had accused her of in the past. I knelt quickly at the small altar I had made under the cross bearing a statue of my Lord and said a hurried but heartfelt prayer for his guidance and assistance in this matter.

I for one knew how it felt to be delirious with fever when upon my death bed at the tender age of thirty, receiving visions which others could have thought were the rantings of someone with a high fever! That was in 1372, over forty years ago now and I am grown to a ripe old age. My heart was now centred in love and empathy as I rose creakily from my kneeling hassock and walked purposefully but a little shakily, towards the tiny door into the garden. I would need to guide her to start at the beginning of her stories, so as not to be confused from the outset with all the detail of her desires. My mind is not quite as clear as it used to be. This was going to be a long but interesting day indeed!

Part 5. Getting acquainted with the mystic, Margery Kempe

Finally, the day has come that I should meet Margery Kempe the visionary and mystic and I am so looking forward to making her acquaintance. "Dame Julian, Mother Julian, please come join me here" she implored as I walked out of my cell into the tiny walled church garden. "I have asked your attendant to bring you the more comfortable chair from your room and am quite happy to be sitting on this bench in the early morning sun. It is so serene here, something I know little about with my 14 children, husband, and a business to run!" Well, Margery Kempe had made herself at home already and was giving me the instructions. I laugh in my wise old way, she is only forty years old and I in my seventies and she has boundless energy it seems.

"Dear One", I begin, "I have heard many, many wondrous things about your good and pious deeds and sincere and deep love for our Lord Jesus. What a very colourful life you have led indeed, it could not be in more contrast to mine own here in solitude these last forty years, from one extreme to another it is surely. Let us start at the beginning, so that I may know you better in person rather than relying as I do here on my own, on the tittle-tattle and tales I am told by the folk through my little window. We know how fanciful such stories can become when handed down through many mouths and I wish to understand everything about you, that I give you the best counsel I am able."

"Oh, Mother Julian that would be wondrous indeed. It be true that I have a husband named John Kempe, ran several businesses, and have even more children than I care to count! I have been from the depths of despair after the birth of my first child (what might be called postpartum psychosis or depression, by your audience), but recovered to have the other thirteen, never do anything by halves myself. I would be what the people today would call an entrepreneur, I started a business an ale house but my staff could not make the beer or sell it properly and it failed miserably and then I started another, a mill, but the horses had other ideas the lazy mares and would not work to grind the flour! A lot of the bairns are grown and moved away now of course, and one is abroad and….she trailed off."

Taking advantage of the tiny pause in the torrent of her conversation, I interjected "can I ask you my lovely, how old are you and when you were born, just so I can get it straight in my head." "Oh! Well I don't normally give away my age Sister Julian", she protested, "but as it's you, I will whisper it and no telling anyone, not a soul, mind? I am forty years young my dear, and don't feel a day over thirty"(cue raucous laughter). I laughed along politely too and then it suddenly struck me that she was born in the very same year that I had my near-death experience with the shewings of the Passion of Christ and the 16 visions! "Margery", I exclaimed, "the reason I think I asked you is that by a very strange coincidence that means you were born in 1373… am I right?" "Yes, I believe I was" she answered" cackling. "Well, I continued, that is the very year that the Lord came to me on my deathbed when I was but thirty years old and shewed me the visions of his crucifixion and his unconditional love for us all in his merciful sacrifice, so many visions were there, that I had to write them all down in short form and then over the last fifteen years I have been working on the long version!"

"Oh, how many years it did take you, but how wonderful", she shouted and stood up in the garden and almost jumped around for joy, "we are for certain sisters of the soul Mother Julian. I had wondered what you could be doing with yourself cooped up in this tiny room for forty years with nothing to do except pray, read and stitch! Marvellous! I am so excited to hear of this, as it is exactly what I also wish to do with my visions and messages from the Lord. So, where was I in my story, oh yes, I began to have these sightings of the Lord more in my latter years and for a certainty, would love to capture these in writings as you have done. To be honest I think my own story would be rather bawdy as I feel to tell the story in a bald and frank way about my wayward way of life, the terrible clashes I have had with the people and priests over mine own lowly way of worship, of which not all approve and for which I have been dragged into court after being thrown unjustly even into prison, one time.

Of course, when I give my testimony they cannot fault me for I do not wear white to exalt myself in social status as a nun, but because I feel I am as a virgin to my Lord Jesus and promised to him only, furthermore they cannot condemn me as a Lollard and send me to the pit in Norwich to be burned at the stake, as I do not preach or teach in public or in contrariness to any of the holy writings of the church. I simply relate what visions I have seen and cannot control my emotions and burst out in laments about my own sinful state with loud tears and crying, even during Mass and it irritates many to the point of exasperation, so that they call for me to be sent away and locked up!

I am not mad, Mother Julian, and this is the reason for my visit to you, please tell me I am not a crazy one when I relate the wondrous things to you that I have seen of sweet Jesus! I think of all the people in England, you are the one to fully understand the sightings I am deeply honoured to have received and to know if they are indeed holy or from the Devil. Oh and going back to my writings, I will write honestly of my many struggles and failings as well as the visions. I have a deep yearning to pilgrimage to the holy places and far-away lands, to repent of my many sins and imperfections, as a way of giving something back to the Lord in any way that I can, for I am a lowly sinner and I am constantly beset by terrible lamenting and sorrows." As she said this she started to beat her chest and call out to the Lord for forgiveness, with tears streaming down her face.

I hobbled to my feet and put my arms around her for comfort, not something I do lightly in these times of recurring plagues, but it is currently safe. You will know now during COVID19 how it feels to be unable to hug and kiss a dear one during quarantine and social distancing. "Dear Margery you are a beloved child of God and he is all good and all-forgiving of each and every one of us, I know this for sure, that "love was his meaning". We will talk of your spiritual inspirations, your works of chastity and the holiness of your tears in the days to come, there is time enough for me to hear about all of these holy things." Margery veritably swept me up in her arms and said that these conversations would normally take many weeks to relate but that she thought she may be able to shorten them into a couple of days for me and laughed again, in her raucous way and the sun came out on her smile again.

I then encouraged her to take a turn around the garden with me, to calm her. As we approached the hazelnut tree, I slowly bent to pick up a couple of nuts of which I gave one to her to behold. This trick of distraction worked handsomely and she looked at me with a smile on her face. "Oh how wondrous that you should have your own supply of nuts", she laughed, "you could make a merry business of selling these at your little window to the world!" Margery was back in business mode and was grounded again. I began to tell her about my thoughts of God and the little hazelnut that I had written about from mine own visions, in order to change the subject.

"Margery, can you believe that Jesus even thought it important to give me a vision of this humble hazelnut, so how much more are you also valuable to him in his love? I will quote to you my understanding of this little nut from my writings:

> And in this he showed me a little thing, the quantity of a hazel nut, lying in the palm of my hand, as it seemed. And it was as round as any ball. I looked upon it with the eye of my understanding, and thought, 'What may this be?' And it was answered generally thus, 'It is all that is made.' I marvelled how it might last, for I thought it might suddenly have fallen to nothing for littleness. And I was answered in my understanding: It lasts and ever shall, for God loves it. And so have all things their beginning by the love of God. In this little thing, I saw three properties. The first is that God made it. The second that God loves it. And the third, that God keeps it. - 'Revelations of Divine Love'

Many of you dear ones worry about your work situation during the virus pandemic and how you will feed yourselves, in light of impending food and fuel shortages. This chaos threatens to sweep many nations into poverty and seems to be reaching a tipping point. Due to the sanctions against President Putin in Russia, economic and financial collapse seem imminent, but have faith and trust that you are as loved, as this hazelnut. With God all things are possible.

I continued my conversations with Margery, "for if God feels like this about this tiny thing, you can rest assured he has you warmly in his heart dear one and you can safely rest in this knowledge and be comforted by it if you should ever doubt it." Margery brightened up in her countenance considerably at this thought and I could see she loved the illustration, so simple but profound. Suddenly she snapped out of her reverie as she was wont to do and verily demanded that she be fed as the thought of the delicious hazelnuts was making her fiercely hungry and she had not yet partaken of her breakfast. "Margery", I apologised, "I am a poor hostess indeed, so caught up was I in these fascinating conversations, please be my guest and come and feast upon what I have. You have luck today, you will not guess, but my attendant especially baked you a cake to celebrate your arrival here and by chance, it is one made of delicious hazelnuts!" Margery looked ecstatic and we walked arm in arm to the little door and entered my room where the smell of freshly cooked hazelnut loaf wafted through the air to greet us!

Thank you for your attention my dear ones and I trust you will want to find out more about Margery's visions in Part 6.

Part 6. Margery Kempe's visions and portents

"Well, it certainly looks as if you enjoyed your hazelnut loaf for breakfast Margery, the mice will go hungry today" I laugh. "Still, Amelia the cat will keep them in line." "Oh she is adorable", said Margery, "I do love a fur fix. I always had a cat when I ran the brewery for the self-same reason. You need a cat for company Lady Julian otherwise it would be intolerable lonely for you, with only your attendant and the ragged crowds outside your little window, for company."

Yes, she is a good companion it's true, and keeps me warm when it is cold. I am sure she can see things that I cannot though. When I kneel and pray here at my little altar, I sometimes see her head turning back and forth when she is looking up in the air at nothing in particular. Maybe it's the angels flitting around or those little light balls people call "orbs" these days."

"Oh yes!" said Margery, "I had a dog called Eddie once who was always staring at things no one else could see. It began when I had my breakdown after the first child was born and I was beset by darkness and it seemed that demons were attacking me from all sides. Eddie would start growling and all the hackles would go up on his back and I knew it wasn't just my own imagination. I was praying incessantly for the archangels to protect us, especially St. Michael and I would feel the room filling with a beautiful golden light and then Eddie would calm down again and I would be able to slumber for a while until the baby woke me again.

I would always ask for a sign that the angels were there when I went out for provisions, as I was terrible anxious and it's a funny thing, but I always spotted a white feather or a tiny coin and knew that they were from the angels, giving me a sign that they were protecting me. I know I sound crazy, but it's happened countless times and I think that if only people would implore and beseech as you and I do, that they too would have their prayers answered. God loves us all does he not, whether we are sinners or religious folk, his love for us is unconditional. Pray tell me what you think on this subject Lady Julian, for I am all ears regarding your opinion of me, a lowly and imperfect sinner."

We continued in conversation for the next hours about the events in Margery's colourful life and why she felt so unworthy. She told me about the constant floods of tears and was openly distressed by them, but could not seem to prevent them, even in church during Mass, which annoyed the friar no end. I could discern a true and pure soul in her, not one possessed of demons as she had been accused. Yes, she was eccentric but I did not think her crazy. I resolved to question her more deeply on her understanding of the scriptures and her devotion to our Lord, so that I may discern the intimacy of her relationship with Christ if she were to be his representative on her planned pilgrimages.

Whilst we talked about the various prayers, readings, and contemplations we each preferred to use, which brought us inner joy and a sense of peace in turbulent times both within and without, I could tell that Margery was becoming agitated again as she started to wring her hands and was pacing around my little room. "Dear Margery, you seem to be troubled, pray tell me what is on your mind that I may console you." Suddenly Margery burst out, "I do not know how to tell you this Mother Julian, but I have something of great import that happened during that time I described with my first child. I fear that you will reject me if I tell you what it is and then I will be dashed to pieces, as you are a beacon of hope to me, that I am genuinely in my senses and one of Jesus' devoted disciples. I could not bear to be judged as a mad woman by you, of all people, as you are so pure and enlightened in your devotion and I am a mere businesswoman of the world, who has come to the Christ later in life."

"Well there is no time like the present," I answered in a calm voice, "you have travelled many miles to visit me here and now it is time to have your questions answered. Please come sit next to me again and tell me what is weighing heavily on your mind." Margery began, a little tentatively for her, to tell me about the time that she had her very first vision of the Lord Jesus. "Oh Lady Julian, it was a trifle scary at first in the middle of the night, my husband was snoring to my right and the baby was snorting to the left and I had lain there a while feeling a bit annoyed not to be sleeping. I had taken my rosary and was saying some Hail Marys and the Lord's Prayer to soothe myself back to sleep, praying for forgiveness of my sins as I always do, when of a sudden Eddie got up, and instead of growling, he started to whine, very softly. I thought to myself, well if you think I am going to get up and let you outside at this hour, you've got another think coming Eddie, but it wasn't that.

He went away from the door and sat in the corner still whining slightly but with his head lowered in a most peculiar way. I don't recall ever seeing him do that. Suddenly I heard a whooshing sound, like the air being expelled suddenly from the bellows at the fireside and it woke me up properly, so I sat up and as I did a bright light appeared above the bed and in the midst of it I could see robes appearing, for all intents and purposes like the one that sweet Jesus wears, and then a woman dressed in white with a blue over-robe materialised next to him and I knew for sure, it was the Christ and Our Lady Mary, Mother of God. The room was suddenly filled with the most beautiful scent of roses I had ever smelt in my life. I must have looked a fright with my hair sticking out in all directions and eyes wide as saucers as I gazed upon them, but then Jesus reached out a hand to me as he sat on the end of the bed and began to speak in the most exquisite gentle voice I ever did hear, on a man.

"Beloved, why have you forsaken me, when I never forsake you? We are come to bring you the love and comfort you have prayed for these many a month. You are a dear child of God and we feel to shew you that your sorrow and tears are not in vain. Dear one, take comfort in the unconditional love we bring, as a reflection of Father Almighty, for he has looked upon you favourably and found you to be a true and humble servant, willing in service to him.

We bring you news of a mission, he is most pleased to announce to you. It is his divine will that you tread that holy path of light and that as you go you may bear witness to those you meet along the pilgrim's way. Bring them comfort and hope in their struggles and assure them of his great love for all his creation and that he never forgets a single soul through all their trials and tribulations. Then Mother Mary turned to me and her gaze was of pure love as she smiled her serene smile and I could feel it emanating out from her and reaching over the bedclothes until it settled around me like a beautiful blanket of bliss.

I will never ever forget that moment for the rest of my life, so astounding was it. I was no longer afraid and I just stared back, I expect with my mouth hanging open like a fool, but I did not care. Here finally, was my comfort during the darkest night of my soul and I wanted to throw myself at their feet in obeisance, except I was hampered by the patchwork quilt and thought better of it. Instead, I lifted my arms out to show my sincere gratitude and bowed my head. As I raised my gaze again, there was nothing there, all was dark again and even Eddie had quietened down and was fast asleep. Deeply in awe, I could not sleep a wink for a long time, but I did not feel tired at all, I felt I could still feel the warm cloak of love Mary had wrapped around me and it comforted me to the core of my soul. When I finally did fall asleep, all I could dream of were angels and cherubs and thrones and golden things. It was wondrous and amazing to me, the like of which I had never seen before.

Well, all good things come to an end and I was rudely woken by griping and a screech from the baby, but no longer grumpy I turned to him in his cot and gave him the biggest smile you could ever have seen on my face. He looked at me almost in surprise and then beamed back a toothy smile at me and it was the first time in my life that I finally felt, all is well in my world."

"Oh how wonderful," I exclaimed, holding both of Margery's hands. "How blessed you be and what loving a portent for you to hold dear to your heart, in your greatest time of need. I have tears in my eyes at the beauty of the love the Lord has bestowed upon you and am greatly encouraged to know more of the unfolding of this pure manifestation of love from our Mother. It greatly warms my heart and has ignited a burning fire in my chest, too. This gift is one to treasure for all time and I feel it will be your way to lead others to the Almighty and his unconditional love for all beings. I am truly and deeply moved."

Margery also had tears in her eyes, but as she turned to look at me, her eyes were burning bright and shiny and her countenance had taken on a glowing appearance as she smiled that special smile again. "All is well my child," I said, quoting from mine own writings, "and all shall be well and all manner of thing shall be well" I whispered and we hung our heads in prayerful thanks. Thank you for listening my dear ones and I trust you will want to find out more about Margery's visions in Part 7.

Part 7. Julian of Norwich and Margery Kempe discuss life

"Lady Julian, that was an amazing luncheon indeed! I do adore a peas-pottage, so warming to the cockles of the heart. Something has been pressing on me to ask you if I may" Margery enquired. "Why yes" I replied, "now that we have been refreshed, let us return to the little garden outside and air our thoughts in the sunshine. I am all ears, my dear."

We gathered our skirts and shawls against the spring breeze and made our way through the tiny door into the high-walled leafy courtyard, scattering blackbirds as we went. Amelia the cat was still inside hoping to be thrown some scraps from my attendant Sarah, who was clearing away our lunch. Margery began with one of the most difficult questions that thousands of souls before her have asked, and millions would ask themselves, in the future. "I, as you Dame Julian, have many poor lost souls coming to me for solace, motherly advice, and a hearing ear. In fact, they call me The Mother in Kings Lynn. They demand that I pray for them and even ask me to tell them if they are saved or not! I do not set myself up to be a teacher, as it is forbidden by St Paul for women to do so in the congregation, but I cannot turn these poor and desperate souls away without some hope. Just as there are many of your audience out there, in the year 2022, who are in a similar situation with the virus, the repeating plagues starting in the 14th Century have decimated half the population of Norwich as we both know, and have left so many with hardly a means to survive, if they did not die of the bubonic plague."

Margery was building up to her big question with the usual preamble... ."Your Lady, the most difficult question I find of all of them to answer is thus: If there is an Almighty God of love, why does he allow such pain and suffering? There are many ways to look at this, but I would love to hear from thine own inspirational visions, not just the Holy writings, how you would explain this seeming contradiction from an all-loving Lord?"

"Well Margery, I have brought my hidden and nearly finished manuscript with me, (I said furtively looking around before I pulled it out from beneath my over-robe), just in case you should ask me this crucial question, which I myself also asked of the Lord Jesus when he appeared to me in the visions on my sick bed, those forty years hence. I was shewn thus: that the outer body feels pain and suffering and it is the way it is on earth, as we know. But if we can accept this, not rail against it and ask "why me, why me"…then our acceptance can assist the inner self to rise to a height of bliss, peace, and love. This is where we find the strength, wisdom, and will to survive and become sovereign over the outer self, living fully in Grace, despite our circumstance."

Margery questioned further, "oh what wise words, yes acceptance is the key to the kingdom of peace and love dwelling within, of course, of course, that is a marvellous way to look at it I must say. But then, I am always asked a second question by the wretched, who are barely eking out an existence and are in a terrible way, covered with fifth and fleas, scratching like a dog, the shreds of clothes hanging off their gaunt pale limbs. That question is "why did God allow sin into the world in the first place if he can foresee all things perfectly?"

I paused a moment to find the place where I had written about this very same question regarding fate and destiny. "Ah here is where I recorded my own conclusions, Margery, after mulling it over in my mind these scores of years since he spoke with me, and believe me, I do not say this lightly after so many years, to come to this conclusion. He shewed me that it was necessary. It troubled me greatly and I did not understand until the Lord explained to me that "all shall be well; and you shall see, yourself, that all manner of thing shall be well.

We are set at naught and not always good in our understanding, but we look to his perfect example of love and it humbles us, just as the suffering does. Through our trials we are purified in a kind of alchemy of our soul and then, no longer slaves to our earthly bodies and inward passions, we become forever grateful for his generosity in suffering and pain. This inner knowing brings forth gratitude, just like beautiful gold that has been smelted and refined and begins to shine, knowing that one day, we will truly understand this all more fully. We are melted down, as the gold, to pure faith and trust that we are beloved, no matter what."

"Well, well, well, I didn't think to compare it to jewellery making indeed, but it seems a gem of an illustration if you get my meaning." She laughed in her hearty way and her face lit up again in that wondrous smile, that I had begun to love already about her. "Well yes, now don't be getting any ideas about selling gold to save their dear souls now will you", I countered in a teasing way. "I know you are a businesswoman, but it wouldn't be seeming for a holy woman of God" I giggled and we both burst out laughing together. "Too true, imagine!" she said, "the priests are already fleecing the sheep with their money-making for prayers and services for the dead". I added more gravely, "but we shepherdesses give them direct confirmation from our own divine revelations of his love to our own person, through the visions, we were blessed to receive, and this we pass on to the people freely without charge."

"You know Margery, I suddenly have an inspiration through our conversation, I will call my book 'Revelations of Divine Love' – now that really will set the cat amongst the pigeons and I shall truly have to guard it with my life, in secrecy, until I can pass it to the Nuns upon my death." I smiled at Margery and she beamed from ear to ear "oooh I do love a secret," she said "and I promise upon me very life that I will never tell a soul of what you write, if you can promise me the same about the one I plan to scribe, of my own visions and travels. I, like you, have been storing these up in my mind over the last twenty years since that first wondrous visitation from Jesus and I am no longer sure I can recall them in the correct order after raising so many children in the meantime. I know God will guide me to make some sense of it all despite the "baby brain" as they call it today."

"I promise you upon the Holy Bible, I will keep yours a secret too," I said "and I admire you for your great tenacity in the face of all the family obstacles to your becoming a woman of God" and we laughed and continued our walk around the old oak tree as we chatted into the late afternoon. I had questions of my own to pose to Margery, I wanted to understand how, despite all that was against her living a life of devotion, she was able to arrange her affairs to give up so much, to become a pilgrim. The only options in these times were to become a virgin nun or wait until your husband died and you were free to dedicate your life to the church. I wanted to know the depth of her desire, despite running a household with 14 children, handing over her business, and leaving her husband and if you join me in part 8, you will find out how and why she was determined to move heaven and earth to do this."

Part 8. How Margery paved her way to pilgrimage

In part seven, we began to see how Margery Kempe and I were truly bringing back the power of the feminine mystic, for healing and nurturing the wound of the patriarchy although at the time we were unaware of the momentous work we were doing and the far-reaching effects it would have. We made valiant efforts to return the balance of the sacred feminine and divine masculine by our hard-won life choices, decisions that were based upon our direct connection to our God or what you may call the Source of all that is today.

This morning it is a new day with more sacred sightings to discuss so we begin the story at the break of dawn and will find out what happens. Margery coughs and I wake with a start. I have rarely had a visitor in this little cell in the last forty years and am unaccustomed to the noises of another human being in the night, especially not the light snoring! I glance over to the mattress on the floor where she is tucked up in a mound of blankets and realise that she is still slumbering. As my eyes close again, a smile creeps across my face. It is delightful to meet and commune with a "sister of the soul" as she had called me. What a wonderful thing, to be in the company of one with like mind, heart, and spirit. A dear soul who has experienced the religious ecstasy of the Lord firsthand, as we both had.

We did not think ourselves mystics at the time but this is now the understanding of these shewings today. We simply felt absorbed or as one with Christ and other angels or saints in these moments of pure bliss when all notion of "self" fell away and a chasm of empty space opened up all around us. We both had a daily practice of devotional prayer and meditation and from this close communication came a drawing close to the veil of the seen and unseen worlds. Although some things we saw, felt, or heard were different from each other, there were also many similarities in the bond we felt with the Lord in these precious moments.

I recalled some of the amazing things Margery had recanted later last night. The way that the Holy Spirit whooshed in, sounding like the rustling of the wind with an air pop like the bellows, and then Jesus would materialise in front of her eyes. Sometimes she would hear such beautiful music that she knew it had come from paradise and it was so lovely that it would touch her heart deeply. She would be overwhelmed by emotion and sympathy for others as it opened her heart to devotion, and this was always the reason she would then begin to sob uncontrollably and wail out loudly.

Or indeed she would sometimes hear the call of a robin or a dove as a precursor to a messenger from God and the more recent of these, she clearly heard the voice of the Almighty as if he were standing right beside her, when he asked her to come to Norwich to visit me. I thought how marvellous a coincidence it was that my favourite bird was Robin Redbreast and felt a surge of gratitude well up in my heart. Now whenever I see him in the future trilling his beautiful song, I will always be reminded of dear Margery whilst she is away, travelling the world as a pilgrim, treading footsteps of light and devotion. She will be healing her own soul, the land she walks upon, and the minds and hearts of those humble ones through to princes and bishops in far-off holy lands. I see her intention is to regale those who will listen with the signs and portents that Christ had given her. With these wonderful thoughts floating around in my mind I drifted back off to sleep again until morn.

Margery jumped and groaned as she swore at the rat that had come sniffing around for crumbs. "Out you foul thing" she hissed as she brushed away the late-night cake crumbs that had attracted her furry visitor. We both laughed and stretched and reached for our rosaries in order that we might pray together whilst still in the warmth and comfort of our beds. As we softly chanted our Hail Marys, the sun shone in with that sharp beam of light across the room. The golden orbs danced around the cell in joy. Today Margery and I expected a more sumptuous breakfast than was my usual meal. She had paid my maid Sarah a sum of money that she might source some lighter, softer bread and even some eggs for our breakfast. Despite her young age, Margery was troubled with her teeth and admitted that too many years of indulgence had rotted them somewhat.

"Oh Lady Julian I am so looking forward to breakfast this morning, I do hope that Sarah knows how to scramble the eggs just so. I love them when they are not like bouncing rubber balls, but soft and creamy". My mouth watered, I couldn't recall the last time I had partaken of eggs due to my simple lifestyle. "It was so kind of you to provide so generously for our comforts these last days" I exclaimed, "it has been a veritable treat and I will miss you sorely when you are gone on your travels."

"Ah, about that," said Margery as she picked her way out of the layers of coverlets and blankets and stretched her arms above her head, yawning. I forgot to tell you how it was that I convinced my husband to let me go travelling and agree to a vow of chastity into the bargain. She laughed heartily as was her wont and that beaming smile was on full display. "I do love your mischievous spirit, Margery, pray tell how on earth you managed to arrange such an audacious thing."

"Well as you know, over the last twenty years I have been the devoted housewife, mother, and business-woman. My husband Mr. Kempe on the other hand had gotten himself into debt, not being as canny as I, with his money. I used to be quite the lady in my younger years, jealous of the neighbours if they should sport some finery I thought better than my own! I was raised with money as you know because my father John Brunham was mayor, five times over. I thought nothing of adorning myself in the best fashions of the time" she said, strutting around the room feigning superiority. I laughed and she continued, "I suppose you would call me a materialist and I expected to be kept in the manner to which I had become accustomed. Poor Mr Kempe could not keep up with me and it wore rather a large hole in his pocket feeding fourteen hungry young mouths as well.

The more visions and conversations I had with the Lord over these years, the more I realised that I needed to reform myself, to become more devoted to Jesus (not my husband)," she burst out laughing. The neighbours were also keen to wag the finger and tell me that my failed businesses were a sign that I was out of favour with God. So I started to attend church regularly three times a day for confession and to atone for my sins I would fast on a Friday. As I became more and more convinced of the joys of heaven and the love of God, experientially, it overtook my need for all these creature comforts, even to the point where I decided, I did not want to sleep with my husband anymore."

"Oh dear," I said, "that must have been a trifle difficult" and blushed. Margery was always brutally honest and I was unused to discussing such things, but secretly I was more curious than ever to know what happened next. We were almost finished with our toilette and the maid would be back from the kitchen soon, so I wanted to hear the story before she arrived with the breakfast. "So how did you persuade him you wished to lead a chaste life as a woman of God?" I inquired.

"As a businesswoman, Lady Julian, you learn to haggle. Everyone has their price and I had John over a barrel. I had the means to pay off his debts and I tempted him to continue a lavish Friday of food and wine, as we used to have before I started the fasting. Eventually, he caved in and agreed to sign a vow of chastity, upon which I promptly announced that I would be off to Norwich to visit you for your permission and blessing, to travel to the sacred sites and holy lands as a pilgrim.

Well, you should have seen his face! He knew he had been tricked good and proper, but a vow is a vow, and stick to it he must!" Now we both burst out laughing and could not contain ourselves until Sarah knocked at the tiny window with our breakfast. It was as wonderful as I had hoped it would be, the eggs were soft and pillowy, the bread warm and scented and there was even a pot of honey! What utter luxury! We laughed as we carried it to the heavy oak table and ate to our hearts' content and suddenly the world seemed to me to be the most beautiful place it ever was, so content was I.

Part 9. Julian gives her blessing for Margery's pilgrimages

"Margery that was the most delicious breakfast I think I have ever partaken of in my life" I crowed "I feel set up for the day ahead and I am looking forward to hearing more of the spiritual meal you received from our Lord, the details of which I am fascinated to hear from you." Margery lustily wiped her chin with the hemp napkin, where a dribble of milk and honey had run down, and thanked maid Sarah heartily for the delicious preparation. Sarah thanked her through the tiny window and cleared away the earthenware plates and mugs we handed to her with a pleased demeanour. It was fun to have such a bold character as this lady to visit Sarah thought, after all these years of serving just Lady Julian alone. She had heard some truly amazing tales as she had pressed her ear up against the oak flap over the serving hatch.

"Now Margery" I began as we exited into the courtyard garden again, where we could talk more privately behind the tall stone walls under the hazelnut tree, "I understand your deep desire to be a servant of the Lord, to follow him wherever he shall lead you and to put your full faith and trust in him to protect you on your pilgrimages. You have paved the way over the years in devoted prayer and confessions and testified daily to the people, of the wonderful revelations you received, about his unconditional love for his creatures, but my concern is that during all this time you were in relative comfort and had the money to feed and clothe yourself, as you wished. Although you have sufficient funds to take you far, it may be that life will seem a lot more challenging and not always as safe as you would like it. I have written much about this in the long text of my book, 'Revelations of Divine Love' and I have been thinking to quote you from a passage that came to mind for you."

We sat together on the bench and chair against the flint church wall, which was now beginning to warm from the rising sun. I reached inside my outer robe for the manuscript I kept hidden from prying eyes and read:

> All men and woman who wish to lead the life of contemplation, need to have knowledge of it; they should choose to set at nothing everything that is made so as to have the love of God who is unmade. This is why those who choose to occupy themselves with earthly business and are always pursuing worldly success have nothing here of God in their hearts and souls: because they love and seek their rest in this little thing where there is no rest, and know nothing of God, who is almighty, all wise and all good, for he is true rest. God wishes to be known, and is pleased that we should rest in him; for all that is below him does nothing to satisfy us. And this is why, until all that is made seems as nothing, no soul can be at rest. When a soul sets all at nothing for love, to have him who is everything that is good, then it is able to receive spiritual rest. - Quoted from an article written by Paula Marvelly, for The Curriculum. [16]

I responded "Yes indeed Margery you will be setting an example for all those who labour in vain, both now and in future generations. I am

---

[16] https://www.theculturium.com/julian-of-norwich-revelations-of-divine-love/

so glad to hear that it seems you have done the inner work and drawn the right conclusions in preparation. Eventually one is ready for the sacrifices that are necessary and only we ourselves know in our hearts when that might be for us. Hence we cannot judge another when they have their own timing and pathway to tread. I, of course, had nearly to die of the plague, to be brought to my senses and dedicate my life to sweet Jeshua. It was only then, when he shewed me the extent of his intense suffering to the point of his feeling almost forsaken by his Father, that I could truly understand what he sacrificed for us."

"Indeed Lady Julian" Margery eagerly responded, "these fine words you have written speak directly to me like an arrow to the heart! I have wasted so many of my years striving for material things and never felt the true satisfaction that comes from having nothing, but the Lord and his bliss in my heart. I feel I cannot truly know what it is to demonstrate my love for him, other than to put my material life to one side as you have done and become a pauper or a vagabond, for Christ. I understand it will be an adjustment of course, but I have been preparing and altering my thoughts and attachments to these things, for many years. I expect your audience may be feeling similarly now that many are unable to work and accumulate material possessions. They may not even know where their next meal is coming from due to the pandemic but are becoming richer in their inner world and closer to God as a result. Perhaps they are also thinking as I do, that these things are not the meaning of life for them anymore and they are hatching a plan like me, to turn their lifestyle around and find a more heart-led way."

I responded "the little sacrifices we make to serve him more fully may seem trivial in comparison but each of us does what he feels able. Your own plans will bring you into hardship and toil walking thousands of miles along dusty terrain, but your heart will be purified by the simplicity of your way. You will have many hours of solitude along your journey to connect your heart and mind to Christ in walking prayers and songs, as a moving meditation where your feet become at one with the earth, your hair at one with the wind, and your face at one with the sun. How wonderful to be immersed in nature and at peace with your God in his beautiful creation. Your footprints made in pure intention will leave steps of light with every tread. I feel somewhat envious as I sit in this cell and will be thinking of you every day, dear one."

I clasped both of Margery's hands and looked her full in the eyes with that smile that had grown between us. You are truly beloved dear sister, you have come to know your Lord and he sees you for who you truly are, a beautiful and shining soul. Those that hear the wonderful things you have experienced of him, will be healed if their hearts are open to hear it. If not, you are free to keep walking on your way with his sweet music in your ears. This will be the adventure of a lifetime and a refining of your soul to the purest gold. I wish you well on your travels and beseech you to write to me when you can through your scribe, that I may come to know something of the wondrous lands you will be travelling through and the glorious churches and holy effigies you may see. Things I have only read about and never seen except through my mind's eye, you will now experience. I will wait in expectation of your return to hear of all of it firsthand. I bless you my child and pray that Jesus keep you close every moment of the way. I hereby bestow upon you my miniature cross with the Lord upon it to keep close to your person in this little pouch and may it bring you protection and blessings along The Way."

"Thank you, thank you a million times my dear Lady Julian. How beautiful it is. I feel deeply blessed to have your permission to follow The Way. I am also honoured you think me worthy of this undertaking and that you have the faith in my true motivation for making it. I will ensure that my scribe records each and every twist and turn in the journey, that you may enjoy and gasp in wonder at the wonderful things I encounter. I wish that your heart may go out to me when you read of my temptations and foes and how I overcome these too. For where there is light there is also darkness and where happiness is also deep sadness and grief and like yourself, I am no stranger to that. But as you have instructed me these days, the alchemy of my soul will be clarified over and over until I beam a light forth from the inside.

You may not even recognise me when I return so ragged and haggard will I be from the dusty roads, my leather sandals will have been changed a hundred times for new and I may have many holes and tears in my garments. My skin shall be full of wrinkles from the wind and sun. But I hope you will still recognise my soul and the things we will always share now in our hearts, about the wondrous mysteries of God that we two have directly experienced and his will for us mere creatures here on earth."

I hugged Margery then for a long time and we both had tears rolling down our cheeks as we rocked back and forth. It was a bitter-sweet parting indeed and both of us had been so enriched by our sharing that we hardly wanted it to stop.

Although I was unaware at the time, this would become a famous moment in recorded history. All the world would read about this from both of our accounts of the first women to write a book and an autobiography in fair England in these times. We did not fully appreciate the emancipation both materially and spiritually that we had consciously fought for, but although our stories were to lay hidden for hundreds of years, and many women would be tortured and burnt in the future witch hunts, our writings were to come to light in divine timing, in an age where many other women were being spiritually emancipated and allowed the freedom, at last, to become fierce in their love of their Lord.

They would now have the culture and tools to throw over the shackles that had been binding and gagging them in silence, in order to stand and shine in their light in front of their God and his pure and unconditional love. This influx of refined souls would awaken and remember their hard-won faith. Trust would finally overcome their fear, acting as a beacon of hope to all beings living throughout the virus, financial turbulences, the chaos of the planet, and the possibilities opening up to change through these things to live in renewed relationship with all beings on earth in harmony and love.

Conclusion

And now I bring to a close this series of short stories having so enjoyed sharing with you dear ones of these wondrous things and I wish you God's rich blessings on your own pathway to inner peace and tranquillity, resting in the bosom of the dear Lord Jesus, to all eternity. Thank you for following me on this journey and farewell to you all.

Postscript I: Scholars pose the question these days if Margery's visions are from God or demons. This is the clarity that she sought here:

In the Middle Ages, phenomena such as voice-hearing were often understood as spiritual experiences, moments of communication with divine or demonic beings. Almost 600 years ago, Margery Kempe visited the anchoress, Julian of Norwich, to tell her about the 'grace that God had put into her soul', including 'many wonderful revelations'. The encounter lasted several days, confirming Kempe's belief that her experiences were given by God. As Margery's words suggest, it was not uncommon, particularly in hagiographies (biographies of saints), to find such experiences ascribed to demonic causes. The phenomenological richness of these very different experiences, described in multisensory terms (including visions, smells, and tactile elements), speaks across the centuries in offering constructive and non-pathological ways in which voice-hearing can be understood.

Margery consulted Julian to confirm that her hearings and conversations with God were real, and the anchorite affirmed her understanding of her spiritual experience. The inclusion of the work of the two women in this exhibition "send[s] an incredibly important message …. That hearing voices isn't new, and that it has been interpreted in more positive ways in the past," said Charles Fernyhough, who helped put the exhibition together.[17]

Postscript II. Rose had heard about the current-day Burning Man festival in the American desert. She was interested to think that the idea wasn't a new one. She knew of The Desert Fathers and Mothers from the third century AD. They built a veritable city of hermit monks and ascetics living in the desert. They saw themselves as "alternative" Christians and followed the principles of Hesychasm described below.

Hesychasm

Hesychasm (from the Greek for "stillness, rest, quiet, silence") is a mystical tradition and movement that originated with the Desert

---

[17] https://www.episcopalcafe.com/julian-of-norwich-and-margery-kempe-are-reunited-in-special-exhibition/

Fathers and was central to their practice of prayer. Hesychasm or the Desert Fathers was primarily the practice of "interior silence and continual prayer." It did not become a formal movement of specific practices until the fourteenth century Byzantine meditative prayer techniques when it was more closely identified with the Prayer of the Heart or "Jesus Prayer". That prayer's origin is also traced back to the Desert Fathers—the Prayer of the Heart was found inscribed in the ruins of a cell from that period in the Egyptian desert. The earliest written reference to the practice of the Prayer of the Heart may be in a discourse collected in the Philokalia on Abba Philimon, a Desert Father. Hesychast prayer was a meditative practice that was traditionally done in silence and with eyes closed—"empty of mental pictures" and visual concepts, but with the intense consciousness of God's presence.[18]

I knew personally of many others, some anchors and other devotees in Norwich who had made this type of vow as well. One such is fellow anchorite, Katharine Manne who passed me messages by word of mouth, via the passers-by. More of her in the next book! For now, let us turn our focus to gaining an awareness of all that we have discussed in light of its relevance to your day. To find out how we are all actors of a sort, living out parts that we preordain and write the script about, in Chapter 3.

---

[18] https://en.wikipedia.org/wiki/Desert_Fathers

CHAPTER 3

We are Actors on the Stage of Life

You may know of the English playwright, that lived a couple of hundred years after I, Julian of Norwich and who was a poet and actor. William Shakespeare was born in 1564 during the early modern period in England. He was a famous writer and wrote the following poem as a monologue, contained within one of his many plays, and I quote :

> All the world's a stage, and all the men and women merely players; They have their exits and their entrances, and one man in his time plays many parts. - Shakespeare, 'As You Like It'

If I can coin the phrase "all the world is a stage" I would like to add my own interpretation to Shakespeare's words (which were meant to describe the seven stages a man experienced in one lifetime). This same idea was philosophised about by the Greeks in much earlier times. I would apply the same adage about the 'stage,' to the many lifetimes in which we seem to be more than just actors and appear to have more lines to remember, than just those in a play! Why it matters that we hone our memories and remember certain incidences from other lives, will unfurl. I will speak with you about the ancient wisdom mysteries, the Akashic records and what we are bound and self-contracted to learn from them.

Rose was not fully aware until she started thinking about past lives seriously some years before she completed her book, that an estimated twenty percent of the world's population believe in reincarnation. In 2022, it was estimated that there were approximately eight billion people on earth, out of which surveys showed that fifty percent of them share similar ideas about a God or higher force, man's origins, the cycle of many lifetimes and where people might find themselves after they die.

Rose had been raised in a fundamental Christian religion in Western society and reincarnation had not been a philosophical concept that she was very familiar with. The idea that the soul, spirit, or consciousness after biological death, carries over into a new life elsewhere or returns to earth in a new physical body, whatever form that may take for whatever reason, was foreign to her. Jehovah's Witnesses do not even believe that the majority experience returning as a soul to heaven, but feel that death is a place of non-existence. This is unless you were one of the human hierarchy that were chosen when on earth, to rule with Christ, known in the bible as the 144,000 elite. She was aware of the Indian beliefs about past lives, returning as various animals or creatures or even a lower caste system, depending on how you had led your previous life. She learnt vaguely that other ancient and modern religions held different versions of this belief, but that was the sum of her knowledge.

In her initial years in Norwich, Rose had read a curious book called "Rising from the Ashes of Jehovah's Witnesses"[19] written by Isisi Allthings, about her journey out of the strictures of a fundamentalist Christian religious cult, to becoming a free spirit. The book describes how her curiosity opened up a few years after 'escaping.' She had made a friend who introduced her to Spiritualism and she learnt much about the loving relatives and ancestors that could communicate with her, through a psychic medium. This belief liberated her from the idea that there is nothing after death for the common folk and brought her the comfort of her grandparents. She had sadly been separated from Poppy and John at the age of ten and was unable to see them before they died, many years later. She began to learn that they were still there in spirit form, supporting her and giving her the strength to fulfil her soul's purpose. One aspect of her path she became aware of through the years, was, to tell the truth about her earlier religious experiences and bring light to what needs to change within organized religion.

Further to reading this book, Rose felt she wanted to do something to contribute to the improvement of life on this planet. To do this she

---

[19] https://linktr.ee/isisiallthings

was drawn to self-development in the form of art, music, therapy and spirituality, which eventually led to her deeper discoveries about past lives. In recent decades, many in the Western world have developed an interest in reincarnation. Rose had not read much on the subject as she wanted to develop self-sovereignty with regard to any thoughts that might fill her head with others' ideas.

She hadn't joined any groups for long periods, just ducking in and out of various belief systems and gleaning what she thought the best principles might be. Curiously though, she seemed to keep stumbling upon information that pointed her towards people she knew or became acquainted with, who seemed to be reincarnated in groups of souls. These teams were based on their shared karma, emotional attachments, and joint projects, rather than through her familial ancestry, although some of these connections were part of her bloodline too.

Another book that had made a huge impression on Rose many years previously, was The Celestine Prophesy, by James Redfield.[20] This was the first in what was to become a series of books. It is an adventure story which speaks to taking heed of energy clues and non-coincidences. It tells of synchronicities that led to spontaneous meetings with like-minded souls with whom we have something to share or engage in. This idea fascinated her, as she could still be a free spirit but also meet with others who were somehow drawn into her orbit, for a reason. This opened up her curiosity and sharpened her skills of observation. Life seemed to gain more purpose again, perhaps even a spark of the curious.

Initially, Rose started to take notice of little signs and symbols which would have passed her by before and began to wake up to the mysteries of life all around her. A world of this nature is magical and brought back the innocent wonder of early childhood to her, remembering the delight in each new leaf discovered and wondering at each tiny creature that crossed her path. She began to understand from reading this book about non-coincidences. That she could take more personal responsibility for her own experiences here on earth. This she grasped, was because she had somehow lived these circumstances before and then spent time away from this planet, processing what she had learnt. She could relate to the idea of planning with her spiritual team, for her return, with a core soul group of

---

[20] https://en.wikipedia.org/wiki/The_Celestine_Prophecy

'actors' in a new 'play.' Some of her team would remain in heaven, agreeing to help her from the unseen realms, to achieve her lessons. They were like a clutch of invisible cheerleaders. This meant that if she remembered what she had come back for, she would be armed with deeper learning upon her return to the spirit world once more, the idea being to eventually break the cycles and remain in spirit. This is a similar idea to that of Nirvana, a completed state of enlightenment.

The idea that she had chosen her religious parents and cult-like lifestyle before she was even born, was a sobering thought. It started to make sense when she understood the broader picture of what this experience had taught her and how she had grown from it. This naturally led to looking at how this might work if we have repeating lives in many different circumstances. Each one perhaps teaches us something new, refining our soul in a process of alchemy, which I will discuss further on in this book. Many topics came up for scrutiny on this pathway, deeply religious lives of devotion or oppression, betrayal and abandonment. These seemed to be repeating themes in her own past lives, which were different from the challenges of others in her soul group. She realised that each soul was on its own unique learning curve and proceeded to dive deeper into these realisations to open up the details for her readers to ponder.

Rose decided to narrate this book as if she was her own over-soul or the part of her that had never been a human existence, but only a form of awareness in heaven. Some would describe this as another dimension where time does not exist but where one's consciousness knows all that has happened to us. A place where we exist in a pure state of bliss. Our Higher Self.

When she was last on earth, Rose had begun to wake up to a remembering of past lives when she was around fifty and living in London. There she enjoyed talking and practising with various shamans and psychic mediums. Not something that would have been approved of in many of her past incarnations as a devout Christian, including mine own. Some of her key lives, you are going to find out about in these pages, because these are the ones that came up the most strongly for healing in a shamanic reading.

Eventually, hundreds of years after her incarnation as Julian of Norwich, she learned to expand her understanding of spirituality over time, which was very liberating for her. I smile wryly at the freedom she had found for herself, that we had not been privy to in the Middle Ages and I was glad that she was not taking her hard-won religious liberty for granted. I watched with great interest as she enjoyed discussing reincarnation more and more and how she slowly discovered that humans can repeat ancestral or past life trauma patterns, which may be impacting their current personal and global life, in strange ways.

I, Julian, undertook a lot of research on her past lives in the years following her move from London to the Norfolk countryside. I constantly had my head buried in her Akashic records where each lifetime is imprinted in a virtual library. Rose had needed some respite from the hustle and bustle of the big city and now she had begun to understand why she needed to move to medieval Trowse Newton. I was calling her gently, like the whispers of her soul.

As with the dance of a spider on a web, strand after strand was being spun and stretched, making the connections needed to weave the web of her life and perceive the whole story. Of course, it's so easy to see it all in hindsight now, up here on my fluffy cloud, but at the time, it was a steady evolution. Many have the experience of seeing their whole life flash before them if they have an NDE (near-death experience) or indeed when they are on their deathbed. Rose felt she didn't want to regret being unconscious during her lifetime, she wanted to understand and heal before it got to the point of her own passing. Perhaps she didn't want to have to come back and deal with her unfinished business.

Rose was not only an author but had taken up songwriting many years previously which had also assisted in alchemising the deepest, saddest feelings and thoughts she had throughout her life and transforming them into lighter perceptions. One such inspiration came from a lovely lady she had contact with that was able to channel Light Language. This is a form of coding from the spiritual realms that had become a strong practice up to and during the pandemic. Many were being called to bring through beautiful sounds, codes and hand mudras along with messages in foreign tongues or ones that they translated into their own language.

These codes seemed to be tips for weaving the best tapestry in our daily lives and Rose felt inspired to arrange these thoughts into a little song, with lyrics which read:

'Life's tapestry'

Verse 1
Letting go of the old
Breathe....
Welcoming in the new
Breathe....

Chorus
Take each day as it comes
Each day's a new day now
No final destination
Merely one chapter
in your life's tapestry

Bridge
Enjoy sewing your magic thread, make it good, make it good
Enjoy sewing your magic thread. happily making it loving

Verse 2
Connecting into nature
Breathe....
Seeing the magic around you
Breathe....

Chorus
Take each day as it comes
Each day's a new day now
No final destiny
Merely one chapter
to your life's tapestry

In its simplicity she understood that these thoughts encourage us to live now in each moment, remembering we are just like an actor on the stage of life. Yes to learn from the past, and to hold a vision of a bright future, but to just allow the tapestry to unfold in all its glory one day at a time, in this lifetime. Only by looking back at the completion of our life, would we see the beauty of the whole garment and understand it, in all its intricacy. Hindsight is a marvellous thing. How beautiful to have woven a luminous cloth of love, peace and happiness.

Now to get into the nitty-gritty, in the next chapter we will take a closer look at the curious breadcrumb trail Rose was drawn along. She will explain using the keys she gives us, what the clues were, not only to her medieval past lives but the understanding of them. These in turn helped her release her past patterns and finally heal from the repeating patterns in her life cycles. In the chapters following this, I will take you on a deeper dive into a handful of the most intriguing medieval characters and what she came to learn from them.

CHAPTER 4

Keys to understanding past lives

In this chapter, I will list many key clues and synchronicities. These are likened to beads of light that I scattered along the winding paths, for Rose to discover. Many of these brief insights will then be developed in the following chapters. I wish for you, dear reader, to garner a deeper understanding of the assumptions Rose made about her own past lives and how she developed a far deeper understanding of their significance as the years unfolded and she began to heal. May this in turn inspire you to similar exploration and insights, for your wellbeing and awakening.

ʔ Keys to understanding the Trickster archetype

The first tough lesson Rose had begun to learn eight years ago, was the Trickster energy. She left her frenetic lifestyle, having lived in London for sixteen years. Initially, her first home in Norwich was with Jade, the daughter of her childhood friend Julia. I, Julian of Norwich, had guided her to the lovely flat in a converted old mill. Trickster energy had already started to cause issues when she was preparing to leave London – on the way home from Rose's leaving drinks, she and her sister Annabel had toppled and fallen drunkenly on an escalator. Rose's knee had been wounded on the grilled metal stairs. The two sisters had to call a paramedic and go hospital that evening and have themselves checked over. This had turned into an all-night session in the emergency unit! Once she had moved up to Trowse Newton, in the summer of 2015, Rose had to visit a local walk-in surgery to have her knee dressed every couple of days. It took a long time to heal and needed antibiotics to stop the infection.

Rose had then signed up to her local surgery, which also happened to be just a little way up the street from my shrine. It is next to St. Julian's Church, in Rouen Road, which she often walked past. This location will be significant as you will see later in this chapter. Subsequently, more things had begun to go awry, as if there was a weird energy around her. She had left the bath running one evening when talking to a colleague, and the overflowing water had flooded the whole corridor, running through into her bedroom and draining through to the four flats and corridors beneath, shorting out the electricity. Then the toilet broke and took an age to get the landlord to fix it. A month or so later she developed an abscess and had a tooth extracted and then the molar on the opposite side crumbled a week later, so she had to have it capped. She hadn't even found her dentist yet, so had to go to the emergency dental hospital. I felt compassion for her during this time, but I knew she would have to overcome these challenges, to learn about the Trickster energy.

By this point, Rose was lonely and pretty stressed. She looked online for mind, body and spirit events and saw that there was a coffee morning over at the Swaffham Spiritualist Church. She needed some support and resolved to get the bus there. Setting off a little late she was hurrying along and suddenly tripped over. Propelled forwards onto the pavement, she had broken her fall by landing right on her almost healed knee! Although she had been wearing jeans, her wound had started to bleed and she was in tears, but still determined to get to the bus on time. When she arrived in Swaffham, I watched her stop off at the chemist's and buy some plasters and wound disinfectant to clean up. Then, despite her tears, she put on her bravest smile and walked along the high street, until she found the little spiritualist church tucked away in a side street.

As Rose approached, the lady that runs the church, Jayne, gave her a very warm welcome and a hug. She had really needed and appreciated that. Walking into the hall a little early, the first lady she saw, she had felt drawn to and asked if she could have a tarot reading with her. It was a woman who called herself The Number Witch[21], a good numerologist. She said "of course" and Rose took a seat whilst she organised the sets of tarot cards on

---

[21] https://vikkifosdal.wixsite.com/thenumberwitch

the tablecloth, along with some beautiful crystals. She seemed such a kind lady and Rose could sense her healing energy washing over her. She began to slowly calm down. As the reading progressed it was very uplifting for her and the lady reached across to get the other set of cards she worked with. At that point, she caught the tablecloth as she leant over and all the cards from three decks were scattered all over the floor. Rose helped her to pick them up and when they had finished, said "oh, I recognise this energy. It's the Trickster energy!"

Rose hadn't heard this term before, so she went on to tell her a story about a man she had been involved with that had used the same energy around her, once. She explained how she had protected herself and thwarted his interference in her life, even preventing him from astral travelling into her flat. Rose was fascinated and told her that before she came here today, her flatmate Jade had screamed out as she had discovered a huge spider in her bedroom and they had captured it in a glass it was so big and hairy and had taken a photo. When Rose had spoken with her healing friend May from Portugal on Skype that same evening, she was relating the story of the spider and sent her a photo of it and May explained immediately that it was the Trickster energy.

The second mention of it that week had made her prick up her ears. The Number Witch had explained that Rose would need to get some help with clearing this Trickster energy. She had already tried this several times with the forensic healing methods she had learnt previously, but it was obviously still hanging around. For example, when she had a Skype video with Julia or May, as soon as they began talking about a certain person in London who she suspected was carrying the archetype of the Trickster energy, their wifi connection would become erratic and the call would drop out, even though there was good bandwidth.

Rose then received a third confirmation that this was indeed what was happening. A dear friend of hers, Jasmine, had mailed her a mind, body, and spirit magazine during that time. Coincidentally it had contained an article about Trickster energy. It explained that things would go wrong when this energy is in play and that the signs of the presence of this energy were often spiders or beetles! She began to realise why some people have a fear of spiders if this shapeshifting were true!

Armed with this knowledge, Rose searched the internet and discovered that there are shamans who can shape-shift into animals or creatures and use them as their muse if you like. This is what The Number Witch had explained to her. She was canny enough to know that the ex-boyfriend was spying on her when she caught sight of a beetle on the beach, where she was sunbathing in Spain. She picked up on the energy and blocked him. It wasn't until she got home and he called round and accused her of being a witch, that she had her confirmation. She tried to remain as innocent as possible and, keeping him on the doorstep, she asked him why he thought that. He answered that he could no longer astral travel inside her flat when she was away! She definitely was not inviting him inside anymore after that, and bade him a final farewell!

Trickster energy is mischievous and seems to cause chaos, Rose discovered. It's a disruptor, which is sometimes needed to bring about a shift or change. As she researched further it seemed it was a sign of things being shaken up, going against convention, breaking the rules and greater awareness being stirred. Even Wikipedia writes about this archetype which has played out in many well-known movie characters over the years. I quote from Wikipedia regarding the meaning of Trickster:

> In mythology, and in the study of folklore and religion a trickster is a character in a story (god, goddess, spirit, human, or anthropomorphisation) which exhibits a great degree of intellect or secret knowledge, and uses it to play tricks or otherwise disobey normal rules and conventional behaviour.[22]

In the present day, Trump, the recent US President, could personify the trickster energy. Considering all those previous instances, led Rose to ask for help, as she felt something needed clearing energetically from the flat where she lived. It is an old converted mill but she felt there were even more ancient connections beneath the foundations and perhaps some negative entities from centuries past. She since discovered that there was an early Scandinavian church on the site and wondered if some of the disturbances were due to these ancient energies. The church had been in existence around 1186-1210 but there didn't seem to be anything traumatic written about events around it except for the Viking conquests, which

---

[22] https://en.wikipedia.org/wiki/Trickster

started in 840 ad. It didn't have a cemetery so there probably weren't any ghosts haunting the site.

Rose was left to explore the possibility that a connection to aspects of this negative person she had moved away from in London, had come up here with her 'in spirit' as an attachment. A Shaman she knew well, with whom she had worked on previous clearings in London, tuned in and said that yes, some of this person's entities had attached themselves to her energy. This was all rather a steep learning curve, but Rose felt that this person personified the Trickster energy in the way that he behaved. She also remembered that energies and entities can attach themselves to physical objects and thought about all the times this person had sat on the sofa that she had brought with her when she divided things up with her sister during the house move!

All in all, she decided to go back to Swaffham Spiritualist Church for help and was given the number of a "ghost buster" called Kevin. When she called him, he explained that he is actually a Catholic and conducts exorcisms. Rose told him that she wasn't a Christian anymore, but he reassured her that it wasn't necessary and that his methods could still work.

Kevin 'tuned' in over the phone to see if it would be necessary to come over to do a clearing. He decided that there wasn't a poltergeist at the flat and that Rose could simply clear the energy herself. He told her that the most effective way would be to get a cross, holding it up in each corner and room of the flat and to say "in the name of Jesus Christ and Archangel Michael I command you to leave this flat, this apartment block and this street and be dissipated out to the universe in unconditional love." He explained that the name Jesus Christ had a powerfully pure and compelling energy to it (as is the same of other ascended masters) and it had never failed to work for him when stated with authority and without fear. Rose was already familiar with this type of clearing, having recently learnt this method at the healing course she had attended six months before, with her childhood friend Julia.

Rose then discovered a key clue and started to understand how past lives could be impacting current life circumstances. Another of her psychic friends had 'tuned in' and thought that she had a past life with this person in South East London, who was in fact, her sister's boyfriend. She said that in that past life they were a couple, in medieval times. When they separated, he took Rose's child away from her and had a curse put on her. Rose felt out of her depth and realised she was in her spiritual apprenticeship and had better start putting some of her recent learning into practice, in her own life. She conducted the clearing, holding up the crucifix and scattering salt into the corner of each room for good measure. She had heard that this also helps clear negative energies. Further on in this book, I reveal many more details of the past lives that Rose discovered in medieval times, that weave together to fit the psychic's description. This particular instance is reflected upon in Chapter 6 in the story of Mary Boleyn when Henry VIII cast her aside and had her son sent away to a college to be educated.

Returning to the house clearance of the Trickster energy, later on that day Jade returned home and immediately noticed that the energy in the flat had lifted. Rose told her about the little clearing ceremony she had conducted with the cross and salt and Jade was really pleased it had worked. Maybe there was something in it after all! So this was the start of Rose waking up to the idea that we are in control of what can and cannot affect us and that so much more is going on behind the scenes, than just our day-to-day circumstances, with their frustrations and hardships. Perhaps it was all a mirage, she thought, like a holographic universe.

She began to realise that challenges seem to be thrown at us, but that it is all part of a Matrix-like computer programme. Our role is to stay present in the moment and have our spiritual Ninja virtual reality glasses on, or be like the movie hero Nero, played by Keanu Reeves! For her, it was also the dawning realisation that here was a story of female oppression, which was deeply prevalent in medieval times, when thousands upon thousands of European women were named as witches at the drop of a hat and burnt at the stake or drowned on the ducking stools. According to her psychic friend, that past life partner's shunning actions towards her were in Tudor times and had left an ancestral imprint, which could still be carried in her auric field or spiritual DNA for centuries to come! Strange thoughts indeed.

The old patterns are difficult to release, although not impossible, as Rose was starting to find out. Later in this tale, you will find the ways and means discovered, to set ourselves free from religious and other oppressive regimes past and present. Also, how to learn to step into the sacred feminine goddess energy, without anxiety. But for now, knowledge and remembering, are the first important steps on the path to recovery.

⅔ Keys to location coincidences, between past and present lives

Returning to the account of Rose's earlier days in this medieval city in her 21st Century life, during the first few months of living in this area of Norfolk, she had heard tales from a good friend about a shrine to Julian of Norwich, mentioned earlier. Coincidentally, it was just a stone's throw away from where Rose was living, but she hadn't thought much of it at the time. Although everything was bombed in World War Two, the chapel and a replica of Julian's anchorite cell were rebuilt. Further information is available on the Norfolk Churches blog entitled: St Julian, of Norwich.[23]

Some months after clearing the trickster energy, Rose moved away from The Mill to another area in this ancient City of Norwich, to a tiny alleyway opening onto the middle section of Magdalene Street, Golden Dog Lane. She had found a little attic flat to rent in Brent House, above an ancient courtyard in the Colgate area. It seemed so magical at the time and had a special energy about it. There is something historically interesting about this particular location and this was also to be a significant location synchronicity, as she was to find out later.

⅔ Understanding key clues from psychics and shamans

A few months later, in March 2016, Rose had booked a shamanic reading with The Wayfinder[24] from London, whose website is linked in the footnotes. This was pivotal to her awakening to her past lives, the time was ripe for her to take notice. The whole journey, which he conducted remotely, was about medieval lives with unjust passings and deaths that needed clearing and healing. I will summarise the events he saw because much of what he said hadn't made sense to Rose or himself at the time. The keys to understanding them quickly began to unfold for her afterwards, as I made sure in spirit. A week later I started giving Rose clues about the

---

[23] http://www.norfolkchurches.co.uk/norwichjulian/norwichjulian.htm
[24] https://www.andrewwayfinder.com

mysterious meaning of the visions he had for her, which led her on a rich historical journey into this fascinating medieval city of Norwich. They revealed that the places she had lived or worked near, had been a series of locations where her own past lives had lived too. Following this discovery, she was then to begin to grasp the relevance of remembering, for her healing and growth.

Shamanism is the oldest form of spirituality known, dating back over 35,000 years and is found in its different forms in many indigenous cultures around the world. Traditionally if you are having a 'journey', reading or clearing with a shaman, you will lie on the floor and the shaman will lie next to you and go into 'Dreamtime'. This will be done in silence and the client does nothing except relax and allow themselves to drift. Rose was drawn to this practice and had a few such experiences when she lived in London and always found them to be very cathartic and healing. In this case, Peter was tuning in from London. She had only met him once at a shamanic workshop he ran and that was a few years earlier, so he may not even have remembered her personally, but she remembered and trusted him. Peter conducted the journey on his own and then sent it to her electronically.

He knew Rose had moved away from London and was now living in Norfolk, but that is all. In his opening sentences, he asked for a blessing and healing for her and saw himself fly up in the sky from London and be transported over the land, which from his description, sounded like Norfolk with a coast to one side and flat marshy or boggy lands in the other direction. This she supposed would be the North West of the county underneath The Wash, which used to be marshland going back thousands of years. He was brought down next to the coast and saw a solitary building with a coastal road which then joined a road from inland. At the junction was a street lamp or lantern. He could see Mother Bear in the shadows, which would be a power or spirit animal in the Native American culture. When Rose researched the Bear animal totem for its meaning she discovered that Bear symbolised wisdom, diplomacy, and healing. Just after Rose wrote this paragraph, she noticed an email in her inbox from The Shift Network and as it was totally relevant, she quoted it here:

The images in our night-time dreams are powerful… and when they're animals, there can be all sorts of interesting ways to explore their meanings, and gifts. Today's dream-worker knows that a tiger, cow, or dove that emerges in our dreamscapes holds particular qualities, gifts, even "medicines" that –– should we choose to explore and bring them to life within ourselves –– can help us to transform for the better…exploring the spirit animals that appear in our dreams can illuminate characteristics, habitats, and "personalities," which can bring us more courage, healing, joy, and creative spark. In this video the shaman, master dreamwork teacher, and bestselling author Robert Moss, shares amazing stories about his own healing experience with the Bear, insights on your connection to the Bear's warrior and goddess energies, how the animal spirits in your dreams help transform you, and more."- Ben Hart, The Shift Network. [25]

Rose realised this was an important synchronicity. She had previously become aware of these recurring events which seemed to be more than mere coincidences, as they were happening over and over again. She found that when she focused on something, other information seemed to appear, like another piece of the jigsaw, leading her towards completion of the puzzle. Although the puzzle seemed a never-ending one, an ongoing process rather than a finite goal.

So, returning to the reading, as Peter the Shaman walked towards the medieval crossroads on the lonely Norfolk coast, in his visions he noticed a tall wooden pole with a basket hanging off it. When he looked closer, it contained a skeleton. He was met there by Gandalf, who is commonly known as the wizard character with the pointy hat and long grey beard of The Lord of the Rings fame. It is conjectured that he could symbolise to some an aspect of Jesus Christ, his death and resurrection. His character came from another land to help people, share his wisdom and uplift them. He travels extensively like a pilgrim and is a healing element in the story. Peter also saw that a third guide was there, Anke. The Egyptian spelling is Ankh and symbolises the cross with a loop above. It seems that these

---

[25] https://theshiftnetwork.com

guides Peter was seeing had religious symbolism and were present to do with death and healing in some way.

Sure enough, Gandalf had come to help. In Peter's vision, Gandalf blasted a bolt of lightning at the base of the wooden pole and it came crashing down along with the hanging cage or gibbet as it was known, containing the skeleton of a dead person inside. This would probably have been a condemned highwayman or bandit, serving as a warning to others to prevent theft on the roads. Gandalf then dragged everything along some secret smugglers' paths until he came to a moonlit pond where he deposited it all into the water. Everything sank except the wooden pole, so Mother Bear approached and taking it in her mighty paws, dived to the bottom of the pond, burying it in the mud.

The scene that followed is one in which everything is dissolving and returning to nature. The metal quickly rusted in the healing water and returned to the elements too, as a form of alchemy. Mother Bear swam to the end of the pond and they followed her up a stream, an underground drain and through brick tunnels. Eventually, they clambered up through a grating into a small graveyard, in a larger town. The three were then observed placing a bunch of yellow flowers, and daffodils, onto a gravestone where a mother and child had been buried. It seems they had died of an illness but had been forgotten and the flowers were an act of honour and remembrance for them.

The shaman then became aware of a freshly dug hole by the side of the grave, which he thought was a second grave, but he observed Mother Bear carrying a tree over to it, burying its root ball in the ground. Gandalf took a watering can and poured a milky crystalline liquid onto its roots. As it became night, the tree seemed to soak up the liquid and start to glow from the base upwards until the whole tree was illuminated and shining golden, in the night. The guides now took Peter up above the churchyard, which is in the centre of the city and as he looked down, he saw a huge triangular energy line of connection between this church, the lonely cottage on the coast and the pond in the fens to the West.

They came back down and this time he saw stone steps leading down to the undercroft of the church, where there was a crypt. Once in the basement, he saw a sarcophagus or carved coffin which was medieval, containing a lady buried there. There was a sword symbolizing power and protection on one side and around the other sides were jewels, big white pearls. The sword seemed to be that of someone who had pledged his life to this lady and had taken care of her. The pearls were glowing brightly. The three guides then left the sarcophagus, climbing back up the stairs and closing the door, they re-sealed everything within.

Peter felt these scenes depicted unfinished business and improperly buried souls that had not been at rest or had been betrayed. The healings bestowed upon them had now put them to rest and had given them a chance to heal. These could have been soul agreements or contracts that needed resolving and had now been symbolically alchemised in the element of healing water or buried in mother Gaia. The tree had been planted and watered, symbolising new growth. The golden glow of the tree and pearls seemed to denote a beautiful healing of these particular events. Pearls could also have symbolised that she came from wealth, but in the spiritual community today they are seen as signs of inner wisdom and consciousness.

Peter had now come to the end of his journey for Rose and said that he had no idea what any of this meant for her, just that there was a lot of healing energy. Having listened to the recording eagerly, she also had no idea what it all meant for her either. It all seemed very strange, but since listening had piqued her curiosity, she undertook some research to see if she could undercover any matching stories in the annals of history.

What she fairly quickly realised, was that she may have had a strong religious past in the county of Norfolk, in fact, more than one lifetime and very unusual existences they were too. The other fascinating thing is that she also started to realise that some of her friends had parallel lives alongside hers, in those times. The more she researched, the more she became convinced that some of them had several medieval lives, back-to-back. This also led to Rose awakening to the thought that we are all just flowing in and out of repeating cycles, in multiple lives with a chosen set of souls, for some reason. The task she now set out on, was to find out what that meant for them all as a group and to see if she could heal this seeming "glitch" in the system, where unfinished business caused repeating pain and suffering.

A week after Rose's reading, she stumbled across her first key coincidence. She was scrolling through her Facebook feed when she came across a photo by a talented local photographer, on which he had posted beautiful shots of medieval Norwich. As she looked through the many stunning compositions, one image suddenly caught her eye. It was taken on a hill above Norwich with a tall wooden pole and a metal basket on top. She saved the photo so that she could return to look at it again.

'Basket on a pole, Kett's Heights'

Although it was similar, this example was a lookout shipping brazier and not the gibbet cage that Peter saw, it piqued her interest and she started reading the description of the image, at the bottom of the picture. It seems the photo was taken from Kett's Heights and the old basket or brazier would have been filled with burning wood as a beacon. At night this would have been seen by passing ships, in particular, to guide them along the East Anglian coast. There was a reference to Robert Kett which interested her, as this was a character she knew nothing about. She began some research and soon found out that he had been a very influential character from Wymondham, a yeoman farmer who led a peasants' rebellion in 1549. He and his brother William Kett had died a hero's death afterwards, being hung in chains on Norwich Castle and Wymondham Cathedral respectively.

Suddenly, Rose realised that there was a connection to the gibbet cage that Peter had seen swinging above the wooden pole. Being hung in chains was the device that some criminals were punished with at that time. They would be trapped in a cage and left to die, out in the elements for weeks afterwards, eventually eaten by carrion. It was horrifyingly fascinating how barbaric those times were. Perhaps his was one of the improperly buried souls Peter had mentioned, with an unjust passing? Rose resolved to find out more and there was no shortage of interesting information about Kett's life and why this had all come to pass. This we will delve into further along, in Chapter 12.

⑀ Keys to understanding image links to past lives

During that summer in 2016, Rose went along to the Swaffham Spiritualist Church again to sit in a spiritual development circle. The group were asked to choose one tarot card from a pack and then another person in the group was to take it home for a week and see if they could read anything energetically, as a message for the person they were allocated. A young man named Steve took Rose's card which was "The Queen of Pentacles." Here is a transcript of what he wrote down after he had tuned in and meditated on it for her, over the course of that week. The pieces of paper he wrote the information on were small and scribbled in pencil so it was not that easy to read. Rose took photos of them displayed below. One shows a small image where he drew a dome with some flowers next to it. Here was his explanation to her of what he saw:

Page 1 - "Tarot card for Rose. I meditated and asked my guides for information about Rose on Friday 8 July at 11.20 pm. The Tarot card was the "Queen of Pentacles". Visually I could see the number four on the back of the card and the word Shalom (this means peace). I could see silver/blue colours then a small circle of bright pink/purple. There were podiums numbered one, two and three, PTO. Shown a pink teddy bear" (Rose guessed that the bear was a message and reference to the Mother Bear in her shamanic reading).

So far this didn't ring any bells with her particularly, but then he turned over the little piece of paper and this is what he had drawn on the other side. Page 2. "the picture of a dome shape. Shiny in appearance with yellow flowers in a bunch above it to the right. Looks like a daffodil shape." The image that drew Rose's attention immediately, was the dome with the yellow flowers. It seemed to her to be the same as the vision that the shaman had, of the grave of a mother and child in a churchyard. If one looks at the image, what Steve calls a dome, is in fact, a tombstone. The shaman had seen a bunch of yellow daffodils being given to the grave, exactly the same as Steve. Steve also referred to it being shiny in appearance (perhaps the golden tree the shaman had seen was lighting it up in the night?) Now Rose had to unravel the mystery of who was buried there and why they needed this healing. What did the tree symbolise and the yellow flowers? Which churchyard were they buried in and was it in Norwich? This was to become clearer in due course, but all in Divine Timing.

Rose attended this same spiritualist development circle again a week later. This time she was working with a different older gentleman who gave her the name "Julian" as a message. She thought about whether she knew anyone named Julian and could only think of an-ex boyfriend from years before with whom she had no more contact. It wasn't until a couple of weeks later that she was reading about my character, Julian of Norwich and she suddenly realised that the name was connected to Dame Julian: the Anchoress. I was doing my best here in spirit, to inspire the idea that I, Julian, am around her watching over her or even that I was her, in a past life. At this stage, she didn't know what to make of this information but she knew somehow it was important. She kept the little papers, making a mental note to listen to the shaman's reading again. She was now avidly following the paper trail that I was laying out for her.

₹ Keys to understanding bodily or experiential symptoms

A couple of weeks later in July 2016, Rose was invited to a birthday party by her new friend Teal, whom she had met at a soul rescue circle and meditation they had both attended. They were camping out in the countryside and Teal invited her to sleep over, as they had put up some big tents for the guests. It was a fun night and a gaggle of Teal's girlfriends stayed over too. The next day was hot and sunny and a group were sitting around talking over a BBQ brunch. The subject of healing came up and Rose offered one of the ladies a Reiki healing.

After she finished the energy work and had cleared her aura, the woman sat up and wide-eyed exclaimed that she'd had a religious experience. Rose had noticed a family wounding timeline in her mind's eye which she had asked for permission to clear with the woman. After giving her consent, Rose felt the energies clearing like reflecting mirrors going into infinity both backwards and then into the present day. She wanted to know if the lady was prepared to break this pattern now so that her future timeline could also be cleared. She consented and that is when she had seen the faces of all her relatives and then older ancestors come in for healing.

Rose was amazed that this was such a powerful experience and still glowing from it, got chatting to Teal about writing her autobiography. Teal said that she also wanted to write her biography, so they agreed we would discuss it further. Later on, over lunch, the conversation turned to Rose's discovery of Julian of Norwich and how she had been thinking about her own past lives. For instance, she explained that she had drawn the comparison with herself to Dame Julian, who had written an account of the passion of Christ's visions that she had experienced in her early thirties, in the late 14ᵗʰ century. She related to Teal that it had then taken Julian twenty years to write the full account of the visions she had of the passion of Christ. She told her that the account had begun when she was on her death bed at the age of thirty and she was being served her last rites. Rose said she thought it was similar to her own story, as it had taken her over twenty years to put her thoughts down on paper and publish this book. This is the account of her own awakening and its significance for all that read it.

Rose told Teal that she had also read about the previously mentioned Christian mystic named Margery Kempe. This fascinating character had come to visit Dame Julian to ask her if she thought her visions and loud weeping were true signs of inspired messages from Christ if you remember from the short story series A Day in the Life of Julian of Norwich in Chapter 3. Rose related how Margery had employed a cleric or scribe to write for her and was planning to go on several pilgrimages to holy shrines and sites in other lands. Julian had assured her that she thought her visions were from Holy Spirit and so Margery had left to go forth on her travels, with Julian's blessing. After many years Margery eventually finished her book, when she was around sixty, four years before her death. Rose began to draw comparisons with her friend Teal and many parallels seemed to arise over the months, as she put pen to paper for a second time.

Whilst Rose was standing in the hot sunshine recanting these tales to Teal, she suddenly had a thought and expressed that perhaps if she had been Julian, maybe Teal was Margery, in a past life. All of a sudden, they both felt full of goose-bumps, truth bumps or angel tingles as Rose liked to call them. Despite the heat of the day, all the hairs on their arms raised up, like an electric current passing through them, simultaneously. This experience began occurring more and more with a few friends such as Teal and Julia over the following years and only seemed to occur when Rose was talking about things of a mystical or spiritual nature, especially in connection with their past lives. It is what Teal and Rose came to recognise as "experiential" bodily proof, that what they are discussing is of import for them or is a personal truth. It has also been described by others who experience this as a 'shift' or using one's body as a pendulum, instead of holding one in the hand. The body conducts an energy impulse as if it were answering a 'yes' the same as a pendulum would swing to a 'yes' or a 'no' position.

Rose had experienced these physical phenomena before when she attended a week-long healing training workshop in 2014, with her friend Julia. They learnt there that when they were on the right track with something, they would get these body shivers as a confirmation, which the trainer called a body "shift". Rose felt very excited about this. It meant that she had met Teal for a reason and had probably lived a medieval past life at the same time as her. Why was this significant and what did they need to remember? Observing their reactions in the heavens, I then gave Rose further keys helping her to draw a deeper understanding and conclusions about these past lives.

Teal's past life as;

Margery Kempe (b.1373 – died after 1438) was an English Christian mystic. Margery was known for writing through dictation 'The Book of Margery Kempe', a work considered by some to be the first autobiography in the English language. Her book chronicles Kempe's domestic tribulations, her extensive pilgrimages to holy sites in Europe such as Rome and the Holy Land, as well as telling of her mystical conversations with God. She is honoured in the Anglican Communion but has not been canonised as a Catholic saint.

ⱬ Location synchronicity

Margery the mystic pilgrim hailed from Kings Lynn on the North Norfolk coast of England. Her counterpart in this life, Teal, was born and grew up just half an hour away in Fakenham. She spent many years working and living in this area, in particular near the famous pilgrimage destination for Catholics, Walsingham Shrine and nearby Castleacre.

ⱬ Character synchronicity

Margery Kempe came from a middle-class background, her father was the Mayor. Margery had started up at least three businesses once she was married, one of them being a tavern. She liked her nice things, especially her fashions and this correlates to Teal's upbringing and tastes. Her parents had run several taverns along the North Coast of Norfolk too. Margery was a bold character and was tenacious once converted to a deep faith in God. After her many visions, she would constantly regale her audiences with the holy details of the apparitions of angels, Jesus and Mother Mary that she saw and relayed the messages they passed on to her. Likewise, Teal would tell similar fantastical stories of the spirits she experienced.

ⱬ Book writing and life circumstance synchronicities

The obvious connection for Rose was the writing. She felt that she and Teal had both been oppressed. Now they each felt that they had to write their life story and speak their truth in some way. Not only for their own healing but as a support for those that would read and listen to their words. Also, both these medieval mystics became independent in their faith and emancipated from normal womanly duties, without children. Julian as a reclusive Anchorite, who may never have had children and Margery as a mystic and pilgrim, whose husband she left in charge of their many children. Teal and Rose had both left the mainstream religions they were raised in by their parents, each having a brush with a cult and then moving on to find their direct connection with the Source of all that is. They had also both been separated from their children for differing reasons, which you will hear more of later.

ⳤ Postpartum depression synchronicity

Other parallels Rose had drawn since these initial musings, were that Teal had postpartum depression after the birth of her son, as did Margery Kempe. In fact, Margery felt that she was being attacked during the night by demons, for many months. Teal had also experienced malevolent spirits accosting her even as a young child, during the nights. Many times she had sensed and even felt spirits in the room with her throughout her childhood and to this day. Margery then had a series of visions of Christ, Mother Mary and others and overcame her depressions. It was about her colourful and eventful life and struggles and then her many visions over two decades, that Margery wanted to write.

Mrs Kempe became well known as The Mother in her area, not only because she had fourteen children, but because many of the poor downtrodden ones would come to her to listen to her speak of the visions she had. The crowds would implore her to prophesy if they would be saved and if their souls would be safe when they died. Teal has also battled her depression and various mental health issues over the years but has shown great strength in overcoming these adversities and keeping her goals in sight. She will also tell anyhow who will listen, about the many signs and portents that she receives on a daily basis. She makes it a practice to pray for protection in the morning and asks for a sign that the angels are with her and she loves to explain how she then sees a white feather, or picks up coins as confirmation from spirit, that they are around her.

૨ Court Hearings synchronicity

Once Margery became fully aware of her relationship to the holy ones, this caused quite a stir in Kings Lyn from whence she hailed. She was well known for her wailing and lamentations about being a sinner, offering up loud prayers in repentance to Jesus. These outbursts she could not control in public places or even during Mass in the church services. She made enemies, as those that were irritated by her wailing and tears, conspired to have her thrown into prison and dragged before the courts, many times over. She was always acquitted as their accusations that she was forbidden to teach as a woman, were dissolved when she could prove that she was not preaching to others. She would testify that she was simply calling out to the Lord in lament and relating the visions she had of him. These were personal experiences rather than teaching, they decided.

The parallel with Teal's life was that she also had to go into court time and again in order to try and gain custody of her son Lee, who had been taken from her unjustly, at the age of seven. This caused her much lamenting and sorrow too, as she felt that her heart had been ripped out. Recently she had described to Rose that when she was walking up the stairs of the Norwich court building, it had felt like going to the gallows each time. It was terrifying, especially as she was mostly unaccompanied by a lawyer and had to stand there alone before the judge and jury.

Rose immediately drew another comparison to the feelings she must have had as another past life of Teal's which she had discovered afterwards, that of Anne Boleyn. Despite her putting on a show of nonchalance with her head held high on her way to the gallows, she was inconsolable the night before her death sentence. The fact that Queen Anne gave the most graceful speech about King Henry VIII just before her beheading in front of the crowd, showed her strength of character in wanting to protect her daughter Elizabeth and her family, from any repercussions. Teal also showed huge strength and courage and refused to give in and agreed with Rose's conclusions. She explained how she had faced the same kind of trauma and injustice within the court as Anne had, who was falsely accused of adultery multiple times.

In Teal's efforts to gain custody of her only son, Lee, she had fought for him over twenty times in the dock, which is fairly unprecedented. It seemed uncanny how similar the challenges were in both of these past lives, although the circumstances were different. Also, people either love or dislike Teal, just as Margery and Anne had both experienced from the people of their day, but it did not heed them from forging ahead anyway. Rose will open up the story about Teal's past life as Anne Boleyn in Chapter 7. Suffice it to say that the Magistrates Courts where Teal fought her battle, were just over the river from the undercroft and plaque to Lady Eleanor Talbot. Also contained within the entrance today, is the Arminghall Arch which had once been a part of the monastery where Eleanor had spent her last years. Here was another location synchronicity between the friends, which you will read more about in Chapter 5.

⅔ Pilgrimage parallels

Teal had travelled extensively abroad just as Margery Kempe had done, without knowing where her next meal was coming from and sometimes running out of money. You could call it 'flying by the seat of your pants' in your day. Teal had journeyed and worked in Australia and also hitchhiked all through West Africa when she was younger. Margery had relied in full faith on the monasteries and the goodwill of those dotted along the famous pilgrimage "The Way" on the long route to Spain, leading to the shrine of St. James in Santiago des Compostela, in the North West. If one carried the sign of a pilgrim, a seashell, it showed people that you were following The Way and they would give you sustenance and shelter for the night.

These repeating stories I had seen in their Akashic records and then brought into their consciousness. Here was obviously a soul learning for Teal and an opportunity to heal and release a pattern in her current lifetime. Rose was amazed how the pieces of the jigsaw were starting to come together and resolved to do some more research on these ancient medieval sites of Norwich to see what other secrets they held. During this process, she realised that she had lived right on top of or near various churches or monastic sites where she found others of her own past life connections, as we will now discover further.

ꝛ Keys to home location synchronicities

The Grey Friars

The first place Rose moved into in Norfolk was an ancient Mill. This old building which was used for weaving silk sits right on top of an ancient Saxon church. It is also very near the Franciscan Friary (The Grey Friars who arrived in Norwich in 1226) and the mill is also a stone's throw from Julian of Norwich, where her sanctuary can be found at the Church of Julian (in-between King Street and Rouen Road). It is conjectured that Julian may have been a nun in her earlier years, at The Grey Friars monastery. At any rate, Karen the psychic had been given a vision of a nun dressed in grey, with a big white collar similar to the garb of the Grey Friar nuns.

The Black Friars

In Rose's true travelling minstrel style, she then moved to Brent House, in Golden Dog Lane which she afterwards discovered is actually on the original site of the Black Friars (Dominican monks who wore black robes). They moved the early monastery over to St Peter's Hall later on, when more money was available. The old map illustration shows the square cell right where Rose was living if looking at the old map on the left, just down from Brent Road where it's marked "Old site of the Black Friars". The modern-day map shows Golden Dog Lane in Colgate, her front door in this narrow little alleyway, it was actually called Brent House.

The Dominican Black Friars came to Norwich in 1226. The original monastery was built in Colgate in 1270 where they stayed until 1307. They had to move back there briefly when the new site at St Peter's was burnt down by fire. It was not until December 2017, that Rose's psychic friend Karen said she could 'see' that she had also had a past life as a monk. She saw him dressed in brown with a rope around his middle and with bare feet. After some research Rose found that at the original site of the Black Friars, there had been a small group of Sackites, who as their name indicated, wore brown sackcloth. They were also barefooted and were called Mendicants, who would preach and teach as they walked the streets begging for alms in return for their readings of scripture.

Interestingly, Karen had mentioned that in this past life of Rose as a monk, she had become very knowledgeable and wise and had pleased the King. She said her guides were showing her that he used an inkwell and ledger, perhaps he did the accounts or taxes for the order. Certainly, if the monks were given any money by the people, they had to make a note and declare it, only taking the alms, scraps of food and bread which the people would throw at their feet and water given to them in wooden cups. The Sackite mendicants represented penance. She said she could see that Rose had been very thin and frail but glad to be alive. When Rose did some research she came across a monk by the name of William de Hoo. She had found the result of researching a particular monk that sounded as if it could fit:

> A new but short-lived order of friars appeared in the city. The Friars of Penance of Jesus Christ, commonly known from their **rough brown habit** as the Friars of the **Sack**, or Sackites, had their origin at Marseilles in 1251, and first appeared in London in 1257. In the next year a party of them arrived in Norwich, and a site was secured in the parish of St. Peter of Hungate. Notwithstanding various small benefactions enlarging their site, and such occasional windfalls as the 6d. bequeathed them in 1272 by Thomas son of Peter of Aldburgh, these Friars of the Sack never flourished, and at last there was only left the prior, William de Hoo, 'broken with old age and nearly blind.' In 1307 the end came, for Clement V suppressed the whole order. - British History Online (BHO).[26]

If this was one of her past lives, it would have been under forty years preceding her next life, as Julian of Norwich. It would also have been another connection to writing, that Rose had been tracing through other past lives too. Rose's friend Karen's guides also directed her to the Bible scripture 1 Corinthians 4:9, quoted here:

> For it seems to me that God has put us, apostles, on display at the end of the procession, like those condemned to die in the arena. We have

---

[26] http://www.british-history.ac.uk/vch/norf/vol2/pp428-433

been made a spectacle to the whole universe, to angels as well as to human beings. - the New International Version (NIV) of the Bible.

The Sackites certainly would have fallen into that category being so visible to the people on the streets. As a description of the Friary at Brent House itself (where Rose had lived), she found the following:

These early buildings, built of brick and dating from 1270 to 1307 mostly still survive and are now The Crypt and the covered remains of the Thomas A' Becket Chapel 'wilfully destroyed' in 1876. A friary was established on this site by the Penitential Friars in 1258 but was later taken over by the Dominicans and occupied until the Dissolution of the Monasteries in 1538. A friary was an institution housing a community of friars. The friars (from the Latin 'frater' meaning 'brother') were a religious movement which advocated a 'mendicant' lifestyle, of absolute poverty, supported exclusively by begging and the gift of alms.

Friars lived in the community, preaching and undertaking charitable works, often moving from town to town. Nevertheless, they did establish permanent bases; friaries, from which, unlike monks, they emerged to fulfil their mission. The buildings centred on a church and a cloister and usually contained a refectory (dining hall), a chapter house and an infirmary (for the care of the sick). Five orders of friars established friaries in Norwich: the Dominicans (known by the colour of their robes as 'Black Friars'), the Franciscans ('Grey Friars'), Carmelites ('White Friars'), Austin Friars and the Penitential Friars ('Sack Friars').

The Dominicans were founded by St Dominic in 1218 as a religious order committed to learning and preaching. They arrived in England in 1221 and reached Norwich five years later, establishing a friary to the north of the river Wensum, between what is now Colgate Street and Golden Dog Lane. In 1307 they took over the buildings of the Penitential Friars, south of the River Wensum after that order was suppressed by Pope Clement V. A church and other buildings already existed; the C13 chapel (originally dedicated to St Mary but subsequently re-dedicated to St Thomas-a-Becket) and an adjacent vestibule (now known as 'The Crypt') still survive today. The Dominicans re-modelled these buildings; inserting brick vaulted ceilings to support upper floors. - Historic England [27]

The Black Friars then moved to a new building which is still in situ as Blackfriars or St Andrew's hall. Rose was very taken with finding yet another highly religious past life and one who was entrusted with teaching and scribing, as she had done in her current life. Rose had preached on the street at one time and had also felt a bit of a spectacle to the world. This work was voluntary and unpaid, which meant that she had to scrimp and scrape for the basics in life, just as the Sackites had done.

The White Friars

The Carmelite Monks were based at Whitefriars, at St. James Close, Norwich. These monks were from Mount Carmel of biblical fame, in Israel. The medieval St. James Church is right next door. Rose came to believe that this is one of the churches on the energy triangle that Peter the Shaman had seen in his vision over Norfolk, which will be described in more detail in Chapter 13. along with another past life connection to this very spot, in Chapter 5. Lady Eleanor Talbot.

ꝛ Manifesting and location coincidences

Rose realized that she had secured a job exactly where she had wanted to work a year ago, at St. James Close. We will see how she came to realise her dream in the next chapter. This was to be right on top of the site where she would have served in St James church and the monastery as Eleanor Talbot all those centuries ago and where this Lady had ended her life. Rose had plenty of time to explore the area and think about healing this timeline over the next two years. Once again, she had landed on a location of a past life quite by coincidence! Or was it? The story unfolds in the next chapter.

---

[27] https://historicengland.org.uk/listing/the-list/list-entry/1220456

₹ Psychic channelled evidence

Evidence for the past life of Rose as Lady Eleanor Talbot in Chapter 5 was channelled by Karen sometime later, giving the following names:

Richard
John
Parker (in connection with a woman)
King Henry in Tudor dress (he held banquets with silver goblets, tables laden with fruit and roast hog in his castle).

Rose eagerly went away and surfed online with her new past life clues and the story that unfolded is told in the next epistle. Below are a couple of the synchronicities that emerged in a later sitting with Karen, which we will unpack from Chapter 6 onwards.

₹ Psychic evidence of further soul family past lives

I fed more channelled evidence through in another sitting with Karen on 6 January 2018, evidently for a further group of past lives connected to Rose, as follows:

John
Canterbury
Belgium or a French connection
Catharine of Aragon, a Tudor lady
Castle with a moat
Manor House
Rose was a Lady in Waiting (a most senior position in the Privy to the Queen)
Anne
Thomas
Cardinal Pope I
James

This set of keys was a little easier for her to piece together as history tells us that Queen **Catharine of Aragon** was married to King Henry VIII. It seemed that these past lives were going to be of great interest indeed and the next several chapters will deal with this Tudor scene, as Rose's realisations unfolded over the following years.

⟩ Location synchronicity

Mary Boleyn (b. 1499/1500 and died 19 July 1543) was probably born at **Blickling Hall** in **Norfolk**. This is only twenty-six minutes drive from **Cromer** on the north **Norfolk** coast, where Rose was born. Her sister **Anne Boleyn** (born 1502 and died 1536), may not have been born there. They were of English aristocracy and Anne became the mother to the Queen of England, Elizabeth I. They were both educated in the French court, but all the Boleyn family later lived in **Hever Castle,** which has **a moat,** in Kent as Karen had seen. **Hever Castle** is near **Seal** where Rose used to live.

Rose had initially visited Hever Castle many times throughout her twenties, when living in West Sussex and again when leaving Bavaria after her divorce and landing in Seal, Kent in her early thirties. In her twenties, a group of family and friends often attended open-air Shakespearean plays or classical music concerts such as Vivaldi, at the castle grounds. These were held in front of the Italian gardens on a stone platform with beautiful sandstone columns and arches, framing the ornate fountain and the lake behind it.

Henry VIII also courted Anne Boleyn at Bolebroke Castle which was a **manor house** or 15th Century hunting lodge in Hartfield where he hunted in Ashdown Forest, five miles from Hever **Castle**. Her father was Sir **Thomas** Boleyn and her mother was Lady Elizabeth Howard. **Anne** was the maternal niece of the Duke of **Norfolk!** The Norfolk connection, she discovered, was where Rose and many of her soul family were now based.

⟩ Physical appearance synchronicity

It is said that the appearance of Anne Boleyn was dark-skinned, dark eyed and dark-haired - the total opposite to the Tudor pale, fair-skinned vision of beauty. She had a sixth finger growing from her small finger and a large mole on her neck. She disguised these imperfections by creating new fashions - long sleeves to hide her six fingers and a black velvet ribbon around her neck, hiding the unsightly mole. These 'deformities' were said to be the sure sign of a witch. - Elizabethan Era[28]

Once Rose was on this trail, comparing her friend Teal to Anne Boleyn, she realised that there was a match between Teal's character and Anne's appearance. Teal had lustrous, long dark hair too and when tanned, an olive skin and is also a great beauty, as Anne had been. I will look at her character more in Chapter 7. Rose had dark golden hair and this was more similar to the much adored Tudor red-gold hair that Mary Boleyn was alleged to have, with the fairer skin.

₹ Family synchronicities

Mary was the oldest of the three Boleyn children as was Rose. Mary was taught many skills when she resided at the family home, Hever Castle in Kent. The skills she acquired were typical of an aristocratic upbringing and were many as listed below:

> Mary learned the feminine accomplishments of dancing, embroidery, etiquette, household management, music, needlework, singing, and games such as cards and chess. She was also taught archery, falconry, riding, and hunting. - Wikipedia, Mary Boleyn[29]

Rose's mother had also passed on her knowledge of needlework in the modern form of sewing, knitting, table manners and cooking, which included music and singing, as they had a piano at home. She also paid for her daughters to have horse riding lessons, ballet and tap dancing tuition and even ice-skating classes.

---

[28] https://www.elizabethan-era.org.uk/anne-boleyn.htm
[29] https://en.wikipedia.org/wiki/Mary_Boleyn

℞ Life circumstances synchronicity

After this fine education, Mary was sent to Paris, France when she was fifteen, as a maid to King Henry VIII's sister Princess Mary when she married the French King Louis XII. King Louis died on 1 January 1515, but Mary stayed on when King Francis came to the throne. She had certainly found her feet in her new environment and by all accounts, may have become quite promiscuous by the sounds of it:

> Mary was joined in Paris by her father, Sir Thomas, and her sister, Anne, who had been studying in France for the previous year. During this time Mary is supposed to have embarked on sexual affairs, including one with King Francis himself. Although most historians believe that the reports of her sexual affairs are exaggerated, the French king referred to her as "The English Mare", "my hackney" and as "una grandissima ribalda, infame sopra tutte" ("a very great whore the most infamous of all"). - Wikipedia, Mary Boleyn

Although Rose had changed her ways in her latter years, once she was free of religious and family strictures in her early thirties, she also wanted to fully experience a whole new world, as Mary had. She was also excommunicated for her 'sins', and had returned to her homeland. Shunned by her mother and step-father now meant that there was nobody to criticise her morally. We could safely say that she fully explored her freedom during the years to come when she discovered the glittering lights of London and the music industry. You could compare this lifestyle to attending the French court in Mary's day. Anything seemed possible and there were so many new things to try!

Mary Boleyn was recalled to England and soon afterwards was married to William Carey at King Henry VIII's court. As Karen had channelled, she became a lady-in-waiting to the Queen, Catharine of Aragon and was then enraptured by the King and became Henry's mistress in secret, whilst still married to William Carey. Eventually, after four years, Henry was to replace Mary in his affections with her sister Anne Boleyn. She though, refused to sleep with him unless he married her, having seen how her sister had been manipulated. He, therefore, courted her for six years, as she refused to become his mistress or concubine.

As Henry was still married to Catharine of Aragon and could not seek a legal divorce, he applied to the Pope of Rome (another clue Karen had given), for a dispensation. We will see how he employed Thomas Cranmer the Archbishop of Canterbury in this dastardly deed in Chapter 9. Eventually, after much team research, Henry presented the excuse that he had married Catharine because she was his brother's widow! Therefore the union was null and void. Obviously, the real reason being, that he had fallen in love with Anne and he also desperately desired a son and heir. Catharine's only surviving child was a girl, Mary, who through a twist of fate later became Mary I. More of her and her soul connection to Rose, in Chapter 11.

Lord Chancellor Thomas Wolsey failed to obtain the Pope's assent. Anne became pregnant in 1532 and the situation came to a head (Mary had a child but he was not recognised by the King as he was a bastard). At any rate, he was in love with her sister Anne already. Thomas Cranmer, the Archbishop of Canterbury granted the annulment of the marriage and Henry promptly divorced Catharine and married Anne in 1533. Pope Clement VII excommunicated King Henry VIII for marrying her. Anne was hated by the people and called a "witch" and a "whore" as they still loved Catharine of Aragon. When Anne gave birth court astrologers had predicted a boy, but she gave birth to a girl, the future Elizabeth I. We will look at her soul connection to Rose in Chapter 8 and which of her friends shared this past life.

⅃ Birthday synchronicity

Anne became pregnant again but miscarried three times and Henry began to think she was cursed and not right for him. He became paranoid that he would not have a son and heir and as the political climate was turbulent, he felt a sense of urgency to produce one. Gradually Queen Anne's men at court disappeared one by one and were arrested and then finally she was arrested on trumped-up charges of adultery and taken to the Tower of London and executed in 1536 by Henry (another raft of unjust passings). Rose realised that five young men (one of which was her brother George) were executed on 17 May, because of the accusations against Queen

Anne. This happened to be on Teal's birthday which is 17 May. Anne had been scheduled to die on that day, but due to a delay, had to be beheaded two days later on 19 May. Rose discovered that Henry has specially ordered an excellent swordsman from France and surmised that this could have been the reason for the two-day delay. On the other hand, it could have been because of the executions that preceded hers, forming a queue!

At any rate, 19 May became an infamous date over the centuries, when hauntings reportedly occur at Blickling Hall annually, on the anniversary of Anne's death. Countless people claim to have seen her riding in a carriage and then roaming the halls, with her head under her arm. Teal and Rose conducted a clearing in the grounds with a selenite wand as they began to realise that one of her past lives seemed to be matching up to Queen Anne herself. More of this is in Chapter 7.

ꝛ Experiential body signs

On 9 January 2018 Teal visited Rose on a bitter winter's day. When they started talking about narcissists and a man that had arranged a date with her and then subsequently had let her down, she realised he was trying to dictate when they would meet and being quite controlling so she decided she was going to put her foot down and say no. They discussed how they were learning their life lessons about loving themselves enough not to get hurt by such people, but to put the boundaries in place and not allow men to treat them like dirt.

As the conversation unfolded, Rose mentioned Karen's reading and that she thought Teal could be connected in some way to the history of Anne Boleyn and King Henry VIII. Rose had been reading about the way Anne had kept him waiting for six years as she would not sleep with him unless he married her. As the two friends talked Rose suddenly realised that she had been Mary Boleyn and that Teal had been her sister, Anne Boleyn (also a brunette). They looked at each other and immediately all the hairs went up on their arms as confirmation and they both had those familiar energy tingles coursing throughout their bodies. Here was another experiential body sign that they had unlocked another key to a past life!

As they took their hot mugs of coffee into the lounge, they talked about King Henry VIII allegedly being a narcissist and got more truth bumps, confirming that Teal was still learning the lessons around becoming involved with narcissists. As soon as Anne Boleyn had capitulated and married King Henry VIII when he divorced Catharine, he started to fall slowly out of love with Anne over the next couple of years. She could not provide him with a son and heir and his narcissism came to the fore. He was becoming insecure and felt less of a man because he could not produce a boy that survived. With the political instability at the time, he felt he needed a man to rule England after his own death. Within three years she was dead, beheaded.

This is a good lesson in not getting involved with narcissists. Even though she kept him waiting all those years he still betrayed her as he had no empathy. The lesson for Teal was just to walk away, to value herself. Also Rose realised that there was a piece of release work to do around this unjust passing due to that past life. The lake at Blickling Hall where Mary was born, is said to be haunted not only by the ghost of Anne. Henry VIII is also seen passing by and therefore Rose and Teal decided to visit the estate which is open to the public and do a clearing ceremony, to lay these souls to rest.

⅊ Losing children synchronicity

Teal's past life pattern often seemed to be one of losing young sons. When married to King Henry VIII she had three miscarriages, one of whom was a son and only bore him a daughter, Queen Elizabeth I. Rose had also lost or been separated from children during three of her past lives, which was reflected in this lifetime. As Julian of Norwich, she either lost them to the plague or did not have any before she became an Anchorite, with Lady Eleanor Talbot she is reported to have lost a four-month-old child and as Mary Boleyn, she would be separated from her son, who was to be educated under her sister's wing as Queen Anne.

⅊ Body pain related to a past life trauma synchronicity

The next day, Teal visited Rose at home again. She had been for some healing at a group and was excited and wanted to relate what had happened. A man was standing giving her non-contact energy healing with one hand at the front and one at the back of her body at a slight angle. After a while, she started feeling discomfort and pain in one of her should blades, where he was holding his hand, slightly away from her body. She eventually mentioned that it was getting more and more uncomfortable and he said that yes, he could feel like something was coming into her body from the front and going out through her back at the point where she had the pain. She wondered if it was a spear or arrow and he said he felt it was a thick spear. As the healing progressed he said he was pulling it out through her back and healing the wound.

She mentioned that she had been discussing past lives with her friend Rose the previous day and that she may have had a past life as Anne Boleyn. He agreed that when there is such a death as this, symbolised by the spear, it could often mean the person had died by hanging, were pierced or beheaded. Queen Anne was of course beheaded. Teal felt that this healing could have now broken the curse of this past life and she may be able to move forward now in her life. Rose realised that this is the reason they were discovering these past lives and why it is so important to acknowledge them, understand the lessons to be learnt and have the necessary past life healing in order to clear the lines and patterns. As time went by Teal explained that she had constant problems with her throat since a child with tonsillitis and with Glandular Fever and even now swollen glands were still troubling her. Rose decided to do a Quantum Timeline Healing on her throat, as she connected it to the beheading.

ঽ Key clues - visits from spirits

Having read up on the history of various claims to Anne's rumoured final resting place, into which I will do a deep dive in Chapter 7, in the summer of 2019 Teal and Rose visited Salle Church in Norfolk and walked around the graveyard to see if they could pick up on anything around Anne's spirit. Normally Teal could be quite sensitive to energies, which she had been since childhood. There was a spot in the graveyard where she felt something, so we put down our rug, did a rattling and clearing prayer and had our picnic. Later that evening something quite astounding happened but I will save that for later in these tales. Suffice it to say she had a visitation from the ghost of a very broad man, wearing a wide-brimmed flat hat, wearing a richly braided jacket in autumnal shades. Teal intuited that he was troubled and tried to communicate with him about why he seemed so puzzled to be there. He didn't answer her, but as she had often seen spirits over her lifetime she didn't think too much of it. Being very, very tired, she fell into a deep slumber, but more of this tale later.

₹ The act of shunning, synchronicity

As Rose studied this fascinating chapter in Tudor history more deeply, she noticed another parallel with her own life. She was reading about the way that Mary was treated when she fell in love secretly with one of Henry VIII's soldiers on a royal trip to France. This was after the death of her first husband, William Carey, and a fair while after her long affair with Henry VIII, during which she may have produced two more children with the King. The boy and girl were attributed to William Carey, who was no doubt bribed to keep quiet. Eventually, after all the secrecy, intrigue and manipulation she had been subjected to in the court, Mary had deeply wished to find a true love, someone who loved her as much in return. Her wish came true but she paid a terrible sacrifice for her choice.

This reminded Rose of the way she had been forced to choose between her own family with all its expectations and religious strictures and her own personal freedom and happiness. She had left her husband at the age of thirty-two and never looked back. This is a very similar scene that we see unfold in the annals of history with regard to Mary's fate:

> In 1534, Mary secretly married William Stafford. He was the younger son of land owner Humphrey Stafford of Blatherwick in Northampton. This marriage was a disaster for her, excepting her personal happiness. Mary undoubtedly loved Stafford, a soldier she had met at Calais (he had been part of Henry VIII's retinue.) But her relatives – all newly ennobled and very self-conscious about their status – were outraged. He was a commoner, not fit for the queen's sister. Accordingly, Mary and her new husband were banished from court, (It is quite possible that her relatives planned to wed Mary to a nobleman, further cementing their rise to

prominence; instead, her marriage was a step backwards socially). Mary did not visit her sister when Anne was imprisoned in the Tower. Nor did she visit their brother George, also condemned to death. There is no evidence that she wrote to them. - Wikipedia, Mary Boleyn

It appears that all of the Boleyn family had disowned Mary and even her own son Henry Carey had been taken away from her by Henry VIII earlier and placed under the care of her sister Anne at Court, for his betterment.

In her past life as Lady Eleanor Talbot in Norwich, Rose experienced being jilted at the altar, as she was secretly betrothed by his bishop, to the young King Edward IV. He then abandoned her and married The White Queen, during the War of the Roses. We will find out which of Rose's friends played this role soon.

Lady Eleanor Talbot was aristocracy but then became a nun at The White Friars (where Rose had worked), possibly as a way of dealing with the betrayal of King Edward and maybe because, not marrying again, she conceived a secret child by him and needed the support of the church. She and her child died when she was only thirty-two and they were buried in the church next to where Rose worked St. James. This is the grave that the shaman had seen with the golden daffodils being offered as a healing. The undercroft where Eleanor was buried is preserved onsite at St. James Close with a plaque to her name. If this was the mother and child that Peter the shaman had seen, then appeasement of their souls was needed.

Some years later and before this book was completed, Rose had seen Eleanor's face clearly in her mind's eye, when she partook in a psychedelic mushroom ceremony in May 2022. Rose described her as very pretty with light blue round eyes and a bubbly personality with dark blonde curly hair. She knew now that she not only had to recognise who this was, but that she must acknowledge and feel the pain of her betrayal, abandonment and separation in order to heal and finally release, this unjust passing. If Eleanor and her child had survived, then her progeny would have been the legal heir to the throne when King Edward IV died. Instead, his brother Richard III became King. The whole story reveals itself in the next chapter.

ꙋ Channelled name synchronicities

The proof that Eleanor must have been involved with the King, came in the form of her will, kept in the **Parker** Library, which showed her bequeathing all her properties to her sister. This was yet another of the words that Karen had channelled. This act of keeping the wealth in their family would have been common amongst female aristocrats. Her will included manors that she owned and there was even a property in **Savernake** Forest which would not have been inherited through her family line and which belonged to King Edward. **Savernake** Walk is where Rose used to live.

King Edward IV may have gifted her property because he took away several of her father's mansions when he had died, which left Eleanor with only one home when her husband died, which the King also appropriated. The young Edward had then abandoned her and may have given her the distant properties in order to bribe her not to speak of their secret betrothal. Again, another past life where a woman had to keep monumental secrets and not speak out or be authentic.

ꙋ Fear and deception synchronicities

Finally, Rose understood the bigger picture for herself in seeing and feeling these emotions, held back by secrecy, betrayal and abandonment. She knew that she had overcome her own family pattern of forbidding free speech by breaking with the traditions of their faith and therefore being shunned. She had turned this to the good by writing publicly of it. The deeper healing had come slowly in the realisation of her fear of betrayal and abandonment in romantic relationships. In her mind, Edward IV represented the experience that she had in this lifetime as a seven-year-old child, of losing her father through a divorce and being prevented from knowing him for all those years. This was a situation she had also grasped hold of and turned around, once again becoming courageously reunited with her birth father and the lost bloodline of her family, her half-brothers.

Then had come the longer journey to rebuilding trust and allowing this to flow into her own life in the form of closer relationships, which she could allow to blossom. She knew this was the hardest of the lessons that she had to learn. To truly open her heart. It was far easier to do what Julian and Eleanor had done, become a nun and bury themselves in spiritual work, until their death. Rose wanted to approach it differently, live life to the fullest and find a long-term loving partner with whom she could reciprocate love, peace and happiness, as Mary Boleyn had with her soldier love, William Stafford. Perhaps, she mused, this was the Lady in the underground casket with the sword of a loyal gentleman by her side. The devoted Knight in shining armour with whom she had lived and loved to the end of her days. True love had been so elusive up until Rose's middle age. She had learnt so many lessons so far, but would this be the one challenge that she would carry to the grave? We will look more deeply into this in the following chapter.

CHAPTER 5

Medieval past life, Lady Eleanor Talbot

I left this earthly plane as Julian of Norwich, in around 1416 when I was in my early seventies. Twenty years later my soul was reincarnated as Lady Eleanor Talbot, also from Norfolk. With regard to this next of my medieval incarnations and to give you an overview, I would like to tell you the curious tale of how Rose followed my breadcrumb trail to connect to another of her past lives.

Lady Eleanor Talbot (married to Thomas Butler) born c. February 1436 - 30 June 1468. Her father was John Talbot. Eleanor died in Norwich aged approximately thirty-two and was an English noblewoman and oblate, buried at St James Church, Whitefriars.

Eleanor was an aristocrat and it seems she had a four-month-old child who died and was buried next to her. She was originally married to Sir Thomas Butler and was also jilted by King Edward IV which led to her keeping a huge secret, which I will reveal. It is alleged that she was secretly betrothed to Edward (whose brother was Richard). We will see how Richard III became inter-connected to her metaphysically.

Psychic channelled evidence

Evidence channelled through Karen for Rose, later confirmed her assumptions about Lady Eleanor Talbot. To recap from an earlier chapter, she was given the following name clues:

Richard

John

Parker (in connection with a woman)

King Henry in Tudor dress (he held banquets with silver goblets, tables laden with fruit and roast hog in his castle).

Location synchronicity

As listed in Chapter 4, Rose had previously connected this past life to a location synchronicity because she discovered she had worked directly on top of the medieval Carmelite monastery site Whitefriars, which was connected to Lady Eleanor Talbot. This was at the office block called Carmelite House! As mentioned previously, there is a relic named the Arminghall Arch which has engraved royal figures on it and dates back to the 14th century. This arch was moved from the Black Friars Monastery to Whitlingham Park. There was a priory there next to the broad and a confluence of three rivers, where royalty and bishops would stay over and take rest, like an ancient retreat. Only scant ruins remain and so the Arminghall Arch has since been returned close to its original position and rebuilt into the Magistrates Courtyard. As we will see in Chapter 7 these courts played a huge role in the life of Rose's friend Teal. The Magistrates' buildings are just the other side of the River Wensum, adjacent to Carmelite House. Here stands another restored and rare archway or undercroft, which bears a green plaque, dedicated to Lady Eleanor Talbot.

A little while before Karen's channelling, in 2016, Rose had joined a recruitment agency, which had secured her an interview. As she scrutinised the map it dawned on her that the address was St James Court in Norwich. Her heart did a little jump and she was suddenly alert and curious. This was the very place she had been attracted to a year ago, for some odd reason. She had walked past Whitefriars then and just felt that she would really like to work there one day. Her life had moved on and she thought no more of it, until now! A year later here she was, smartly dressed and excited, as she walked briskly along the River Wensum on her way to her interview.

As she approached the building, she noticed a sign, the modern office block was called Carmelite House. Afterwards, she had discovered that it was named after the monks that originally immigrated there from

Carmelite, in Israel, or The Holy Land as it was known, eight hundred centuries ago. There were still fragments of some medieval ruins in the flint facade, which had been restored and set into a brick wall and also a beautiful and well-preserved arch, an ancient undercroft with a green plaque entitled "Lady Eleanor Talbot". It seemed magical somehow, but she didn't know why, yet.

'Undercroft & plaque to Lady Eleanor Talbot'

Rose entered the spacious reception and a bright young lady came to greet her. She seemed lovely and very friendly, which gave her a good first impression of the department. She was introduced to the boss and he also seemed very kind and welcoming. She had a good feeling about this. The interview went really well and Rose just knew she had secured the job! Call it instinct if you will. Sure enough, a couple of days later, she received a call confirming that they wanted her to start working there; as soon as possible. This suited her perfectly and she worked there happily, for a few years.

This gave her the time to walk along the river at lunchtime and explore all the ancient history in detail. Cow Tower was another significant past-life landmark which we will learn more about in Chapter 12, in relation to

Robert Kett. Also, the Magistrates' Courts on the opposite side of the river adjacent to her offices, was a significant spot. Then there were the golden daffodils lining the way along the beautiful walkways weaving their way along the River Wensum. These bright blooms served to link to another key she had been given, to unlock the mystery of Lady Eleanor Talbot, to be discussed in more detail in due course.

Date synchronicity

In Rose's past life as Eleanor, she was married at the tender age of thirteen to Sir Thomas Butler. He died on an unknown date before Edward IV overthrew the House of Lancaster, on 4 March 1461. 1961 just happened to be the birth year of Rose's incarnation in this century, a numerical key linking the year '61 to this Lady, who came to be called The Secret Queen.

Channelled location synchronicity

It is claimed that Lady Talbot, may have borne a child but when Eleanor died at only thirty-two, her child also passed away, at just four months old. This could of course have been from the plague. She had been a benefactor of the White Friars at Carmelite, Norwich (next to St. James Church which is one of the three churches on the sacred triangle the shaman had seen). The plaque bearing her name, says she was buried at the Carmelite Priory Church. As she had no heir, the deeds were signed over along with all her property to her sister Elizabeth. These are now preserved and kept in the **Parker** Library at Corpus Christi College. So now we see one of the random words that Karen had given Rose was **Parker** and how that had slotted into the story.

Past pain and wounding synchronicities

Could the grave with the woman and child depicted in Rose's shamanic reading from Peter, be that of Lady Talbot and her young child? Were the yellow daffodils given as a symbol, to heal the unjust way she was treated?

She was from an aristocratic background, she lost her considerable property and then promised in marriage to King Edward IV, but he betrayed her. Was this the same vision that Steve had drawn on his scrap of paper when he saw the grave with daffodils being given to them? Could it be the grave that Peter the shaman had seen concerning the unjust passing? Rose pondered these things as she walked along the River Wensum during her lunchtimes.

Rose was aware of the symbolism of the golden daffodils sprinkled along the river banks and pathways and had made the connection to the healing needed here. She conducted some healing ceremonies during this time, praying for any souls still not at rest to be blessed and released to the light. She even took along her shamanic rattle and cleared the energies a few times. She was to delve even deeper into the synchronicities of their lives and look at the betrayal, abandonment and unjust passing parallels and how to heal these also.

I will relate an experience Rose had just before finishing the writing of this book, when she experienced another awakening, in May 2022. Rose had never partaken in a sacred mushroom journey before but decided to see if any messages came to her under the influence of this psychedelic 'schroom' ceremony as they are nick-named. She employed a healing woman with experience of holding space in a shamanic journey, who used hands-on healing during the protected time and space. Apart from the usual things you would expect, feelings of love and forgiveness, seeing bright multi-coloured points of light and beautiful shapes and images, suddenly a lovely face appeared to Rose. The image was so clear and was of a beautiful and vivacious-looking young woman. She had honey blonde, tightly curled hair arranged in a halo around her sweet upturned smiling face. Her eyes were china blue and engaging and she seemed to be full of mirth and the joys of life. Rose had the overwhelming feeling that this was in fact Lady Eleanor Talbot showing herself. She didn't say anything at the time, but it was to her a brief shewing as if to confirm to Rose that Eleanor, was there. Looking at historical images and paintings of Eleanor she hadn't found any direct resemblance to her, but she was convinced it was her energy.

I will explain what was a gradual unfolding of discoveries for Rose. Her past pain patterns or soul woundings were slowly emerging into view, with the realisation that there were shared feelings and parallel life events that linked these past lives together. So far Rose had discovered from her avatar as Julian of Norwich, that she had needed to hide things, in order to survive. Now here was another life in which she was bound to silence, by the King himself!

Upon Thomas Butler's death, the hapless Eleanor lost one of the two manors her father-in-law had settled on her and her husband when they had married, even though his father did not have a license for the return transfer to himself. After her father-in-law's death, King Edward IV had then seized both properties after he became king. This is a significant titbit of information as you will discover. Around this time, Edward IV took a fancy to Eleanor but she must have held out, as it seems that she was then secretly betrothed to Edward, England's first Yorkist King, by Bishop Stillington.

The legal pre-contract of marriage was not honoured by the King later on, but it would have allowed him the intimate privileges of a married man with her! He swore her to secrecy and she, needing a place to live, capitulated. At any rate, it is surmised by historians that she was one of three famous lovers of his, and probably the one nicknamed The Holiest Harlot, as she was very devout. The other two had been known and quoted in the King's own words as:

> The merriest, the wiliest, and the holiest harlots in his realm, (hellfire and holy water, depends on how you treat me as to how I taste)

It is also commonly argued by Ricardians, that Bishop Stillington, also sworn to secrecy, was later imprisoned by Edward IV in 1478, ten years after Eleanor's death, because he incautiously spoke of the pre-contract to George, Duke of Clarence. To add to these machinations, it is thought but cannot be proven, that she had borne King Edward a child, shortly before her early death at the age of around thirty-two. Another grave secret indeed. Her child was also thought to have died, possibly from the plague and was buried next to her. This, it turned out, was one of the unjust passings that the shaman had seen, the grave of the mother and child being proffered yellow daffodils in their honour. These flowers were as a blessed healing from the heavens, for the bad treatment meted out from the King, her tragic losses and untimely death. Her secrets had gone with her to the grave, just the same as Julian's writings had.

Rose had by contrast thrown over the traces of religion, soaring like a bird escaping from its gilded cage. Although she was not sentenced to death on a stake, she had been cast out of that metaphorical 'gated' community in which she had grown up and was subsequently banished by her puritanical parents.

As for Eleanor's previously betrothed, although a remarkable military leader who decisively won the bloody, dynastic conflict known as the War of the Roses, King Edward IV's love life was a mess. Shakespeare wrote two plays about him, but gave him short shrift in 'Henry VI', Part 3 and 'Richard III'. It may have been that he considered Edward a shallow and fickle man, being overshadowed first by the heroic Warwick 'The Kingmaker' and then by his own villainous younger brother, Richard.

At any rate, Edward IV had moved on and later quickly fell in love with a beautiful young woman named Elizabeth Wydville (as the surname Woodville would have been spelt in those times). She became known as The White Queen, due to her connections to The House of York, which was represented by a white rose. Their subsequent marriage would have invalidated his hidden betrothal with Eleanor. Later on, there was to be another cruel turn of fate when Richard III was killed by Henry VII (Henry Tudor).

Prior to this karmic twist, Richard had used the knowledge he gained of Edward's pre-contract to justify his actions, claiming that his brother's marriage to the Queen was fictional. This led therefore to Richard usurping the power to become king and the probable murder of Elizabeth and Edward's two oldest sons. Eleanor would no doubt have turned in her grave knowing that her simple act of secret betrothal caused so much political turmoil and had changed the shape of history! Luckily she knew nothing of it, slumbering in her grave in the Priory Church in Norwich. That was until her next incarnation, an even more prominent figure in history with a huge secret to be kept, at all costs. More of that repeating karmic pattern, in the following chapter!

So, to recap, due to the previous losses of her properties, Eleanor had feared that Edward would take away the mansion he had bestowed upon her as a type of bribe, in order that she would sleep with him. He was known for behaving in this fashion, pleading sexual favours with other needy widows. This reputation could have been one of the reasons Shakespeare thought ill of him. All of the finer details of this affair had only come to light when Edward IV had died suddenly at a young age, having sired seven children with Elizabeth Woodville, The White Queen.

Bishop Stillington, who had betrothed them four years before the royal marriage, had eventually found his opportunity to crawl out of the woodwork. The urgent question now was, who would inherit the crown after the King's death? Elizabeth had borne Edward an elder son and a second son who were the presumed successors to the throne. When Stillington had revealed Eleanor's secret betrothal, despite her untimely death and that of her child, the consequence of this information had then deemed the two young princes to be illegitimate bastards! They had previously been confined in The Tower of London, allegedly for their own protection, but had unfortunately found their secret and sorry end. It was never discovered who had murdered them, only that they had 'disappeared', never to be seen again! The crown then fell conveniently to Edward's younger brother, who became Richard III.

There are two camps amongst historians, those for Richard III and those for the alternative story. More information has slowly been revealed through various findings as recently as 1997 which showed that certain properties belonging to King Edward IV had been passed on in Eleanor's will to her sister Elizabeth (also the middle name of Rose). Her will has been preserved to this day, at the Corpus Christi College in Cambridge, in what is called The **Parker** Library, which if you recall, was one of the keyword clues Karen had given Rose in one of her psychic readings.

An article titled "Eleanor Talbot: The Secret Queen" has this to say:

> Ten years ago little was known about Eleanor Talbot; even her parentage was a matter of dispute. Yet Eleanor's surname and her paternity are absolutely key issues. In a fifteenth-century context, the fact that she was the daughter of the first Earl of Shrewsbury was enormously significant. Lord Shrewsbury was regarded as a towering figure and a national hero. When the Act of Parliament of 1484 explicitly characterised Eleanor as his daughter, the effect

was akin to that of a late-twentieth-century writer describing someone as a daughter of Sir Winston Churchill. Eleanor's rank – and her plausibility as a potential royal consort – were immediately established beyond any question.

Why then has Eleanor been so completely neglected? She is, in her own way, a key figure in English history, a veritable 'Cleopatra's nose'. If her marriage to Edward IV had been acknowledged in her lifetime, if she had actually been enthroned and crowned as England's queen consort, all subsequent history must have been different. The House of York might still have been reigning today, in a separate kingdom, never united with Scotland. The despotic, paranoid Tudors would have remained unheard of outside their native Wales. Enormous consequences would flow from these events. The English Reformation, which sprang from Henry VIII's dynastic and financial crises, and was neither generally desired nor supported by the English populace, might never have taken place. England's monasteries, still undissolved, could have preserved their unrivalled cultural heritage to the present day. No Tudors would mean no Stuarts; no Civil War; no Oliver Cromwell. The story goes on and on. It all turns on Eleanor. - The History Press[30]

Rose could now begin to draw other significant parallels with her own life in the form of loss, betrayal and abandonment. Regarding Lady Eleanor Talbot, this particular lifetime had left a deep imprint on Rose's oversoul. During her search for clues to her past lives and those of her soul family, she realised that her childhood friend Julia was most probably The White Queen, Elizabeth Woodville, with whom King Edward IV had fallen in love. He had married against his advisors' wishes for him, four years before Eleanor's death. She would have been distressed at some level by this betrayal, having once been in line for the throne herself, along with her child. The feelings of betrayal and abandonment would have left their stain on her spirit and had been reverberating down through the centuries, certainly playing themselves out in her next life as Mary Boleyn and on into her last life as Rose. The King's betrayal of Elizabeth, must have been

---

[30] https://www.thehistorypress.co.uk/articles/eleanor-talbot-the-secret-queen/

all the more deeply felt by his long-standing wife of nineteen years, after the discoveries she made at his death.

Connecting with soul family past life: Julia, born as:

Elizabeth Woodville (Dame Elizabeth Grey, aka The White Queen of England) b. 1437- died 8 June 1492 aged fifty-two, married to King Edward IV. She had two children from her previous husband and bore seven with Edward. Their two oldest sons were ensconced in the Tower of London by Richard III, supposedly for their protection, after the king's death. Elizabeth was born in Northamptonshire and became Dame Elizabeth Grey. As we know, the chance for one of her sons to become King was wrenched away when they found out that her husband, Edward IV, had secretly become betrothed to Lady Eleanor Talbot (nee Butler) many years previously. Here was a tragic love story with a very unhappy ending!

Julia. b. 26 March. Married to Simon b. 14 December. They have two older daughters, Jade and Lisella.

Religious life synchronicity

Despite Eleanor's death and leaving no possible heir to the throne, Elizabeth's sons were declared illegitimate and disappeared, probably murdered in the Tower where they had been held for safety! It is not certain who commanded this as there was so much intrigue around the crowning of the next King after Edward IVs sudden death. That is when his brother Richard III then grasped the throne and his wife Anne became Queen. Eventually dethroned, Elizabeth retired in safety to Bermondsey Abbey with her children and lived a monastic life until she passed away in 1492. To draw a religious life synchronicity here, Julia was also raised in a highly religious household in this lifetime, from which she eventually escaped, along with her family. With these actions, they had both broken some of the oppressive religious karmic patterns.

On 13 May 2022 Rose resolved to heal what she thought was a deep karmic wound, once and for all. She felt she needed to free herself and her childhood friend Julia from their unwitting inter-dimensional entanglement. The resulting pain experienced due to King Edward's irreverent actions towards them both, some five hundred years previously, reverberated down through the centuries. She and Julia felt a soul whispering to journey once again to Glastonbury in Wiltshire on a sacred pilgrimage. This time, Rose intended to propose they join forces, in a past life release ceremony for them both.

In September of 2018, the friends had visited Glastonbury Tor at the heart of Avalon, with the remains of a church dedicated to St. Michael gracing its summit. Glastonbury is associated with many legends including a connection with the early Christian Church. It is also reputed to be the resting place of King Arthur and his Queen Gwenevere. They had also spent time in the Chalice Well Gardens with its holy springs and secret gardens. This time they planned to visit other sacred sites. Rose had taken the time on the journey to Glastonbury, to explain the keys and clues to Julia which had been detailed in the previous few pages. Once they arrived at the hotel, they rested and prepared their sacred space with crystals, candles, a Tibetan bowl and rose and geranium oil, sprinkled on red and white rose buds. They knew that the archetype of Mary Magdalene's energy is strong in Wiltshire and were excited to join with her and other goddesses of unconditional love more deeply this weekend.

In a sacred ceremony, they dropped the fragrant oil onto the dried flowers and took a rose from the box. In gentle circular motions, they rotated it above their crown chakras. Clearing the energy around their heads. They invoked the power of Mother Mary and Mary Magdalene and her energy began to appear. The first oracle card they picked from the 'The Mary Magdalene Oracle' which had the following message for them both was called 'Our Lady of Divine Presence' – suddenly they noticed that the image on the front was of a beautiful woman with a serene face enshrined with a garland of red roses, all around her head and face.

They looked at each other in wonder, of all the unique cards in that deck, the red rose had appeared as a sign. This felt like a strong confirmation that they were to work with the rose of Mary Magdalene.

> You have been preparing to receive me, opening your heart and clearing away past shame and doubt. You have been asking for the divine light to be with you and I tell you now, I am alive within you. Your wish to serve the world, to be blessed by my light so

that you can assist others, is granted. As you open your heart and mind to me, your every touch becomes my touch. Your loving gaze holds the light of my own eyes within it. My grace lives in you, flowing through you, into the heart of the world – The Mary Magdalene Oracle Cards

Such gentle but powerful words struck a deep chord in their hearts. As they opened up and allowed the process to unfold, they felt the energy rise through the flame of the candle they had placed before them and it seemed as if Mary's essence was palpable in the room.

Next, they rubbed the rose oil between their palms and deeply inhaled, with hands cupping their faces until the spiritual energies began to sparkle throughout their bodies. Using the warmed oil they lightly stroked their own aura field which uplifted the energy further. Rose felt the tingling energy of Mary's presence around the back of her head and Julia felt it descending her crown chakra and moving down her nose to the tip. This is the way that Mary always manifested for her, like a special touch or a signature calling card, to show that she is there, present and supportive. The friends asked that they be guided along a mystery trail to the relevant sacred sites over the weekend. Julia received a message from Mary that she should find fun in this journey and would be light-hearted in her discoveries.

The next card they pulled was from Rebecca Campbell's "The Rose Oracle."[31] It was about the importance of using one's own self-knowing or instinct, in order to move forward. On her website, Rebecca describes the metaphysical qualities of the rose thus: "The Mystic Rose. Compassion. Devotion. Humility. Humanity. Grace. The rose was a symbol of the Goddesses of old, so it's no wonder that when Christianity absorbed large parts of the indigenous Celtic traditions in Europe, the Mother Goddess Mother Mary became associated with the rose. Perhaps the reason Mary is so beloved."

The energies built and Rose also received a message. It was a reminder that there was also some release work to do. As they talked about this theme of personifying love and grace, Rose thought of her past life as Lady Eleanor Talbot and told of how she had appeared to her during a healing shamanic ceremony with mushrooms, a couple of weeks previously. Rose

---

[31] https://rebeccacampbell.me/category/oracle-cards/

had asked for a guide to be revealed and the lovely face of Lady Eleanor Talbot had come into view. In her mind's eye, she knew that there was something that still needed healing between the friends' past lives, at the time Eleanor and Elizabeth were alive.

Rose reached for the rose quartz pendulum that glittered on its gold chain and requested it to be programmed for an answer to what still needed to be healed in their union. She asked for confirmation of the character she had guessed that Julia had been, Elizabeth Woodville. Was she The White Queen, she asked. As the pendulum began to swing, it answered a clear 'YES' to her question, as affirmation. She knew already the connection for herself as Eleanor.

As they spoke about the way that Edward had rushed into marriage with Elizabeth and caused enmity between the Lancastrian and York houses, the friends realised something astounding. The battle was famously known as The War of the Roses. Rose had unwittingly dried both white and red roses some weeks previously which she had only just realised during their ceremony, represented the White Rose of the House of York, to which Elizabeth Woodville was connected and was the reason for her nickname The White Queen. The Red Rose had represented the House of Lancaster, into which Edward IV was born. This further connection to the roses laid before them could not be a coincidence!

As they delved deeper into the story of the many children Elizabeth begat the king and then his untimely death, it became clear that Julia was carrying the energy of the turbulence she would have been thrown into, as his widow. With her two sons in The Tower of London and having to seek sanctuary in Westminster Cathedral along with the king's coffers, she and her children hid themselves and awaited their fate. Unhappily her eldest sons were probably murdered and the ensuing battle for the kingship had begun. What a great loss she experienced.

Bishop Stillington who had given his blessing to Eleanor and Edward all those years ago had kept his dark knowledge for the nineteen years of Edward's marriage but then went straight to Edward's brother Richard with his forbidden secret. He exposed the betrothal, betraying Elizabeth in her most vulnerable moments. He claimed that this would make the two young princes Edward's bastards, as he had therefore committed bigamy and was not legally married to Elizabeth in light of the secret pre-contract with Eleanor. This was enough to give Richard the upper hand, as we have learnt.

Elizabeth got word of this and would have now felt in mortal danger for her little abandoned family huddled in the cold vault of the cathedral for safety. What would be her fate and those of her two older daughters now? To her huge relief, when he came to power, Richard III was lenient with her and spared her life, promising that he would not hurt her, or the children, but her wealth and properties were taken from her and a meagre annual allowance given instead. The bitterness she felt at the horrid secret of Eleanor's, must have been unbearable in the face of her grief.

One can only imagine the utter betrayal Elizabeth must have felt hearing of her late husband's dalliance with a young woman of whom she had probably known nothing. She was devastated and heartbroken. This was the pattern of pain that needed release between the two present-day friends. At a core level, Julia was still replicating a feeling of fear of loss around her husband's business and also her material belongings and the resulting security they gave her and the family. Also, Elizabeth was no doubt in terror of her children being brutally wrested from her and possibly murdered. This pattern of loss and need for safety had played itself out in Julia's present life too. Holding on to the family business at all costs and keeping her daughters and extended family as a tight-knit unit close by, were of tantamount import to her, even at the expense of her own health. She had been on the brink of exhaustion before the trip and knew that something had to give.

Rose intuited that this was an echo from the past life that needed healing, so that Julia could release any unfounded fears now, for her highest good. To develop a trust that "all is well and all will be well" as I, Julian of Norwich had realised and written about before. The remembering of these past dynamics is a large part of the present-day past life healing work, made more effective by using a physical energy cleanse, which is key to freeing the old blueprint from the body. Rose knew then the part that she had played by keeping secret her betrothal. She knew now that this had caused an unknown block in their friendship several times over the years. She then intuited what they needed to do to release this.

The next morning, armed with this backstory, and open to being guided by their instincts, they arranged to visit St Margaret's Chapel, the Magdalene Alms Houses and Quiet Garden, in the centre of Glastonbury.

This beautiful little church is dedicated to Mary Magdalene and was built in 1215! They, at last, found the little church tucked away down a narrow stone pathway sandwiched between two ancient buildings, at 38 Magdalene Street. As they entered the courtyard they were greeted by the scent of many beautiful flowers being tended by a local volunteer.

Once entering through the ancient doorway to the tiny sandstone chapel, they both lit a candle and moved to kneel and pray at the altar. There in front of them was a beautiful framed example of historic iconography depicting Mary Magdalene dressed in her red cloak, on a gold leaf background. A bunch of deep red blooms with a single red rose at its centre, were placed on a side table, again echoing the theme of the rose. They both prayed to be connected to the loving energy of this beloved saint, who truly represented the divine feminine, that they so strongly linked to. They intended for Mary Magdalene to open their hearts in unconditional love, in order to heal any past wounds between and surrounding them. So much beautiful energy came through during their visit.

After leaving the sacred chapel, they then sat on a little wooden bench outside, with a view of the beautiful garden in front of them. The sun was shining hot on their skin and added to their feelings of relaxation and peace. The friends unpacked their sacred objects onto a little red cloth. They carried with them their ceremonial selection of beloved crystals, the box full of hand-dried red and white rose buds and the Tibetan singing bowl for clearing the energies. They then repeated last night's ceremony, using the oil on their palms. Rubbing their hands together to release the beautiful scent, they raised their palms to their faces and inhaled the essence deeply once again. This brought a shiver of energy through the crown of their heads and they became aware of the presence of Mary Magdalene's energy at once. Rose repeated the stroking of her aura with her rose-covered hands, strengthening the inflowing energies, in particular around her heart chakra. Again she rotated her right hand clockwise over the heart energy vortex and prayed for it to be fully opened. She knew it was now time to implore clearing of all pain patterns from their previous lives and that of the present. She was finally ready to be open to this healing, as was her dear friend.

Another synchronicity the two friends had shared was their chosen self-banishment, into the life of a nun. Elizabeth had chosen to join the monastery at Westminster during Richard's reign and Eleanor had Become a patron and served at Whitefriars monastery after her abandonment from King Edward. In their youth, the two friends had both experienced extreme religious devotion, which is akin to becoming a nun! Both had managed to break the bond of servitude to that way of life eventually and had completed this aspect of healing from an oppressive religious lifestyle, from each others' timeline.

Another present-day synchronicity Rose then realised, was the ray of light in Elizabeth's future brought about by her arrangement for the marriage of her daughter Elizabeth of York, to Margaret Beaufort's son, Henry Tudor. He became known as King Henry VII after he had vanquished Richard III. This final battle in the War of the Roses brought the feuding to an end, establishing The Tudor dynasty. Their marriage had sealed the alliance of the warring houses at long last. Julia's daughter was also to marry later that year and it felt like a happy parallel for her too.

Interestingly, a couple of weeks before the wedding in 2022, Rose did some research on the church they were to be married in, St. Mary's Church in Worstead, Norfolk. She was amazed to see that this church is one of the most significant Tudor examples in the country! Not only is the stunning rood screen perfectly preserved, but one of the sixteen beautiful paintings of various saints and religious figures is a rare image of St. William. Rose determined to develop this story further in her next book because here was another link to a past life in her soul group. St. William was, she had discovered a couple of years ago, the murdered son of a woman in Norwich in 1144 and was a repeating soul pattern for her friend Teal and her son Lee! The roses were doing their work! As a result of this fortunate pairing, Elizabeth Woodville, therefore, became the grandmother of Henry VIII who features strongly in the following chapter about Rose's third medieval past life and the weaving of her emerging soul group.

Birthday synchronicities

Whilst Rose was making further edits to this book suggested by her publisher, she alighted on yet another couple of number synchronicities to her soul family. In her mind, this now confirmed the connections between Elizabeth Woodville and her husband's brother, Richard III with her married friends Julie and Simon. Elizabeth's eldest daughter by Edward IV was named Elizabeth of York. Rose had already linked Julia's eldest daughter, Jade, to Elizabeth of York. As she was reading about her birth, Rose realised that Elizabeth of York was born on 11 Feb 1466. Can you see the numerology? This date links Jade's father Simon (Richard III) to her because his date of birth is 14 December 1966. Hot on the trail again, she read further and discovered the recent and exciting archaeological find of Richard III's remains. The bones of his well-preserved skeleton showed fatal battle wounds from when he died at The Battle of Bosworth Field.

This was the significant war that ended The War of the Roses when he was vanquished by Henry Tudor. Richard was the last of the British kings to die in battle. His bones even showed that he had scoliosis, where the spine was rounded. In Wikipedia, she found a section called 'Exhumation and re-burial of Richard III of England.'[32] As she was reading about the discovery on the former Grey Friars Priory site in 2012 and following the subsequent extensive radiocarbon dating and genetic testing, the remains were confirmed as Richard's. After legal clearance, they were then reinterred at Leicester Cathedral on 26 March 2015. Rose immediately realised that 26 March is the birthday of her soul friend Julie. This tied them both together in this current life and their medieval past lives as well.

Healing past wounds

Returning our thoughts to the present, in Glastonbury, Wiltshire, Rose and Julia's next steps were to take them to the top of a sacred Druid mound dating back to the Neolithic Bronze Age some 5,000 years previously. It was called Barrow Mump and had been connected to the manmade Tor in Glastonbury. Both mumps now had the remains of the chapel of St. Michael built on their summits. As these were strategically placed on the St. Michael and Mary ley lines, Rose found it curious that the Christians must have known of the sacred energy lines running through these sites. These churches had lain in ruins for many years but had hosted an established pilgrimage for thousands every year, dating back centuries. It was a perfect spring day and the meadows surrounding the mump were

---

[32] https://en.wikipedia.org/wiki/Exhumation_and_reburial_of_Richard_III_of_England

heavily sprinkled with sun-drenched buttercups and daisies. It seemed as if they were sparkling against the verdant fresh green of the spring-bedecked meadows and trees, with their bright new green leaves. As they climbed the steep slope to the top they drank in the sight of the deep blue skies dotted with small fluffy white clouds. Rose felt as happy as she had ever been, drinking in these beautiful sights and summery scents, along with the sounds of the birds trilling happily.

'Barrow Mump, Glastonbury'

The St. Michael and Mary Ley line

The aforementioned intertwining ley lines run from St Michael's Mount in Cornwall to the old St Margaret's Church ruins, in Hopton-on-Sea, Suffolk. St. Michael's forms the arrow-like energy line from coast to coast and the female line weaves back and forth crossing the male line intermittently, like a snake and is also known as the rainbow ley line or umbilical cord of the earth. There are many maps and descriptions of sacred sites, to be found along their pathway. We do not know which stars might have been important in Neolithic times but one group of stars, the constellation of Orion, could well have figured in their cosmology. This group of luminaries certainly were significant in Ancient Egyptian times. The star Mintaka in the belt or Orion would have set along the Michael alignment in 2800 BCE and could have provided an accurate sighting measure for a long-distance alignment.

Rose had visited some of the sites along this line. One notable spot was Bury St Edmunds Cathedral ruins. She and a male friend, a medium and a bit of an expert at using the dousing rods had teamed up to explore the energies there. They decided to douse for their past lives there. When asking the question of whether Rose was tried for witchcraft there, the rods noticeably crossed over each other, indicating a 'yes'. He then asked if he had been a priest and again this was confirmed and it seems he may have condemned her to death as a heretic. That is a story for the next book methinks, otherwise, we shall never be finished with these tales. On the subject of further ley or earth lines in Norfolk, I will unfold more about these pathways of energy seen by Peter the shaman, in Chapter 12.

Once at the top of Barrow Mump, on the crossing of the St. Michael and Mary leylines, the view was breathtaking with streams and rolling fields stretching out before them in all directions, a truly three hundred and sixty-degree panorama of the glorious English countryside. Once settled on their picnic blanket they thoughtfully ate their lunch and relaxed more deeply on the lush thick grass. Rested they then prepared themselves for another ceremony, this time one of deep gratitude to the elements and four directions of the North, East, South and West. Calling in their loving ancestors and power animals they determined to work on the release of any darker emotions tied to their unhappy past lives and Rose rubbed the rose oil in her palms once again and prayed for healing.

Rose continued to sweep Julia's aura from top to toe, brushing the energies down each of Julia's legs and out through the soles of her feet. She invoked all traces of sorrow and fear to be swept clean and dissolved into the atmosphere. Eventually, she gently placed her hands on the soles of Julia's feet to complete the healing. These were Reiki techniques that they were both familiar with and as the heaviness of the long-carried emotions left her body, she repeated the affirmations of peace and love that Rose chanted. These intentions were to take the place of the fear and bereavement held over the centuries. At the close, Julia's body felt relaxed and peaceful and she grounded herself into mother earth with gratitude and thanks for her part in the healing.

Finally, it was time to descend and make their way back to the town for the herbs and potions they wished to purchase in Glastonbury. Culminating their inspiring day, they enjoyed the nourishing food the restaurant that they chose had to offer. Once back in their room, they cleared their auras by taking a shower each, which included a salt foot bath sprinkled with rose petals. As they rested, they enquired of the rose quartz pendulum if the healing was completed. Too tired to do anything more than slumber, Rose knew there was just one more aspect to their healing journey that still needed completion. As she drifted off into peaceful slumber she was inspired as to what they needed to do, on their last morning.

Upon waking refreshed and thoughtful, she suggested to Julia that they say the Hawaiian Ho-opono-pono prayer to each other and the energy tingles flooded back into their crowns at the mere suggestion. With legs crossed and arms outstretched they held hands and looked into each other's eyes, chanting this ancient prayer of love and forgiveness. It is known to be a very powerful agent for change and they repeated it many times singing "I'm sorry, please forgive me, thank you, I love you" until they felt that the energies were completely cleared and released. What a wonderful conclusion to this karmic life cycle and preparation for a fresh way of being, for their onward journey.

The final destination after leaving their hotel was the Avebury Great Circle, in particular the corridor of standing stones at the southern entrance named the West Kennet Long Barrow. They had read that Avebury is the largest megalithic stone circle in the world, consisting of a large henge with an outer circle of stones, and two smaller stone circles situated in the centre of the monument. The causeway they visited, near West Kennet, had only recently been discovered in 1999 and they chose to walk through the entrance to the huge rocks. From here there were one hundred pairs of stones along the avenue creating a corridor fifteen metres wide and running for over a mile. Rose's idea had been to connect to the energies of the St. Michael/Mary ley lines which were said to cross here. She felt that if they placed their backs against the rough surface of the stones they could tune in to these neolithic energy conductors, placed there thousands of years previously, during the Bronze Age.

Julia felt the cold stone behind her back and jolts of energy coursed through her body. They knew they had connected to the spirit of the land and were grounding down the energies from the heavens. It has been said that those who are conscious of healing will experience a feeling of being like a human bridge between the sky and earth. Rose visualised a column of pure white and golden light beaming down through them, the rock and into the ground. This felt like a satisfying conclusion to their pilgrimage and they happily picked their way back through the dappled black and white cows lying chewing the cud nearby, who seemed to also be soaking up the earth energies. Finally, the two made their way back to the car, happy to drive home in the knowledge that they had re-connected to each other, the land and their own inner bliss.

Around the time that Rose had discovered these older timelines between herself and Julia, she had also thought about Julia's husband Simon and whether he might fit into the story somewhere. It struck her that he may well have been King Richard III.

Connecting with soul family: Simon's past life (Julia's present husband)

Richard III(1452-1485). Although Richard III's crooked advisors were possibly responsible, (unknown to himself), for the death of the Queen's two sons, they were declared illegitimate due to Edward IVs secret betrothal to Lady Eleanor. He did act more leniently with Elizabeth and her older daughters and swore that they would not be hurt so that they could come out of hiding. This respite could also find its equivalent energy in Simon's protective nature with regard to his two daughters and could explain his behaviour towards keeping his family safe. This is something that Julia and Simon could explore in the future when the right time came. At any rate, Simon definitely has a kingly air about him, Rose grinned to herself.

Whilst Rose was staying with her friends Julia and Simon in August 2022, she took a break from editing. Lo and behold, she was to discover another clue to the connecting past of their second daughter Lisella, to the second daughter of Elizabeth and King Edward IV. First, she asked

Lisella what her middle name is and she said it is Maria. This name is also known as Mary in England. The second daughter of the King was Mary of York b. 11 August 1466 and died on 23 May 1482. Rose could not find very much detail about her as she died when she was fourteen without being married or having any royal children. There was though, another date synchronicity which Rose was excited to find. It was Lisella's birthday whilst she was staying there, so Rose decided to research her date of birth to see if there were any bonds to the family's royal past life. She was a bit disappointed to learn that their birthdays were different dates. Lisella's is on 9 August 1992 and Mary of York's on 11 August 1467. The trail went cold and Rose decided that the middle name Maria and the fact that she was the younger sister in both scenarios, would have to be enough. The family circle now seemed complete.

Now, having discovered that Julia as The White Queen was the grandmother of King Henry VIII through the marriage of her daughter Jade (Elizabeth of York) to King Henry VII, we will turn our attention to one of the most notorious British royals in history, King Henry VIII and the secrets kept by his wives and mistresses!

CHAPTER 6

Medieval past life, Mary Boleyn

I, Julian of Norwich, in spirit, would like to take you forward again, this time thirty-two years later to another medieval and very well known character, Rose's third significant past life in a row. To re-cap, the first in this series was mine, Lady Julian, born in 1342 and died in 1416 at around seventy-four years old. Twenty years later I incarnated as Lady Eleanor Talbot in 1436 and died of a mystery illness in 1468 at the age of thirty-two, as detailed in the previous chapter.

Thirty-two years later I emerged as:

Mary Boleyn, (born c. 1499 - 19 July 1543). She passed away at the age of forty-four. The first born child of Thomas and Elizabeth Boleyn, she had a sister, Anne and a brother George. Mary was probably born at Blickling Hall, Norfolk not long after which the family moved to Hever Castle, in Kent. The family, most likely Sir William Boleyn, (b. 1451 – 10 October 1505), who was the Sherif of Norfolk and Suffolk, owned other property apart from Blickling Estate. For example, 125-127 King Street in Norwich, close to the area where Rose had first moved close to eight years ago. There are very good videos about all things Boleyn on the Tudor Travel Guide website[33] or their YouTube channel, at thirteen minutes in.[34]

To set the current scene, the Welsh Tudors came to the throne in 1485 and reigned until 1603. They brought peace to England after one hundred and fifty years of virtually continuous warfare. The War of the Roses being

---

[33] https://thetudortravelguide.com
[34] https://youtu.be/KYX8qR-9pYU?t=2

one such battle. The family had encouraged new religious ideas, overseas exploration and colonisation. Later on in her discoveries, Rose came to believe that her sister's boyfriend Stephen was in fact King Henry VIII and that her sister Annabel was his first wife, Queen Catharine of Aragon. I will set out briefly, the evidence Rose gathered here and then explain the third-party situation between them.

Catharine of Aragon - Henry VIIIs first wife from Spain (1485-1536), mother of Mary I, their only surviving child. She came to live at Greenwich Palace upon her marriage to King Henry VIII. Catharine was buried in Peterborough Cathedral, aged fifty-one. After Henry divorced her, she was removed from the King's presence and housed in another abode for the rest of her life.

Annabel Virgin (b.25 July). Rose's younger sister was born in Whitby. She divorced and left her puritanical upbringing, in her early thirties. Her birthday on **25 July** ties her to Katharine of Aragon's daughter Mary I, who was married to Phillip II of Spain on **25 July** 1554.

Significant date and age synchronicities

Another connection of Annabel's life in the present day to that of Henry VIII is that Annabel was married at the age of **eighteen,** the same age that Henry was, when he married Catharine of Aragon.

Then, Rose noticed another date connection. Annabel had married on **24 April,** which is the date that Henry's "Oyer and Terminer" laws were drawn up and used against Anne, to find a reason to trap and accuse her, on **24 April** 1536. Quoting from a blog, "One Response to "**24 April** 1536 – The Commissions of Oyer and Terminer":

> Where these commissions set up with Anne Boleyn and the five men in mind or is it just a coincidence that they were tried for offences in Middlesex and Kent? Was this, in Paul Friedmann's words, "virtually a death warrant for Anne"? - 'The Fall of Anne Boleyn'[35]

---

[35] https://www.thefallofanneboleyn.com/home/24th-april-1536-the-commissions-of-oyer-and-terminer/

This now linked Annabel to Roses's friend Teal (Anne Boleyn), in the same soul pairing, as they had both been dethroned by Henry VIII.

King Henry VIII (b. 28 June 1491– **28 January** 1547). Born at **Greenwich** Palace, London. Henry was King of England from 22 April 1509 until his death in 1547.

Stephen King (b. 22 February) Born In **Greenwich**, London.

Location synchronicities

Stephen was born and still lives in the same location to that of Henry VIII, **Greenwich** in South East London. Rose's sister Annabel, had moved to the area from West Sussex, when she got married at eighteen to her first husband. Although she had left him by the age of thirty-five, she is still living in the same area close to **Greenwich,** to this day.

Birthday synchronicity

King Henry's death on **28 January**, ties in with his only legitimate son's ascension to the throne, as King Edward VI. This would now connect Stephen to his girlfriend's half-brother Terry. Rose discovered sometime later on in her tracking, that Terry's past life seemed to have been as Edward VI because his birthday is **28 January.** She will lay this out for you dear readers in more detail, in Chapter 10. As Rose was to discover, there seemed to often be a certain amount of intensity and discord with soul pattern relationships and Terry's current disappearance from the family scene, was in part due to his sister's boyfriend Stephen, with whom he had very little patience or understanding.

Injury and character synchronicities

Henry VIII was known as an extravagant spender, which could also be said of Stephen. Henry had suffered from various ailments during his lifetime, such as malaria. He was a keen sportsman and he had several accidents, but the worst one was a jousting incident when he was older, at forty-four at Greenwich Palace. His horse fell on him and he was unconscious for two hours. He recovered but became increasingly paranoid and melancholy after this fall. He suffered a leg injury which never got better and his legs became increasingly ulcerated. His mood became worse as a result of the constant pain and this was the real turning point when he became more of a tyrant. It is said that Anne Boleyn miscarried a son and heir because of the shock of him nearly dying after his jousting accident. The fact that he lost his longed-for son and heir did not help his mood either and was a downhill trajectory for the couple.

Likewise, Stephen began to have problems with his leg around the age of fifty and eventually, it became so painful that he had to have a hip replacement. He was certainly very grumpy during that time and still suffers with his back to this day, as everything was put out of alignment.

Forced family separation, synchronicity

Catharine of Aragon's daughter Mary I (Annabel's mother Constance Mary in this lifetime), was demoted from Princess to Lady when her parents divorced. She was sent away by Henry VIII to live at Knole Park and forbidden to communicate with her mother, but they were able to send secret letters between them via sympathetic staff. This is mirrored in their present lives, although the mother/daughter roles are reversed. Annabel has been unable to have more than a few occasional clandestine texts with Constance over the last few decades, due to her mother's religious beliefs, those of shunning ex-members who are disfellowshipped. This subject will be dealt with in more detail soon. Constance has never met her daughter's boyfriend Stephen as a result.

Catharine of Aragon would also have been deeply affected by the dim royal prospects for her only daughter Mary, who was now deemed illegitimate. Henry drew up the First Succession Act when his second wife Anne Boleyn bore him a daughter, Elizabeth, on 7 June 1533 (we will look at the equivalent digital number 15.33 or angelic number 3.33 further on). **Three** years later, Catharine died in January and by 19 May 1536, Anne was also to lose her life, **three years** after her wedding to Henry. Her banished sister Mary Boleyn died ten years later in 154**3**. The new Act now left no avenue to the throne for Mary, or so Henry thought! Twenty years later in 1553, Edward was to be crowned. It proved to be lucky for

Elizabeth eventually, but more of this further on in these shenanigans. Karmic patterns certainly seemed to come in **three's!**

Location synchronicities

Rose loved living in Greenwich and would walk in Royal **Greenwich Park** regularly. It is said that it is still home to a small herd of Fallow and Red **deer**, harking back to its royal hunting past. This reminded Rose of the **deer** park she had enjoyed some years previously when she had lived near Royal **Knole Park**, where Henry VIII had also owned a sizeable herd of royal **deer.** The sisters had also lived along the Thames River, once in Royal Woolwich Arsenal, in a waterside apartment. This would have been where Henry VIII built his naval arsenal and held many sporting and jousting events. As Rose completed this paragraph, she glanced at her Facebook feed and saw a picture one of her friends from Otford had posted. It was of himself with one of the royal **deer** behind him, in **Knole Park**! That, my friends, is synchronicity. The magic of the Universe is all around you at every moment, but you need to heighten your awareness to become conscious of it. It brings joy to the heart, knowing that all things are interconnected at all times, for the highest good of all.

'Knole deer park, Sevenoaks'

Rose's character was being finalised in the final editing stages of this chapter in late July 2022 and she planned a break away to see her long-lost family, down at the coast. She hadn't seen her parents and brothers for over two years because of the virus, lockdowns and her bad health. She was excited to come together, to celebrate with them all and to welcome her daughter from Bavaria, at the airport. They all met at her sister's Edwardian place, overlooking the sea and revelled in a wonderful and uplifting celebration. On her trip down she had visited one of her soul tribe, Harry, who lives in Otford. Naturally, she wanted to walk around the relics of Otford Palace and sing her Ho'oponopono to release any stagnant energies connected to it.

Rose hummed under her breath and as she turned the corner, she discovered to her delight, that the old run-down tower had been refurbished and was looking almost as good as new. Harry mentioned that this last surviving ruin of the once glorious palace was going to be turned into a tourist attraction shortly. He said it was going to undergo internal reconstruction and made safe for people to mount the stone staircase. From the top, they would be able to take in the view of the rural countryside, from the turret. When she walked closer to take photos, she noticed that the sole inhabitants were pigeons, sitting in the window and making their nest together.

The two friends then parked in Sevenoaks and walked down into Knole Park along the little pathway that she had trodden so many times with her daughter nearly twenty-eight years ago. It was like a beautiful trip down memory lane and although the grass was scorched by the unusually hot and dry summer, it took on a magical feel, when she spotted the deer frolicking in the shade under the oak trees. They are very tame and as they watched in fascination, one cheekily stuck its nose into someone's picnic basket.

As they walked in and around the inner courtyards and chatted about her trip, Rose just mentioned that she was to sleep on a couch for the coming week. Her sister had assured her that it was a very comfortable one, with its cushions stuffed with duck down and covered in a stunning gold-hued fabric with embroidered dragons on the puffy cushions. She described the carved double wooden knobs at the back corners held together with silk rope. Harry exclaimed, "you do know that those sofas are called Knoles after Knole Park?" Rose didn't know this and asked "why are they called that?" Harry explained that they were originally commissioned by King Henry VIII, for Knole House and hence all the copies made since then have acquired this very name! Here was yet another synchronicity out of the blue and it made Rose chuckle, as it seemed so surreal that she should be sleeping on one of Henry's sofas all week, at Stephen's apartment!

'A Knole sofa, Roses's temporary bed'

Still visualising the deer that day and as she fell asleep that night, Rose slipped into memories of stately Greenwich Park in South East London, where she and her sister had often walked. Unwittingly, they were very close to the ruins of the old Greenwich Palace, where King Henry had lived. Rose knew little about the palace at the time, as it no longer existed. That was until a recent discovery was made in 2017.

Archeological work in 2017 revealed some remains of Greenwich Palace beneath the Old Royal Naval College. Two service rooms connected to the palace's Friary buildings were discovered; the foundations can still be seen beneath the floor of The Painted Hall. - Royal Museums Greenwich[36]

Special interest synchronicities

Quoting further from above:

Henry VIII was particularly fond of ships and the navy, and Greenwich was well sited for visiting the new shipyards at nearby Deptford and Woolwich

The naval connection with Henry VIII made Rose think about early Stephen's interest in seamanship. He undertook maritime training right there, at the Old Royal Naval College in his younger days. This meant that he would have studied right above the remains of the old Greenwich Palace, unbeknown to him, until it was discovered just five years ago! This was his favourite palace it seems:

Henry made the Palace at Greenwich much larger. He built stables, forges, a new banqueting hall, and armouries to make suits of mail for soldiers.

In his present life, Stephen had wanted to be a naval sailor but at the time he was studying at the college, his circumstances changed and he was unable to finish the course. Instead, he built a career as a plumber and progressed on to becoming a fine interior decorator and designer, a trade which he had practised in that area, all of his life. He loved it, just as Henry had. Stephen also adored character properties and had owned several, which he had renovated to a high standard. One of them had been a converted naval hospital, in Woolwich, called the Royal Herbert

---

36 https://www.rmg.co.uk/stories/topics/greenwich-palace-tudors

Hospital. He had lived there when he met Annabel and it had the most beautiful huge arched window, a real beauty of a building.

He certainly was a man after Henry's heart! It was amazing looking back, just how many character similarities there were between these two timelines, separated by five hundred years, and how they were all drawn to these locations at different times in their lives. Stephen (Henry VIII) was born there, Annabel (Catharine of Aragon) had moved there to be married and eventually, Rose (Mary Boleyn), had joined them.

Despite her happy times in London with her sister, since Stephen had come on the scene, there had always seemed to be a strange and strained energy connection between Rose, Michael and Annabel, right from the start. When she looked at their relationships from the perspective of the past life love triangle between King Henry VIII, Catharine of Aragon (his 'old' wife, as he had called her) and the new young lady-in-waiting, Mary Boleyn, Rose began to understand the present day tensions between them all.

Rose knew from history, that the King had a **three-year** clandestine affair with Mary Boleyn of which Catharine would have been suspicious. We will look at the clues which led her to believe that this was indeed a medieval past life of Rose's. Although she didn't have an affair with her sister's boyfriend in this timeline, Rose had moved to **Greenwich** to live with her sister when she was in her late **thirties**. Likewise, Mary Boleyn had moved to **Greenwich** Palace after her spell in France. All of these events and the dramas that followed in both lifetimes, certainly made sense of the Trickster energy and the medieval curse Rose had learnt about at the beginning of this book. Henry VIII could most certainly be seen as the arch disruptor!

In brief, the affair with Henry had taken place when Mary Boleyn was married to her first husband William Carey. He was one of Henry's favourite Gentlemen of the Privy Chamber and Esquire of the Body to the King. Upon her husband's death, Mary had to forfeit a child that she had borne, which Karen the psychic had 'seen" in the original reading. This was when King Henry had Mary's son raised and educated under the ward of her sister, as she was not deemed a suitable mother, due to her wayward past and reputation. Her first husband William Carey had left her without the funds to educate her son Henry Carey. She never got her son back and was later disowned by the Boleyn parents and siblings for secretly marrying a soldier beneath her station. It was a love match which left her happy, but destitute materially.

Likewise, in true karmic style, Stephen had been separated for most of his daughter's young life with very little contact or visiting rights with her, due to the nature of the strained relationship he has with his ex-partner. He knows very well the pain that this can cause and perhaps this was one of his current life learnings to remember and release. As King Henry VIII, he was infamous for his callous dealings with the unfortunate women and children in his orbit. Annabel seemed to be turning the tables on this pattern and acted as a healing influence in his life, in the present day.

I will dig deeper into this past avatar and the characters surrounding Rose, where we can look at other aspects which mirror her life. We will also compare and learn about the reason for the experience she had when she was 'excommunicated' from her parents' religion. As a consequence, she was also disowned or shunned by her mother and stepfather. Now she could see that the clues to her painful experiences lay in the distant past, hundreds of years ago.

Many years after leaving London and a year after she had started to explore these significant Tudor lives, she met and befriended Teal, who she had originally met at a healing circle at Swaffham Spiritualist Church in Norfolk. That was the first time Teal had channelled through some lost souls, these are ones who die, and have not gone to heaven. These particular 'ghosts' were in the form of a clutch of young orphans. They were dressed in ragged old-fashioned clothes They needed help but were afraid to come forward. Jayne, who has much experience leading such rescue operations, made a psychic connection to the youngsters. She gently encouraged them that it was safe to come into the circle. She explained that it was for their highest good, there is no longer anything to fear and that the group intended to assist in sending them on to their rightful destination in spirit.

Simultaneously, Rose had begun to be aware of an Edwardian governess in the long black garb, bonnet and gloves typical of the time. She piped up and said she had someone materialising who had been strict but loving, who seemed to be connected to these children in some way. Once the circle realised there was a positive connection between the children and this governess they beamed light at them all. Soon this Edwardian lady began to hover and wave a wand and then started to sprinkle fairy dust over everyone as she spun a circle around the group and children. They were then all released to the light. This was an out-of-the-ordinary experience and Rose and Teal had bonded over this unusual soul rescue, keeping in touch afterwards.

Eventually over the next few years, as the tapestry of her life grew, it became apparent to Rose that they had been together in a further past life scenario, in addition to those of Julian of Norwich and Margery Kempe. This time they had returned as sisters, Teal taking the role of Anne Boleyn, which I cover extensively in Chapter 7.

As an aside, Rose discovered that with some well-known royal characters such as The Tudors, many people alive at the time of the awakening in the 21st Century also claimed to have been one of these royals in a past life. I remembered the world-famous hypnotherapist Dolores Cannon's explanation, a lady who came to conduct thousands of past life regressions with her clients. I now reveal the answer she gave to a question often asked, "how can more than one person claim to have been the same famous person in a past life?" I shall quote Delores brief synopsis and you are welcome to research this subject further, in the link given in the footnote, from whence it is derived:

> For example, Dolores Cannon explained that you could have five lifetimes that are real and five hundred lives imprinted from the records that deal with leadership. You could have imprints from various types of leaders, ranging from tribal chiefs to mayors, presidents or leaders of thieves, etc. Soul imprints explain why more than one person may claim to be a historically significant figure in their past life. - Big Picture Questions[37]

Having explained these anomalies, I observed that Rose was always fascinated by these discoveries as she burrowed deep in her research into the wee hours of the night. Slowly, she managed to uncover others' lives apart from Teal's. These were part of what she came to understand were her repeating soul family or group, but not necessarily always from her physical family or bloodline ancestry. As the picture grew, they seemed to have been involved in this and other dramatic historical events, in particular in the timeline which was set inside King Henry VIII's court. There certainly

---

[37] http://bigpicturequestions.com/what-is-a-soul-blueprint-or-imprint/

were some huge challenges and lessons to be learnt in this particular lifetime, for all of the characters involved in this matrix-like play on reality. There were also plenty of clearings to be executed if you will excuse the pun. I do apologise for the poor choice of words, on with the story.

Now I will lead you on this third interlinking soul journey, which had the 21st century Rose seriously considering that she was Mary Boleyn or at least a soul imprint or archetype of her being. However you wish to think of it, there were important lessons to be learnt by her.

Understanding key clues from psychics and shamans

After Rose had established their friendship, Teal introduced her to a friend later in 2016, Karen, who is an excellent psychic medium. As we weave back and forth in time, you will remember that Karen had given Rose a list of names and places a few years previously, like a colourful set of silken threads to bring her embroidered tales to life. These I set out for you in Chapter 4, as an overview of certain 'keys' that can unlock our understanding of our past lives. These lead to our akashic records and Karen seemed to be adept at tapping into these spiritual 'folders' where every single experience is documented, about each and every existence we have ever had. I repeat those clues given here and they will be highlighted in bold type throughout the following texts, as we pick up again the illumined trail of clues:

Catharine of Aragon, a Tudor lady
Anne
Thomas
John
Manor House
Castle with a moat
Belgian/French connection
I was a lady-in-waiting (a most senior position in the Privy to the Queen)
Cardinal Pope
Canterbury
James (see Chapter 11. about the Norfolk triangle of light and St. James churches)

Using the information channelled above, it didn't take Rose long to place these names. One of the clues given was a full name, a very well-known one at that and it also gave her the time period to look for. Therefore, she could quickly put it into the correct historical setting. I have marked the initial clues in bold type where they correspond to the list above. In summary:

Queen Catharine of Aragon (b.16 December 1485 – 7 January 1536), was married to King Henry VIII in Tudor times.

Mary Boleyn (b.1499/1500 – 19 July 1543) had a sister called Anne (b.1502 – 19 May 1536)

Anne and Mary's father was Sir **Thomas** Boleyn and her mother was Lady Elizabeth Howard. There are though, two other significant men by the name of Thomas, she preferred the idea that it also included **Thomas** Cranmer, whose piece of the puzzle was only discovered in the spring of 2022. He was the Archbishop of Canterbury and he links to another friend who Rose seemed to have a present-day parallel life with, Clare. Only just discovered in 2022, her story and the clash with Rome's Cardinal Pope will be detailed in Chapter 9.

Birthday synchronicity

In another link between the Tudors and the Boleyns, Henry VIII's illegitimate but recognised son, Henry FitzRoy, Duke of Richmond and Somerset, was born on 15 June 1519 and died on 23 July 1536, at the age of seventeen. Rose was scouring for date connections and lighted upon a match with her date of birth. The two families were joined, through matrimony, when young Henry Fitzroy married Lady Mary Howard, on **25 November** 1533. If you remember, Rose's birthday is on the **25 November**.

The family name Howard loops us back to Mary and Anne's mother, Elizabeth Howard and her paternal family. Henry Fitzroy was associated through family, with both Mary and Anne Boleyn. He was part of the jury at Anne's trial and he was an illegitimate step-brother, not blood-related. A year after the marriage between Henry Fitzroy and Mary Howard, in 1534, Mary Boleyn secretly married William Stafford, a soldier and was banished from all royal and familial contact. She passed away nine years later, never having seen any of her family again.

> Mary FitzRoy, Duchess of Richmond and Somerset, born Lady Mary Howard, was the only daughter-in-law of King Henry VIII of England, being the wife of his only acknowledged illegitimate son, Henry FitzRoy, 1st Duke of Richmond and Somerset. - The Anne Boleyn Files [38]

> On this day in history, **25th November** 1533 (some say 26th), Henry Fitzroy, the Duke of Richmond and illegitimate son of Henry VIII, married **Lady Mary Howard**, daughter of Thomas Howard, 3rd Duke of **Norfolk,** and the **cousin of Anne Boleyn**. Richmond and Mary were both 14 years of age. They were both born in 1519. Richmond was the illegitimate son of Henry VIII and his mistress Elizabeth Blount (Bessie Blount). Although in "The Tudors" series Richmond died in childhood, he actually died on 22nd July 1536 at the age of **17**, probably from consumption (tuberculosis). Wikipedia, Henry Fitzroy. - Wikipedia, Henry Fitzroy[39]

Fitzroy's death at the age of **17** adds to other numerological coincidences, connected to the number 17. This number seems to manifest a lot in this book, so do look out for this key again later on. Suffice it to say, Rose noticed that she had lived at door number **17** a couple of times, it being the number of her current home. According to numerologists, your door number has a significant meaning, one for you to learn from. In this case, **17** denotes new beginnings, progress, spiritual awakening and enlightenment, amongst other things. To highlight another very recent example, Rose and Julia spent a long weekend at a spa hotel, in late August 2022. The number on the door was **17**. Rose mentioned that she had written about this number recently and Julie confirmed similar door number synchronicities she and her family had experienced with the number 22.

The friends decided to look at their tarot cards that evening and each

---

[38] https://www.theanneboleynfiles.com/henry-fitzroy-marries-mary-howard-2/
[39] https://en.wikipedia.org/wiki/Henry_FitzRoy,_Duke_of_Richmond_and_Somerset

of them pulled a card with a message about **doors.** Rose took the message that things only move forward when one **door** closes and another opens. This, she realised was about her recent romantic relationship. She now understood that in order to move on and meet someone more suitable as a long-term partner, she needed to bring a close to any romantic association. When she was honest with herself, their meetings were still laced with emotion and regrets and she felt this was holding her back.

Julia's tarot card was of an image of a **door,** with a bright light behind it. The tarot encouraged her to shut the **door** completely and walk away. She would find light, blessings and personal growth on the other side, as long as she did not look back. Julia related this to her current work situation and her plans to leave the business and begin another chapter. She had longed to launch herself as a self-employed counsellor, hypnotherapist and Reiki healer. Her studies were just coming to an end and she would have the qualifications needed to begin this venture. The two had already joined forces on their shared Facebook business page @ PeacefulMindsandSouls111 and were planning to promote each others' offerings in the same space as their practices cross-pollinate. They both had Reiki training and worked with healing clients' patterns of past pain, either in this life or in their past lives.

Name, location and circumstantial synchronicities

Elizabeth Boleyn, Countess of Wiltshire (née Lady Elizabeth Howard; c. 1480 – 3 April 1538). Mother of Mary, Anne and George Boleyn. Rose's middle name is **Elizabeth**, giving another link to this family. There will be another name link to **Elizabeth 1** in Chapter 8. Elizabeth Boleyn's father was named **Thomas** and her paternal grandfather, was **John** Howard. Both men's names were clues given in Karen's psychic list. Oddly enough Rose's grandfather on her paternal side was also named **John.** Her paternal grandmother's maiden name, **Howell**, was phonetically close to Howard, too. Another synchronicity was that Rose was also the eldest child, as Mary had been, and Rose was born near Cromer, on the north Norfolk coast. This is only thirteen miles distance and directly North of Mary Boleyn's first home, on the Blickling Estate, another location synchronicity.

Mary's was yet another life in medieval times, which linked to where

Rose had been born in Norfolk. It was in the little abode on the East Anglian coast of England, which the shaman had seen in his vision. In her Tudor life, she was born in a rather more prestigious manor house though, Blickling Hall in North Norfolk. The daughter of aristocrats, she was also known as Lady Mary and her father, Thomas Boleyn, was a rich diplomat and courtier. These were still turbulent political times as the War of the Roses was not long concluded. Her parents met each other in King Henry VIII's court and along with her uncle, made a formidable team. They would push the siblings forward into any opportunity they could scheme up, to elevate their family status. Being linked to royalty by any means, was the best way of climbing the ladder in those days.

Wedding date synchronicity

Another key synchronicity that Rose had only recently discovered, was the arranged marriage of their daughter Mary Boleyn to her first husband, William Carey on **4 February** 1520. This would bring her closer to the King. When Rose looked at the date of her wedding, it surprised her to see that it was the very same day and month that Rose and her husband Robert were married. This was some four hundred years later on **4 February** 1989! Could Rose's husband Robert have been her first husband William Carey in a past life, she wondered? William was 'coincidentally' serving in Henry VIII's court. Rose had always felt hers was strangely similar to an arranged marriage. This tended to happen within the closed community of Jehovah's Witnesses, which forces the dating pool to be small and exclusive.

Family separation synchronicity

It seemed from reading about Mary's marital relationship, that it was an aristocratic arrangement rather than a love match and that they may not even have had much intimacy. Allegedly, the couple bore two children, a girl, and then a boy. It is debated by historians, whether these children may have secretly been Henry VIII's bastard children with her. It is possible that he kept William Carey (who served in his court) quiet with hush money.

He gifted him grants when each of the children was born. The surviving financial records seem to indicate that the dates of the King's payments, match with their births. The male child was sent to live at a monastery, for his education. This was at a later date, when Mary's first husband William Carey had died of sweating sickness and she was left with all of his debts. Anne Boleyn was granted custody of the young Carey by Henry, who re-assigned the toddler, to the monks.

This was evidenced in a letter that King Henry VIII had written when Mary's husband William Carey, had died, as quoted thus:

> William Carey died on 23 June 1528 and Henry VIII promptly granted Anne Boleyn the wardship of her nephew (and possibly his son), two-year-old Henry Carey. In another letter to Anne, Henry remarked upon Mary's easy virtue. He and Anne were concerned that, after William's death, Mary's behaviour would degenerate; in other words, she would be an embarrassment to the king and his intended wife. In November 1530, Henry gave Anne 20 pds to redeem a jewel from Mary; it was probably a gambling debt. - EnglishHistory.net [40]

Well, Rose had chuckled at that. She most certainly had become an 'embarrassment' to her pious parents, once she set foot in 'the big smoke' as London is nicknamed. I would have inserted one of those 'emoticons' as you call them, with the crying with laughter face, but being medieval, it's not my style.

> Mary's husband had left her with considerable debts, and Anne arranged for her nephew to be educated at a respectable Cistercian monastery. - Wikipedia, Mary Boleyn [41]

Rose was relieved that history had not repeated itself in that way, Robert had never been addicted to anything except work.

Carey and his elder sister Catherine came under the wardship of their maternal aunt Anne Boleyn, who was engaged to Henry

---

[40] https://englishhistory.net/tudor/citizens/mary-boleyn/
[41] https://en.wikipedia.org/wiki/Mary_Boleyn

VIII at the time. The children still had active contact with their mother, who remained on good terms with her sister, until Mary's secret elopement with a soldier, William Stafford (later Lord of Chebsey) in 1535....Anne Boleyn acted as her nephew's patron and provided him with an excellent education in a prestigious Cistercian monastery. - Wikipedia, Henry Carey[42]

Child loss synchronicity

Was Henry VIII showing support for his ex-lover, Mary Boleyn, out of the kindness of his charitable heart? Or were his paternal instincts coming to the fore, in the protection of his bastard children? We will never know for sure, historically. As another mirror to this particular experience, Willow, who was Rose and Robert's only child, returned at a young age to live with her father. She had spent a short spell in England with her mother, after her parents' divorce. In Bavaria, Willow was able to pursue higher education in IT and Microbiology.

Here was another repeating theme, Rose, as a mother would have been unable to support her daughter financially to study at college. She had sacrificed her chances of further education on the altar of the Christian ministry before she was married. Once she left her mother's religion, she had no qualifications other than knowing the bible back to front, as an unpaid full-time preacher. She had to start on the first rung on the career ladder at the age of **thirty-two**, in order to put a roof over her head (look out for the number thirty-two as significant to Rose's past lives, later on). There was also a similar sense of emotional loss, separation and lack of funding, experienced by both of these mothers. Rose had not received any money from the divorce settlement. Mary, and likewise, Rose, had kept in close contact with their children after the separation, in order to give them the emotional support and feminine guidance they needed, despite the sad circumstances.

---

[42] https://en.wikipedia.org/wiki/Henry_Carey,_1st_Baron_Hunsdon

Family home move synchronicities

Rose had listened to stories her mother told of her very early childhood. She discovered she was born in the winter of 1961, up on the North Norfolk coast. It had been one of the coldest on record, with temperatures so icy, that waves and breakers had frozen on the shoreline. The bitter cold North Sea wind blew in off the sea onto the beach. Her mother told her tales of how the nappies hung out on the washing line would be whipped dry in an hour or so by the fierce East Anglian winds, despite the sub-zero temperatures. She would walk along the coastal route to the local shops with baby Rose crying in her perambulator, because of her cold hands. Little Rose thought that her gloves were the culprit as her hands hurt so much. She kept shaking them off and they fell into the snow and got even wetter. She described Rose's nearly frozen tears streaming down her face, whilst her mother had tried to secure her mittens again. After hearing these grim stories Rose had lost all interest in exploring her desolate-sounding roots and didn't set a foot in Norfolk until she was in her mid-thirties.

At that time, her visit was just a whistle-stop tour of the seaside village, Cromer, which surprisingly, she had loved. The flint-faced cottages were so quaint, nestled in amongst the bustling high street stores. As it had been in the summer, the shops had been jam-packed with tourists scouring for trinkets and souvenirs in this now popular holiday resort. Over the decades the middle classes and wealthy folk had widened their net, buying up gorgeous properties all along the North Norfolk coast, as second homes. It is a straight two-hour journey out of London, ideal for a weekend hideaway. This had totally changed the nature of the area, transforming it from a bleak little fishing village, into one which was dotted with art and craft shops, artisanal baked goods and organic produce. It was the perfect idyll for jaded city slickers. As she was pondering these memories, Rose made a mental connection between the little place she had been born and the lonely little cottage on the coast, that Peter the shaman had seen in his vision.

A mere six months after Rose's birth in Norfolk, her father and mother had moved the little family away from East Anglia, further north of the country. They settled in Whitby, but were still on the chilly East Coast, as he had been relocated there for work. Just as Rose had not stayed long in

Norfolk, Mary Boleyn's family had moved further South of England when she was but a young child and settled in their permanent family home and seat, **Hever Castle in Kent**. This was where Mary was raised, receiving her elocution lessons and intricate education as any other aristocratic child would, along with her siblings Anne and George Boleyn. As an aside, all of Rose family on the paternal side lived in **Kent,** ever since her birth father left her mother when she was seven. Before this, when Rose was only five, the original family of four had moved back down from Whitby to the South of England. He found a home for them in Sussex when she was six. There she lived for the remainder of her childhood and into her late twenties, when she married and moved abroad to Bavaria.

The town where Rose original family settled in Sussex, was not far from **Hever Castle**. In fact, it is only seventeen miles distant and therefore, she, her mother, and their friends, loved to visit there often. They would attend Shakespearean plays and classical music concerts such as Vivaldi on the beautiful grounds, near the lake. Rose's ex-husband Robert, was a mutual friend of this circle and had attended some of these events when visiting from Bavaria. She remembered the wonderful picnics and the triumphant finales with fireworks lighting up the newly darkened skies after sunset. It had been so magical and romantic. Rose had walked across the bridge over the castle moat many times when taking a tour of the well-preserved interior, just as her counterpart Mary Boleyn would have done. If you remember, Karen had given a **castle moat** as one of the clues channelled through her spiritual guides.

When Rose left her marital home in Bavaria and returned to England, she wished to live near her birth father so she could get to know him better, after all the years of separation. She chose to live in a **Tudor** flat in Seal, near her father in Kent. Here she stayed for several years. Strangely this meant she was still close to her past life location, as Seal is only eight miles distant from **Hever Castle**. Although it is not known for sure, Mary Boleyn may have been buried at Hever Castle. Another location synchronicity was that Mary's second husband, William Stafford married a second time after Mary's death and he along with his wife and children, eventually moved to **Switzerland,** where he later died.[43] This was yet another link to Robert, who also moved to live in **Switzerland** in his latter years.

---

[43] https://www.findagrave.com/memorial/73929565/william-stafford

Disownment synchronicity

Rose loved history lessons at school and was particularly fascinated by the medieval period, poring over illustrations of the beautiful clothes they used to wear and drawing them over and over again. Little did she know then, that she would uncover a far deeper connection to this dim period in history, known as The Dark Ages. As a child, she had felt a creeping horror at the awful way that many had met an untimely end, at the hands of gruesome means. It seemed that organised religion, hand-in-hand with politics, had been culpable of the bloody threat for so many innocent lives.

In some ways, this awareness stayed in her memory and once a young adult of **thirty-two,** she made a bid for freedom from the religious and patriarchal cult she had been raised in. They required members to completely and coldly disown anyone that commits a sin or dissents against the religion. It felt like the black and white strictures of the Catholics and Protestants, being forced to swear allegiance to the right side, or die in medieval times! Of course this changed like the wind in Henry VIII's time.

The consequences of walking away was well known to Rose. She was very aware that her disloyalty in their eyes, meant that she was to be shunned as an apostate (one who speaks against their beliefs, which they consider to be an act of heresy). This rift included her own mother, stepfather (an Elder in the congregation) half-brother, sister and all friends with whom she had grown up, from that time onwards. This had taken place some twenty-eight years before completing this book. Happily, her two siblings took it upon themselves to escape the cult in fairly short succession of each other. Terry left within months of Rose, with Annabel coming out **three years** later. They all suffered the same shunning treatment from their parents for nearly three decades and counting. All three of them had given up any hope that there might be a reconciliation with their parents and had accepted their separation as the high price they had to pay for their freedom and personal sovereignty.

Here again was a key comparison with the way that Henry VIII banished Mary from his court for marrying a soldier beneath her station. Mary's parents had followed suit and completely disowned their daughter for her indiscreet choice of partner, cutting her off from their will and having nothing more to do with her! King Henry added to this tragedy by engineering the cruel execution of her siblings Anne and George, **three years** later. Now she really was alone, but at least happily married to the love of her life, the soldier William Stafford. After her death he had become a knight, but he really had been her knight in shining armour.

Rose and Annabel experienced a similar fate and had now been doubly abandoned, by both father and then mother. After their birth father left the family when Rose was seven years old and Annabel only five, he had been prevented even visiting rights with his two daughters, by their mother and she had also not allowed them to see their paternal grandparents ever again! Due to their mother's manipulation and twisting of the facts, the courts had ruled against him and overnight the sisters lost half of their family. In reality, the trumped up charges against him were just an excuse to prevent her daughters from exposure to any worldly influence or freedom of thought and replace him with a new step-father.

As Rose's father is an atheist, and their mother Constance a new convert to the cult, she was convinced that she had to prevent any undue influence from his wordly way of thinking. God forbid he may provide them the mental support to leave the religion, once they came of age and could be independent, using critical thinking abilities. This ruling had also included their paternal Grandparents, who were bitterly disappointed, but felt that they had no choice but to go along with her wishes in the matter. Their mother consciously engineered this, allowing her new husband in the faith to adopt her daughters and change their surname to his, on their birth certificates. This gave him sole oversight as their 'new' father, a much more suitable replacement, or so she thought. The net tightened around them. The little girls were not ever asked how they felt about being cut off permanently from their lovely Nana and Grandad, or indeed their Dad, after all, children were to be seen and not heard. In effect the sisters had been 'orphaned' said one counsellor, first from one parent when young and then by the other when they were excluded from their mother and the congregation, in their thirties. The past life patterns seem intrinsically interwoven here.

In another unfortunate and cruel twist of fate, their maternal grandmother Sarah had also died when Rose was ten and then not long afterwards, her mother's sister Kathleen and Terry had emigrated with their five children, back to Sri Lanka. Rose and Annabel missed their beloved maternal cousins dreadfully. They had lost another big chunk of their family in the space of a couple of years. This left them no external support or encouragement to make something of themselves in the world. They became well and truly indoctrinated in their new, nuclear family. Even their mother's three, well-heeled and talented elderly spinster aunts had passed away, not long afterwards. One had been a pianist and teacher, one a secretary and the other a seamstress to the rich and famous in the West End of London. This left the young girls truly in the grips of the cult.

So it was that Rose endured another parallel life experience with Mary Boleyn, when Lady Mary was estranged from her parents and even her own siblings. This caused the same kind of emotional shock waves that Rose had lived through in her own family, to the point that Mary's parents had no longer viewed her as their own child and she was cut off from any financial assistance or inheritance. Rose and her siblings had also been excluded from both sets of their grandparents' wills. Why was this pattern of abandonment, loss of custody of children and any financial support, repeating itself again in Rose's lifetime? What did she need to remember and learn from this cruel religious shunning and these heart-breaking family separations? More importantly, how could she heal? This she learnt in time and will be unravelled in these stories, it being the reason for the writing of them.

Coincidence with shunning

To explain the religious background to this cruel 'shunning' practice, as justified by the cult Rose was raised in, we need to see how they felt that they could biblically underpin this ruling. By using an interpreted example in the New Testament of the Bible, the Governing Body of approximately twelve men, in authority over around eight million followers today, use the following scripture from the Bible:

> If your brother sins against you, go and tell him his fault, between you and him alone. If he listens to you, you have gained your brother. But if he does not listen, take one or two others along with you, that every charge may be established by the evidence of two or three witnesses. If he refuses to listen to them, tell it to the church.

And if he refuses to listen even to the church, let him be to you as a Gentile and a tax collector – Open Bible Info, Matthew 18:15-17[44]

The shunning and reviling of tax collectors, who often ostensibly robbed the people by extorting more than was due, was a common practise in Jesus day. Indeed if one was seen walking towards them, so hated were they, that people would cross the street to avoid speaking or even looking at them! The Jews were also instructed not to eat, drink or socialise with them, just as they could not mix with the Gentiles at that time (non Jews). Today this application of The Apostles' words by this cult is being contested by an ex member. In other words, the practise of despising sinners and separating their worshippers from these unrepentant ones. The wrongdoer is likened to a bad apple who would poison the barrel of good apples, if allowed to stay in close contact, even with their family!

These christian fundamentalist rules are also common to many non religious cults, as a form of control. The rebels who escape are labelled as being 'Disfellowshipped' for example, if the sinner is unrepentant. Otherwise, they can choose to be 'Disassociated' if the person themselves does not wish to be associated publicly with the organisation henceforth. The resulting shunning punishment is identical. This course of action is similar to the Catholic practise of ex-communicating someone from the church, but in fact is not as extreme an action, as Catholics who are allowed continued familial contact. They still enjoy being able to eat, drink and socialise with their loved ones and are simply barred from participating in the holy sacraments (taking of the bread and wine) and attending Catholic services.

Cults tend to believe that if a person is ostracised by their colleagues and family, they may have a turn of heart and return to their former beliefs, in repentance. It is one of the cruellest forms of emotional bribery and has led to a disproportionate amount of ex-members living in daily hopelessness and misery. Religion purports to emulate the unconditional love of their God, but could simultaneously be spectacularly hypocritical!

In a recent court case initiated by an ex-member of Jehovah's Witnesses, for example, and regarding their practice of Disfellowshipping, he consulted with his lawyers, and the Organisation is being taken to court

---

[44] https://www.openbible.info/topics/tax_collectors

in Belgium. The case began in November 2021. If you wish to follow its progress, please refer to The Open Minds Foundation website for updates.[45] This case will be of interest to certain Jewish sects and others who suffer from the same religious shunning treatment.

The most recent development at the time of completing this book was that JW.org had contested the case and it was to be revisited in court on 31 May 2022. In this way, the Organisation will metaphorically 'fight to the death' to justify their rules and the right to shun their members. They employ a fierce legal team to prevent them from losing control of their mandates and pour millions of their members' weekly donations and capital from the vast estates and properties they own, into expensive lawsuits. This was reported on the Australian online news channel ABC.[46]

What is it like to experience shunning, when even your friends and family will not speak to you? Read Derek's experience of shunning and his journey through the courts, to challenge this. Learn through his discussions about world-wide coercion, gaslighting and more, on the Open Minds Foundation website.[47]

Rose felt that these cultish issues, previously fairly unknown to the general public, were now being pushed out from under the radar into international awareness. There had been several high-profile court cases and a flurry of movies about them. Rose sensed a lot of similar red flags due to the lockdowns and vaccine mandates taking place around the world. Because of the pandemic, socialising and travel had been squeezed into a little box of compliance with the need to show a vaccine passport. Similarly, freedom of bodily autonomy, self-sovereignty, medical choice and the right to peacefully protest against it in public, was being suppressed around the world.

New and oppressive legislation was being rapidly drafted, both nationally and then internationally in the form of a new medical treaty being drawn up by the WHO (World Health Organisation). Without

---

[45] https://www.openmindsfoundation.org/blog/jw-appeal-shunning-is-a-crime/

[46] https://www.abc.net.au/news/2021-12-03/how-queensland-criminalise-coercive-control-domestic-violence/100670944?fbclid=IwAR00E4v-b9tnk0JRY9VNLn40dvb4mmeM5ywV5rNTJEoc-uaYV8BlnxR8mJI

[47] https://www.openmindsfoundation.org/blog/coercion-at-its-worst-religious-mandated-shunning/?fbclid=IwAR1xfqZT9O52m2YFXHO6FuwVPhklIfDZzaNEp91ASmo7fsTcRBSuQoQ5dRo

public consultation, the heads of governments met with many world players in Davos, in May 2022. They all seemed to be hand in hand with the WEF (World Economic Forum). Those common folk who were aware and valued their freedom did all they could to warn others. Sadly the elites had tight control of mainstream media, which had become a propaganda tool for mass manipulation. Using distraction techniques and censorship in the form of cancel culture, most people were simply sleep-walking into the possible birth of a New World Order.

Those powerful corporations and select billionaires, were using similarly oppressive tools of control, typical of those used within cults. This led to a huge increase in depression, even amongst school children, due to the isolation and lack of human contact. Adopted by countless governments in many countries, the threats used were those of losing one's employment or medical license, if one did not comply with the mandates. Top-down pressure to receive only the recommended medication in the form of inoculations was mandated, without being open about the ingredients or the hidden truths of dangerous side effects. All early prophylactic treatments were heavily suppressed along with any doctors promoting them openly and on giant social media platforms, were threatened with having their medical licenses taken away for spreading 'misinformation.'

These worldwide government restrictions had crept up on the vast majority, using fear-mongering and scare tactics, alternatively, they would try and shame those not complying by calling them selfish, when they should be thinking of the 'greater good'. This sounded so familiar to Rose, who had constantly been brainwashed into thinking she had to preach to others for 'the greater good.' Those asleep to this type of 'undue influence', were unaware that they were slowly losing their freedoms, over two years between 2020 and 2022.

Worst of all, the only choice of medical intervention, experimental at best, was nowhere near as safe as the 'out of patent' cheap alternatives. These had been discovered to be safe and effective if used at the onset of the virus and were being used to good effect in third-world countries that could not afford the jab programme for its citizens. In the wealthier nations, even babies and children were being 'coerced' into having the inoculations, sometimes without their parent's consent. Many scientists were becoming aware after two years of the pandemic, that youngsters were in no danger at all from the pandemic. People seemed to have forgotten that it was not lethal to over 99% of the population from the outset.

Rose had already lived through this coercive type of top-down bullying behaviour, nearly thirty years previously and was older and wiser to these present-day tactics. She saw the red flags and stood her ground. This was not looking good for the future! Keeping this medical example in mind and returning to the subject of religious coercion, it being a centuries-old phenomenon, the charges being brought against the JW's are that they are guilty of 'hate crimes.'

Russia had already banned Jehovah's Witnesses from openly preaching and practising their religion in public some years previously, in some areas. Their shunning practice was one of three major reasons why President Putin claimed that it destroys the community, causing division and hatred. Rose had concluded that putting people in isolation from their loved ones, is a form of domestic terrorism, destroying the fabric of society from within. As supplemental information, please find below, quotes from an article named 'Persecution of Jehovah's Witnesses' in Wikipedia, explaining why President Putin thinks in this way and has made this ruling against them propagating their religion openly:

> Russian anti-extremism laws were extended to non-violent groups in 2007 and Jehovah's Witnesses were banned in the port city of Taganrog in 2009 after a local court ruled the organisation guilty of inciting religious hatred by "propagating the exclusivity and supremacy" of their religious beliefs".... "on December 8, 2009, the Supreme Court of Russia upheld the ruling of the lower courts which pronounced 34 pieces of Jehovah's Witness literature extremist, including their magazine The Watchtower. Jehovah's Witnesses claim this ruling affirms a misapplication of a federal law on anti-extremism – Wikipedia 'Persecution of Jehovah's Witnesses[48]

Although The Witnesses are pacifists and have been persecuted for not signing up for military service for over a hundred years, they could in fact be likened to the Catholic Crusader 'heroes' in the Middle Ages

---

[48] https://en.wikipedia.org/wiki/Persecution_of_Jehovah%27s_Witnesses

who intolerantly silenced those that did not comply with their rigid way of religious thinking. Preventing people from emotional and physical contact with their families, just as everyone worldwide had experienced in the pandemic lockdowns, was in her mind akin to 'killing' their souls. Far too many people within the Organisation, who want to leave but are afraid to do so, or those who have left already and were shunned, end up committing suicide. The average death toll of those taking their own lives, is a lot higher in this mind-controlled community, than amongst the general population.

Even if it doesn't end in untimely death, the feelings of guilt, shame, trauma, and even PTSD are all legacies of this type of ostracism, long after leaving the community. One only has to look back to the Harlow tests with Rhesus monkeys in the 1950/60s in America, to remember how the experiments ended for their young, when they were prevented having contact with their parents. They died – Psychological Science.[49] Distress statistics were of course soaring after the intentional health mandates, as was to be expected.

Fundamentally, we are tribal animals and are wired to desire company and cooperation from a close group. Psychological damage of those less resilient, can last a life-time and had indeed set like concrete into Rose's bones. Over the years it manifested itself as a fundamental lack of confidence and trust in herself, and anyone who came too close to her. This was something she gradually became aware of after her departure and had worked hard to overcome in the following decades. She strove to understand and release these feelings.

Rose could testify to the exclusivity of a controlling religion. As a young woman, she was strongly discouraged from socialising after school or work, or marrying anyone who wasn't a fully active member. Often members do not fully understand the dire consequences or the effect it could have on their mental health, until long after their baptism, which had sealed their fate. If they fall out of line and sin unrepentantly, this will then be announced from their church platform, and the hapless person will be publicly shunned for the rest of their rebellious lives.

Again using the example of Jehovah's Witnesses official beliefs, written

---

[49] https://www.psychologicalscience.org/publications/observer/obsonline/harlows-classic-studies-revealed-the-importance-of-maternal-contact.html

about extensively in their many publications in addition to the Bible, they believe they are the only true religion. Behind closed doors, they call their belief system The Truth. This includes the firm belief that the rest of Christendom is the Harlot or Prostitute spoken of in the last book of the Bible, Revelation between Chapters 11 and 19 - Wikipedia, The Beast (Revelation).[50]

This religious prostitute is depicted as sitting with a cup of wine brandished in her hand, on a seven-headed beast with ten crowns, symbolising (they think) The United Nations. This creature has the mark of the wild beast emblazoned across its chest, the number 666! The drunken woman is then depicted as coming to her sticky end when God brings a bloody and murderous war against each and every individual and organisation on the planet, who is not a member of Jehovah's Witnesses. This authoritarian battle is called Armageddon, also spoken about in Revelation. Jesus Christ is pictured therein, leading his army on the White Horse of The Apocalypse, followed by three other horses denoting widespread earthquakes, famine, disease and death. He leads in this almighty culling of all human sinners, except for the Jehovah's Witnesses. Rose drew the conclusion that this qualifies as a supremacy belief and also a hate crime!

Rose had watched with interest, the unfolding of the 'shunning' court cases and in her heart knew that it was high time that The Governing Body was forced to see the cruelty they are personally responsible for. They were known to claim that their small 'ruling' body of around twelve self-ordained men (women are barred from being ordained) are the only true 'channel' of God to their eight million followers. They seem to take little personal responsibility for the suffering caused by their imposed belief system. It was discovered that there is a top-secret database of 'offenders' of all kinds, which is strictly guarded in their Bethel Headquarters. Many times paedophiles and murderers find a safe haven within the congregations when this information is known only to the Elders and not the rank and file, especially if they were offenders before they converted. In theory children and other vulnerable people are at risk, as this information is not known by the parents, in advance.

A new indie movie "Debutante" has been released, directed by a

---

[50] https://en.wikipedia.org/wiki/The_Beast_(Revelation

young woman, Kamilia Didinya, who escaped the cult. It is also raising awareness of the subject of shunning. The film won the Audience Award at CIFF. [51] 'Debutante' was nominated for an IFTA (Irish Film and Television Academy) Award! The Executive Producers were Scott M. Homan, Chris Stuckmann and four others.[52] Rose remembered that name, Scott Homan,[53] because he had also interviewed Isisi Allthings in 2019 for his project 'Witness Underground,' when she published her book "Rising from the Ashes of Jehovah's Witnesses" whose book Rose had read.

Location synchronicities

Returning to Rose past life, the next clue in the psychic reading with Karen, connecting her to Mary Boleyn, had been a **manor house**. Henry VIII also courted Anne at nearby Bolebroke Castle. This manor house or 15th Century hunting lodge in **Hartfield**, was where he stayed and hunted in Ashdown forest five miles from Hever Castle. Rose had stayed in **Hartfield** once when her musician boyfriend had played a gig there some twenty years ago. Karen also said there was a **French or Belgian** connection. From the annuls of history we know that Mary went to live in the **French court** when she was fifteen, as a Maid-of-honour for the English queen. This she had become, due to her wily father's influence, who was now the English Ambassador of the Embassy in France. He had requested the position on behalf of his daughter, manipulating a situation where she could be closer to Queen Mary, who married the French King Louis XII.

In effect Mary was her father's eyes and ears in that extraordinary royal setting. During her frolics at the licentious French court and in a twist of fate, Mary Boleyn became one of the next King's lovers for a time, as we will find out later. Mary Boleyn was eventually recalled to England when she was twenty and soon afterwards was married to her first husband, William Carey. She then became **lady-in-waiting** (another clue on Karen's list), to the Spanish Catharine of Aragon, Queen for the last ten years. This led Mary into a tryst with King Henry VIII during this time. Here was an indication of a love triangle, as Henry did seem to develop feelings for

---

[51] https://www.KamilaDydyna.com
[52] https://ChicagoIrishFilmFestival.com
[53] https://www.WitnessUnderground.com

Mary. Some years later though, it had fizzled out and she was then replaced in his affections by her sister.

Anne Boleyn refused to sleep with the king unless he married her. He, therefore, courted her for the next seven years. She would not be his mistress, after what happened to her sister. By now, Henry VIII had been married to Catharine for twenty-four years. She was much beloved of the people but had not borne him a son, just Princess Mary had survived. He could not seek a legal divorce, so he applied to the Pope of Rome for a dispensation! Here another of Karen's clues was mentioned, a **Cardinal Pope** and **Canterbury.** We will explore these in depth in the following chapters about **Anne** Boleyn and **Thomas** Cranmer.

Parallel learnings of Rose's past lives

In three back-to-back medieval lives, Rose had to keep enormous secrets in order to survive. She also lost most of her personal possessions in these lives, which could explain her feeling of being a rolling stone that gathers no moss, in this lifetime. Rose had read about the 'vagabond mentality' spoken about in the international spiritual community she followed. In their view, poverty was not always considered a bad thing when one is on the spiritual awakening path. Rose acknowledged this in her daily life, but she did not want to get stuck in Hermit mode or poverty mentality for all of her life.

As we previously learnt, **Julian of Norwich** could have been burned at the stake in nearby Lollard's Pit, if she had dared to publish her religious writings. Rose had become an author. Her books about her religious background were somewhat controversial and downright condemned as 'apostate literature' in certain circles. Despite this, she forged ahead and self-published her works. She was very glad to have reversed this timeline and had her paternal grandparents in spirit, to thank for this. They always appeared, to support her in her endeavours, unlike her living family.

Mother Julian had also sacrificed all the trappings of an aristocratic upbringing, when she became an anchorite. All the funds she was left with, after the plague had devastated her family and home life, were given to the church for her board and keep, in the adjacent anchorite's cell. This had been a life-long commitment for her. Eventually, Julian's dowry ran low and she had to rely on others gifting her a sum in their will, as was documented. Alternatively, she received alms from the commoners who would visit her little cell for guidance. She gratefully accepted contributions through her tiny window to the world. Alms would probably only have been dry bread and water. Rose wanted to feast on life, after her past sacrifices.

Rose remembered back to her days as a voluntary full-time minister of Jehovah's Witnesses. It was unpaid labour, preaching for ninety hours a month and she had only the capacity to work part-time. Fifty per cent of her funds went to her parents for board and keep. She had economised strictly during those ten years, by sewing her own beautiful clothes, knitting and home baking with her mother. Similarly to Julian of Norwich's position as an anchorite and recognised mystic, Rose parents gladly supported her financially. It was seen to be an honour in the congregation to be a 'Pioneer.' This was the reason that Rose did not pursue further education. She was put on a pedestal in the congregation of eighty members, along with her dear friend Julia and a couple of others who were full-time ministers. She considered her preaching role in this community, to be her only and best career.

In her late twenties, she had gone straight from the family home into marriage, where she was also supported financially. Rose felt that she had worked through a lot of healing around this, but still had things that she wanted to accomplish in life. Her music was also important, singing and writing were good for her soul and could also lead to her financial independence in the future. She knew that the responsibility for her success lay solely with her now and was determined to give her all to her music and book projects.

As character **Lady Eleanor Talbot,** she was to take the secret of her betrothal to Edward IV to the grave with her. The previous shenanigans of her previous father-in-law after her husband's death and then King Edward IV's actions left her without her rightful property. After her sham, secret promise of marriage to the King, she felt she had no choice but to live out the rest of her young life at Whitefriars monastery. Here her board and sustenance would have been taken care of by the nuns. That was, until her passing at the young age of **thirty-two** and the death of her only child, likely from the Black Death.

Rose realised that she had reversed roles in this current timeline, having 'died' to her old way of life as a wife, mother and minister when she was **thirty-two**. She had instead liberated herself, and been re-born to a new way of life and freedom of choice. This cross-over timeline had some symbolic meaning, she was sure. It had freed her daughter too, who, rather than live a controlled religious life, had gone on to study and gain her degrees. This, Rose realised, was the reason she loved discovering her past lives and the clues that showed her how far she had already come along her pilgrim's way, to full awakening.

Affair synchronicity

In her third medieval life as **Mary Boleyn**, she was rumoured to have had an affair with the young French King Francis I. She was fifteen when she had been nominated as one of the maids-of-honour to Henry VIII's sister. The eighteen-year-old Mary Tudor married King Louis XII of France, who was fifty-two. He died three months after the wedding on 1 January 1515, when Francis I then became king. Mary was, therefore, four or five years younger than him. There are three trustworthy sources by Claire, author of the online blog entitled The Anne Boleyn Files. In one article she hypothesised that Mary was not an official mistress of the new French king, but had probably been his lover. Claire says that these suppositions have to be taken with a pinch of salt because there were writers at the time, who were apt to malign the Boleyn family, in general. Similar to the paparazzi or celebrity press of today:

> Nicholas Sander's words in "Rise and Growth of the English Schism" (1585):- Soon afterwards she appeared at the French court where she was called the English Mare, because of her shameless behaviour; and then the royal mule, when she became acquainted with the King of France.

> Lord Herbert of Cherbury in "Life and Raigne of King Henry the Eighth" (1649) quotes William Rastall, author of a biography of Sir Thomas More (c1557), who wrote of how Anne Boleyn was sent to France where "she behav'd herself so licentiously, that she was vulgarly call'd the Hackney of England, till being adopted

to that King's familiarity, she was termed his Mule. - The Anne Boleyn Files[54]

Rose felt she had mirrored Mary's behaviour in the celebrated city of Paris, when she had flown the marital nest and thrown herself into life in the party city of the world, London. Free from any shame or guilt about her newfound freedom, she had explored it with unbridled passion and enjoyed all that the world has to offer. Likewise, Mary had kicked over the traces of her cloistered family setting, to revel in the sumptuous royal way of life at the French palaces and chateaux of the king.

Character synchronicities

In June 2022 Rose hatched another hypothesis of her own. After staring at the images of Francois I, it struck her that he looked and acted similarly to a man named James with whom she had an affair not many years previously. Their ages were switched, as she was six years older than her lover, whereas Francis I had been a few years older than Mary. The king was known for his aquiline nose, which one can clearly see in the portraits of him that survive today. He was also a very enthusiastic patron of the arts and music. So much so, that the famous Italian painter, Leonardo da Vinci, was invited to come and live in France, by the twenty-two-year-old ruler. The artist's most historic paintings, the Mona Lisa amongst others, remain in the Parisian Louvre Museum in France to this day.

The young king had shoulder-length, straight dark hair in his youth and was known to be a bit of a dandy with the ladies. So far, all the details matched up with Rose's romantic but secret tryst. She smiled to herself when she read about the king's nose, as her counterpart in this life hated his Roman nose with a passion. He is a professional musician and obsessed with culture and the ladies, so here were further similarities between the two men, James was certainly a player in his time and not just with the guitar.

---

[54] https://www.theanneboleynfiles.com/mary-boleyn-was-she-really-the-mistress-of-francis-i/

Location synchronicity

Interestingly, the country Palace of Fontainebleau where the kings sometimes resided, is only thirty-four miles South West of Paris. In 1923, following the First World War, it happily became home to the *Écoles d'Art Américaines*, schools of art and music, so here was a clear link to their love of culture. Another important link to James's past life is that he feels very enamoured of France. He lived in Paris, in the **St. Denis** district close to the main train station, Gare Du Nord, for a year. This was when he was nineteen and playing in a Parisian rock band. As Rose dug back into the architecture of the time, she discovered that Francis I's royal residence in the city was the Palace Louvre. James said that this was his favourite palace, now a famous museum of course. When she looked at the street map, it was only eighteen minutes drive from where he had lived. After more research, Rose discovered that King Francis was actually buried at the **Basilica of St. Denis,** another location synchronicity. It seemed that there were more glowing gems on the path. Like crystals, lighting the way through the dark passage of time, illuminating the way ahead.

Rose then put two more pieces of the puzzle together when she realised that in latter years, James had developed a yearning to return to France and constantly talked about selling his property and moving to a remote cottage in the mid-South – on his own. He had led Rose a merry dance and being the third spoke in the wheel of a clandestine relationship, had broken her heart. Any future dreams of them being together withered, due to his indecision.

We will never know if that was also the case, with Mary and the fanciful French King, but their affair did not lead to anything either. She was not granted a title, as his later mistresses were, which led to historians having to piece together the mysterious tale of intrigue from various writings and alleged throw-away 'quotes' from the French King:

> If Mary was, indeed, the mistress of Francis, she may have felt she could not refuse the king without repercussions on her family. She may have been in the same situation her sister later faced when Henry was interested in her - as long as the king was pursuing her, no man would offer for her hand and risk offending him. So, she

may have felt it best to give into the king's interest in hopes she might be made his official mistress, or he might find her a suitable husband afterward. Francis did neither. - Under these restless skies, blogspot[55]

Rose felt that in order to move forward in her life and free herself of the player energy, she had to draw a complete line under her friendship with James. It seemed to be blocking her from moving forward and finding herself a true soul-mate and a partner she could rely on and trust with all her heart. Her psychic friend Karen visited her in the final stages of this book edit and confirmed that she would have to shut one door before another opened, the same message she had received when she did her Tarot cards with Julia.

It is questioned, whether Henry VIII would have later commenced a fling with a woman rumoured to have been so immoral in the French court. Kings though, are a law unto themselves and Henry wasn't considering her a serious prospect. She was by now, married at the age of twenty to William Carey in England, when Henry set his cap at her. It is presumed that Mary's affair with King Henry VIII lasted three years, and that during this time she bore him a daughter, and then a son. If those closest to them had known of the secret, it had been very well guarded by all parties involved, unlike some of his other mistresses, who were flaunted brazenly. Here was a repeat experience of that with the French king.

A later and more deadly secret that Mary attempted to keep hidden, was during the time that Anne was Henry's intended and Mary had secretly married her soldier love when they were at court. She had fallen in love with this young man during Henry and Anne's royal trip, where she was to come face-to-face with her ex-lover, King Francois I in France.

In 1532, Mary traveled with Anne on her trip to France with the king to be presented as his consort, so she may have been back at court already as one of Anne's attendants. At the masquerade where Anne not-so-subtly met with Francis, Mary was given the position of honor, walking directly behind the new queen-to-be. If Mary really was Francis's mistress at one point, it's tempting to

---

[55] http://under-these-restless-skies.blogspot.com/2013/09/mary-boleyn.html

speculate about what their reunion meeting must have been like. - Under these restless skies, blogspot

Some years after her affair with Henry and the death of her first husband, Mary married William Stafford in seclusion and she had subsequently become pregnant. This was a secret that would eventually force itself to be revealed of course and she already knew the dire consequences of her actions. Similarly, Rose had known how her family would react when she disassociated herself from their religion.

Reading the sad events that unfolded as a result, Rose noticed this painful parallel with her own life. The website "English History" has this to say:

> In 1534, Mary secretly married William Stafford. He was the younger son of land owner Humphrey Stafford of Blatherwick in Northampton. This marriage was a disaster for her, excepting her personal happiness. Mary undoubtedly loved Stafford, a soldier she had met at Calais (he had been part of Henry VIII's retinue.) But her relatives – all newly ennobled and very self-conscious about their status – were outraged. He was a commoner, not fit for the queen's sister. Accordingly, Mary and her new husband were banished from court. (It is quite possible that her relatives planned to wed Mary to a nobleman, further cementing their rise to prominence; instead, her marriage was a step backwards socially). Mary did not visit her sister when Anne was imprisoned in the Tower. Nor did she visit their brother George, also condemned to death. There is no evidence that she wrote to them. It appears that all of the Boleyn family had disowned Mary and even her son Henry Carey had been taken away from her by Henry VIII earlier and placed with her sister Anne. - Excerpt from Hanson, Marilee. Mary Boleyn: Biography, Portrait, Facts & Information. [56]

Mary graduated from high society flirt, during her highly educated upbringing, to being the mistress of two kings and living in pomp at court, to losing her financial privileges altogether. It was a riches to rags story. She

---

[56] https://englishhistory.net/tudor/citizens/mary-boleyn

hadn't minded living simply with the love of her life, but eventually, she had to beg Anne for financial support, after Henry VIII refused her request for money, desperately needed to feed her young family. Although there was no further communication with her sister or family, eventually, Anne managed to arrange for a goblet of pure gold to be sent to Mary, which would have seen her through till her passing, a few years later.

Anne, of course, preceded her sister's death when she was beheaded after just three years as Queen. These were sad times indeed for Mary but she had made her own happy family and that had counted more than anything in the world. Here was a parallel again with Rose's life and although she had worked hard for twenty-five years, she fell ill and had to be supported by the state in the last few years. She was back to making do, with just enough money to get by. She thought about how she could break this pattern of poverty and mused that perhaps her new book would change her fortunes if it was successful. This would now be her focus, she determined. It seemed that she may suffer the same fate as Mary, waiting until her mother and step-father's death, before she inherited their two properties, but she hoped that she could change her fortune by marrying a man of substance as well as loyalty and reverse her fate. As for Mary, the following happened:

> In March 1539, when her father died, Mary inherited the Boleyn estate, which allowed her to fund her children Henry and Catherine's careers at court. Her daughter Catherine served in the households of Anna von Kleefes and Elizabeth I, and made a fine marriage to Francis Knollys. In 1542, Mary inherited the property of her executed sister-in-law, Jane Parker. But legal wrangling over the property lasted until 1543, and she and her husband acquired Rochford Hall only a few days before Mary died. Most of Mary's property was inherited by her son, Henry, but she did leave some manors to William Stafford. The location of her grave is unknown. She may have been buried at St. Andrews at Rochford, but the church records do not go back that far and no trace survives of her tomb. It's possible the tomb may have been destroyed in the Reformation. - Under these restless skies, blogspot

In the same moment that she was reading this information, Rose received a text from her ex-husband in Bavaria (past life as William Carey). He sent her through a video and some photos of her darling daughter on stage receiving her Bachelor of Science! It would to seal her future career and she had already secured herself a very well-paid role in a private clinic in the city. This was too much of a coincidence that she should be writing about her past life child's good turn of fate with the inheritance and that of her present life daughter. She would now be set for a life of independence, in a brilliant career. Rose prayed thanks to the source of all life and the Universe for bringing gratitude to her heart, on a dark and rainy day.

Estrangement Synchronicity

Having formed the bigger picture of these complex timelines documented in history, Rose could reflect on the mirror with her own life. She had also experienced shunning, loss, betrayal and abandonment. Further to this, she had endured another parallel life experience with Mary Boleyn when Rose, in addition to being cut off from her mother and step-father, was also estranged unnecessarily from her half-brother Terry, for two decades. This was when he had drawn away from his two sisters, even after their departure from the cult. This echoed the painful separation Mary experienced after her second marriage when she was barred from all contact with her full-blood brother George Boleyn. Crucially, this terrible situation was never reversed, as he was executed by Henry VIII along with her sister Anne. Rose wondered how she could bridge the gap again with her dear brother, who she missed terribly. He had been ignoring all her calls and messages until the present day and her heart hurt whenever she thought of him.

Rose reflected deeply on Mary's disgraced marriage to her true soldier love, William Stafford. She wondered about any parallels with her own love life today. She longed for the love and loyalty that had seemed so elusive in all her past lives until Mary had finally found hers in her mid-thirties. This synchronised with Rose's own timeline and bid for freedom and meeting the love of her life back then. As she allowed the thoughts to flow, she gathered nuggets from her research and allowed them to take form in her imagination. Half of the writing of this book was scribed in this way, switching between research, making copious notes and then meditating. Also helpful were walking in nature or singing, to allow her mind time to make sense of the inspirations she was receiving. This process had taken her six years, and still, she was no closer to finding her partner for life. It didn't stop her from dreaming about her knight in shining armour though.

She remembered her discovery that the happy couple had met when Stafford was one of the King's courtiers. He was a soldier, employed in Henry's entourage. On 7 October 1532, William was enlisted to accompany the troops guarding the King and his intended wife, Anne Boleyn. Her sister Mary, who was a thirty-three-year-old widow at the time and probably considered to be 'on the shelf' by now, accompanied them on the royal expedition to Calais, in France. You can follow The Tudor Trail blog to find out more.[57]

Religious self-sovereignty synchronicity

The area around the port of Calais was still the last stronghold of the British in Europe and Henry wished to parade Anne before Francois I, for his open acceptance. Simultaneously Henry had been in open communication with him about his wish to gain the stamp of approval from the French King. This was not only for his forthcoming marriage to Anne but also for his planned religious split with Rome, Pope Clement VII and the Catholic church. Their common enemy was the Holy Roman Emperor, Charles V and Henry wanted to form a stronger alliance with France. Here again, was another parallel with Rose's desire to split from her formidable religious upbringing and transition to self-sovereignty. We will dive into Henry's religious triumph in Chapter 7, about Anne Boleyn.

The rampant affairs of Mary's youth, beginning with Francis I from the age of fifteen or so, then with Henry VIII a year after she was married at twenty-one to William Carey, were now well and truly behind her. Six long years after her first husband's death, Mary would have had plenty of opportunities to smile and nod to the handsome soldier, William Stafford, during this royal trip. Surely they must have had opportunities

---

[57] https://onthetudortrail.com/Blog/2021/03/14/part-1-the-trip-of-king-henry-viii-anne-boleyn-to-calais-by-olivia-longueville/

for clandestine conversations, when no one else was looking? Perhaps she flirted a little with him and dropped her handkerchief in order to evoke a chivalrous response, Rose mused.

At any rate, Mary had been used previously as a royal plaything in the licentious French court and earned herself the unflattering nickname The English Mare. Mary had also lived through a possibly loveless arranged marriage to a nobleman with whom her parents had matched her, William Carey. Unfortunately, he had a gambling habit and after a few years of passionless marriage, she caught Henry VIII's eye and had been bewitched into a dalliance with him for some years, whilst a married woman. This clandestine affair she had to keep a firm secret. Not so long afterwards, her husband William Carey died and left her with nothing to support herself and her two children, because of his gambling habits. This was despite all the hush money in the form of generous grants and oversight of lavish properties he had been given by the King, to keep him quiet. Her love life had certainly seemed like a 'car crash' as you call it these days.

To say Mary was disillusioned with men, at this stage, would be an understatement. It had been an awkward situation having to beg her sister Anne for financial support from the King in the first, and now her second, marriage. What's good for the goose though, should be good for the gander. Mary had surely been in love with Henry for some of those years but was now cast to one side after she got pregnant, when secretly married to her second husband, William Stafford. Remember that in-between husbands, Henry had taken her son Henry Carey from her, not trusting her to be a reputable mother and had made her sister his ward.

After these many disappointing relationships, Mary must have been ready for her forever man. Rose likewise wondered if she had already met her counterpart, or if she was still to encounter her own Mr Right. She remembered the vision Peter the shaman had given her, of the tomb of a lady buried in a casket in the undercroft. He had particularly mentioned seeing glowing pearls and jewels laid around this lady, along with the trappings of a **Knight** and his sword. This soldier would have loyally adored and kept her safe. Who was this mysterious lady? She wondered if this was in fact the secret grave of Mary Boleyn, with the symbol of her soldier husband, William Stafford. When she read the history of their relationship, she realised that they had been very much in love. They had spent her last nine years together, until Mary died at the age of forty-four in 1543. Although not a Knight when she knew him, he had gone on to re-marry some years after her death, and had been **knighted** eventually, for his good services.

As for Rose, there had been a young man she had fallen deeply in love with some twenty-five years ago. Another psychic had picked up on this relationship in the last year and given her the number **twenty-five**. "Either this man, who was your soul mate, **was twenty-five** or it was **twenty-five years ago**" she pronounced. Rose counted back over the years and realised that this special relationship must have been the one she had with Robert. He had felt like a true soul mate right from the start and it was so heartfelt and beautiful to be with him. They had fallen deeply in love immediately, which was often a hallmark of a past life connection. It is an unspeakably strong bond when your eyes meet. There is a sense of familiarity and also a spark of passion during these re-connections. It was impossible to resist and they quickly became engaged.

Robert had taken Rose to visit several ancient residences in Kent when they were dating. These were Leeds, Canterbury and Bodiam Castles, but one had a more significant Tudor connection, Hampton Court Palace in the far West of London. This would link Rose to another of her past life soul family, but we will read more of that in Chapter 8. Robert and Rose had met when she was living in Seal in the Tudor apartment and he accompanied her to nearby **Knole Park** for picnics amongst the 'royal' deer, many a time. This linked in with several others of her soul tribe which we will look at in Chapters 9 and 11. Rose had always felt a magical connection to these locations and had felt so close to Robert when they visited these places together.

Robert was the one with whom she moved into their humble home in **Tudor** Drive. It was also the location of the big party reunion Rose had arranged to get her long-lost siblings Terry and Annabel together along with others of her soul family such as Julia, Simon and Channel. Funnily enough, it was a five-minute drive from the ruins of the **Tudor Otford Palace** she remembered, where they lived happily for a while. Mary and William would have also spent time at **Otford Palace** whilst travelling further afield from their London base. Could William Stafford have been her lost love, Robert? They went their separate ways when he was **twenty-five**, another connection back to the date the psychic had given her.

It struck Rose as interesting at that time, that her new friend Channel had been a **Knight** in her past life and that Robert, as William Stafford, had also been granted the honour of **Knighthood,** after Mary's death. Rose had now connected the Lady with the pearls and jewels around her in her burial casket. She recalled the image of the **Knight's** sword lain beside her tomb. Peter the shaman had said it was someone loyal, her protector till her death. The penny had dropped, she knew for sure now that it must have alluded to Mary's burial chamber and her loyal soldier husband.

Although history does not reveal where Mary was buried, Rose liked to think she would have been buried near her family, either in Kent or in Norfolk. Sadly she remembered that Mary was persona-non-grata, so would not have been given a respectable burial by The Boleyn Family. Most likely, her husband would have found her a suitable grave. Perhaps Mary's was also one of the unjust passings that the shaman had seen, she pondered. Rose thought about her mother and what would happen when she passed over, after all these years of separation. She would of course attend the funeral and cremation. It would be extremely difficult for all three of the siblings because they would be given stony stares from those still within the religion and avoided. She didn't want to dwell on it too much, but this seemed like another awkward synchronicity. Perhaps, Rose imagined, turning her thoughts to lighter things, she would find her own knight in shining armour one day, just as Mary had.

There was a social class difference between Mary and William. With her fantastic education, elocution and her stint in the French court of King Francois I, Stafford would have been viewed as working class by today's standards. He was from a good family, with vague royal ancestry, but he was simply not highly educated or wealthy, being the second son. Robert had also been the second son and was a naive twenty-one-year-old when Rose met him. He was a fellow Sagittarian, his birthday being a day after hers and the energy between them was passionate, fun and fiery, typical of two fire signs together. He was an intelligent young man, but with very little worldly experience. His background was working class but the difference in their thinking wasn't the only reason she started to feel an inequality with him. "Well he is twelve years younger than me," she had mused. Rose, like Mary, had lived abroad and had some life experience.

Rose was open to the new world she had started to explore having won her freedom from enslavement in a domineering household and controlling patriarchal religion. Robert led a protected life and although his spirit was pure and his heart open, he desired to have children and settle down with her. The age gap between them didn't help either, Rose was mid-thirties and didn't want to be saddled with another young family. She wanted to get the bit between her teeth and explore the glittering lights of London. She had met her wild-spirited blonde friend Channel, who wanted to show her the high life, like two white, prancing Lipizzaners. During their high jinx, they visited Harrods for fun, although they usually couldn't afford to buy anything. Channel showed her new best friend the backstreets where many vintage shops sold second-hand designer garments, the cast-offs from the rich, which they squeezed themselves into. Channel's motto had been a twist on the famous saying, "you can never be too rich or too thin" by Wallace Simpson, except she had changed it to end with "or too blonde, darling."

Afterwards, they would gravitate towards the bars along King Street or make their way to the renowned 5th Floor bar at Harvey Nicholls in the West end. Channel was always up for adventure as a fun-loving Sagittarian. This Zodiac sign depicted as half-man, half-horse seemed apt. Here was another horsey connection with Channel. The two of them really sparked off each other, and got themselves invited to the most amazing parties, even a ride in a stretch limo. Rose felt her Sagittarius side coming out, after all those years of religious drudgery. Channel's well-heeled contacts in London City's banking area and the private school she had attended in Seal, meant that she was always bumping into someone she knew from the 'old days.' Rose felt she was learning so much more about her true nature, which had been totally suppressed all those years. At last, she could be her authentic self and explore her true nature.

The girls fluttered their eyelashes at these London Yuppy types, who would happily sign the friends into private nightclubs such as The Roof Gardens, as their guests. Rose lived and breathed this adventure with her lively friend, and any desire to settle down for any length of time paled into insignificance in comparison to this glamorous new lifestyle. She had a tug-of-war in her relationship with Robert because she truly loved him, but the lure of the big city won her heart in the end, and they sadly parted company. Just as William Stafford had done, Robert moved on and married. As was his heart's desire, he had two children with his new wife, unlike William who had six with his second wife, Ursula Pole. Rose wistfully looked back in time, remembering Robert's blonde hair, blue eyes, handsome face and tall lean stature. She knew though, that she had made the right choice for herself, at the time. Her destiny was written in the stars. It seemed though that Rose did like to do things the hard way.

Location synchronicity

Rose had befriended this beautiful young woman, Channel, not so long before she met Robert, which meant the friends all spent plenty of time around each other, in Seal. In June 2022, whilst on the final edit of this chapter, Rose suddenly had a hunch that Channel may have played a role in this past life scenario. When Rose started to talk to her about the finishing of this book and the times they had shared together twenty-five years ago, she asked her friend if she had ever felt any past life connections to anything, back then. Channel had been living in Normandy for the last couple of decades. When considering her friend's question, said she always had a special place in her heart for **Ightam Mote**. Also, her mother had worked there for the National Trust, for some time. Originally it would have been home to Courtiers and Knights in the Tudor period. Rose immediately looked up the description of the property that she had lived so close to when she had been located in Seal. Searching for any connection between this beautiful moated property to the middle ages, she quickly discovered the following character.

The Knight of Ightam Mote

His name was Richard Clement and he was **knighted** in 1529, when Mary would have been single and thirty and living at court. Initially, in his early twenties, he had worked for Henry VII from 1503 as a Page Boy to the Privy Chamber for five or six years. When the King died Richard had stayed at court and served the young Henry VIII, as a Gentleman's Usher. His career didn't progress past being a courtier and so shortly afterwards, he moved to Northamptonshire. Much later on his career had taken a good turn, and he was given the title of Sir Clement. Earlier, he had climbed the ladder and had then been able to afford to buy **Ightam Mote** in Kent. Wikipedia has the following to say:

> He carried out much building work on his new residence between 1521-9 including reglazing the windows of the great hall, adding a long gallery to connect the two halves of the family quarters and rebuilding and re-fronting the private apartments. In the decoration he made liberal use of the royal badges of King Henry VIII and his first wife Katherine of Aragon, thus displaying his loyalty to the Tudor dynasty. - Wikipedia[58]

Here was another link to the Tudor royal family and Rose's soul family. After his **Knighthood,** he served as Sherif of Kent from 1531. In the opinion of Mercer (1995), Clement's patron was **Thomas Boleyn**, 1st Earl of Wiltshire, and owner of **Hever Castle** in Kent. Thomas was of course father of Queen Anne Boleyn, and Clement's career suffered after the queen's execution in 1536 and the downfall of her family. Now Rose saw the cross-overs, they looked at some dates to see if they could find any synchronicities.

Birthdate synchronicity

Channel's birthday is **29 November** and the only important Tudor date Rose could find close to that,was **28 November** 1489. It fitted in numerology terms because the year contained the number **9** of her birthday. This was the year that Henry VII's eldest daughter Margaret was born. The link to the Tudor family was there because Richard Clement secured his position as Page Boy to the King in 1503. This meant he would have been at the royal court and have surely met Mary and also Princess Margaret before she got married that very same year to King James IV.

---

[58] https://en.wikipedia.org/wiki/Richard_Clement_(courtier

She became known as the Queen of Scotts, but she remained in England for a short time. This match was hugely significant, as it brought about the first peace agreement between the two countries for one hundred and seventy years as quoted:

> The Italian historian Polydore Vergil said that some of the English royal council objected to the match, saying that it would bring the **Stuarts** directly into the line of English succession, to which the wily and astute Henry replied: "What then? Should anything of the kind happen (and God avert the omen), I foresee that our realm would suffer no harm, since England would not be absorbed by Scotland, but rather Scotland by England, being the noblest head of the entire island, since there is always less glory and honour in being joined to that which is far the greater, just as **Normandy** once came under the rule and power of our ancestors the English....on 24 January 1502, Scotland and England concluded the Treaty of Perpetual Peace, the first peace agreement between the two realms in over 170 years. The marriage treaty was concluded the same day and was viewed as a guarantee of the new peace. Margaret remained in England, but was now known as the "Queen of Scots" – Treaty of Perpetual Peace, Wikipedia[59]

Ancestral synchronicity

Here was a connection for Rose to her family line of the **Stuarts** of Scotland on the maternal side of her family, her mother Constance Mary's father being a **Scotsman**. Rose had always been proud of her Celtic roots. She took some pride when people had said she had a Celtic lilt to her singing voice. It also linked her to her fiance's surname, **Stuart.** In the above quotation was also a passing mention of **Normandy** by Henry VII, which is where Channel now lives, with all her horses.

---

[59] https://en.wikipedia.org/wiki/Treaty_of_Perpetual_Peace

Location synchronicities

Now that Sir Richard Clement lived in Kent he bought further properties;

> At the same time he acquired further nearby estates in **Shipbourne, Wrotham** and **Seal** – Sir Richard Clement, Wikipedia

Rose's father had lived in **Wrotham,** Kent, for many years and he was living there when Rose had moved back from Bavaria, to settle in Seal. This is where she had met Channel. Channel blurted out enthusiastically that she had been married in **Shipbourne** Church and that she had worked in **Seal**. This was great, the location clues were coming in thick and fast.

The friends thought about the equine connection, with Richard becoming a Knight in his mid forties. Channel reminded Rose that she had always kept horses, in particular Lipizzaners which were white and of Arabic stock, originally reserved for royalty. She had ridden and competed in dressage events and kept ten horses at her own stables in **Hadlow**, not too far from where Rose lived in Seal . She visited them a few times over the years, even taking her young daughter Willow along to have a ride round the field on one of the dancing Lipizzaners!

> In 1534, following conviction in the Star Chamber, he was imprisoned in the Fleet for having used force, in his capacity as a justice of the peace for Kent, during a property dispute in **Shipbourne** between the rector and Robert Brenner of **Hadlow,** a servant of Sir Edward Guildford. - Wikipedia

Here was a further tie between **Shipbourne** where Channel had married and **Hadlow** where she had lived. Other location name synchronicities were that Channel had worked for **Hever** Racing Cars, so the name connected her to Mary and Anne Boleyn's home at **Hever** Castle. He was also at the magnificent Coronation of Anne Boleyn in 1533 (3.33 again), then had a hand in her demise in 1536. This linked Channel to the Boleyn family more firmly now.[60]

---

[60] https://www.nationaltrust.org.uk/ightham-mote/features/richard-clement---ightham-motes-royal-courtier

Channel also remembered that she would ride her horses over to and around **Ightam Mote** frequently, when living in the area during her youth. After their enlightening conversation, Channel sent Rose a beautiful meme, which sums up the sanguine approach to life we need to take.

> *Whatever happens, believe in life, believe in tomorrow,*
> *believe in what you are doing,*
> *but above all,*
> *believe in yourself*

Rose's wounding patterns affecting her Sacral chakra (sense of identity)

Why were these wounding patterns repeating themselves over and over again? What did Rose need to remember and learn from this cruel religious shunning and these heart-breaking family separations? More importantly, how could she heal? Rose realised that she lacked self-belief or the confidence to come out and be seen as a creative and perform or speak her mind in public as a teacher and healer and this was reflected in some of her past life traumas. The chakra associated with asserting oneself and expressing one's creativity and sexuality is the sacral and womb area, depicted as the colour orange. This was the chakra that healers usually picked up on when feeling energy blocks in Rose's aura. Healing did seem to help her to loosen these ties to the past and let go of her unfounded fears.

In her life as a full-time minister, Rose had been celibate until her marriage in her late twenties, unable to express herself fully as a woman, as she was a virgin. Likewise, Julian of Norwich had also sworn herself to celibacy as an Anchorite from the age of **thirty-two** till her death in her early seventies. Eleanor Talbot kept her betrothal and sexual relationship with Edward IV a secret even when he subsequently married the White Queen. We saw that Eleanor then became a nun! Eventually, Mary Boleyn married her soldier love in secret in the king's court. When she became pregnant, she had to make it known and was then castigated and banished from not only Henry and Anne at the court, but by her whole family.

So many of these experiences were about ridicule from men in power around the open sexuality of their lovers. In Chapter 5 we saw that King Edward IV had nick-named Eleanor Talbot "The Holiest Harlot in the

Land" because when she was not in his bed she was in the church. He though, had two other famously named lovers and more besides! Also King Francis I was infamous for calling his young mistress Mary Boleyn "The English Mare" ridden by him and ostensibly others in the flourishing French court! Despite his jesting about her, he had two official mistresses of his own, who wielded quite some political influence.

It seemed as if the pendulum would swing violently from a lack of respect for licentious females due to the Kings' male double standards to the complete opposite. This was the oppression of the true natural expression of a woman's sexuality. The best example Rose could think of was the Catholic worship of the chaste and perpetual Virgin Mary, or the deep respect that was afforded anchorites and mystics. They were literally put on a pedestal, such as Lady Julian of Norwich.

Numerology of thirty-two

Lady Julian had of course chosen to sacrifice her sexuality altogether, being celibate from the age of **thirty-two** till her death in her cell at seventy-four. Here was another age link to Rose's reversal, when she made her bid for religious freedom and changed her present-day timeline, at the age of **thirty-two.** Remember, **Eleanor Talbot** had died at the age of **thirty-two** and Mary was free and single at the age of **thirty-two.** Curious about this number, Rose found the following explanation by Sarah Scoop, of its possible meaning in numerological terms:

> The name number **32** is a very important number, with many important messages, in numerology. There are **32** Kabbalistic paths of wisdom and **32** is the destiny number of balance and harmony. This number in the present name of guardian angels can mean **creativity and joy in your life**. When this number appears in your life even during tough times, it means that you are on the **right path** and things are going to work out for you in the near future. - Sarah Scoop[61]

---

[61] https://sarahscoop.com/the-meaning-and-symbolism-of-the-number-32-in-numerology/

Rose felt that she had brought about the beginnings of **balance and harmony** in her own life, from the age of **thirty-two,** and that she was firmly on the **right path** in all ways now. This applied especially with regard to her creative writing and singing, which had brought her much inner peace. She admitted to herself that despite feeling much **wiser,** the **joy** and romance were somewhat missing at the moment. Still some more work to do there, she thought wryly, whilst editing this book.

Sexuality had always been and still was, a truly feminine dichotomy and one that Rose had become very familiar with herself since her liberation. She had lived life at both extremes and was now realising how important it was to find a deep **balance and harmony** within and in her external life. She was conscious of integrating the **wisdom** garnered over the years and becoming a more complete and balanced human being. Now we will find out how Rose followed my paper trail of clues, to trace other members of her soul family and the lessons that they all had to learn together. We will explore the exciting story of her sister Anne Boleyn and the many parallels this infamous character had in common with her friend Teal.

CHAPTER 7

Tudor past life, Anne Boleyn

Further to Rose's discoveries in the previous chapter about her third medieval past life as Mary Boleyn and from my spiritual vantage point as Julian of Norwich, I now dropped a few more beads of inspiration into her imagination. Very excited to discover yet another pretty piece of the jigsaw puzzle, she uncovered another soul tribe member living in Tudor times, in the form of a sister. A year after she had started to explore these significant characters of hers during the Middle Ages, she befriended Teal, who she met in Swaffham. We saw in earlier chapters, how they found out about their shared lives as the mystics, Julian of Norwich and Margery Kempe. Eventually, it became apparent to Rose that they had also been sisters in another past life. She became convinced that Teal had the archetype blueprint of or indeed had been reincarnated into, the role of the well-known historical figure, Anne Boleyn.

Teal's Tudor past life

Anne Boleyn (c.1501-07 – died 19 May 1536) – Anne was probably born at Blickling Hall in Norfolk, after her sister Mary, if so, she was very young when the Boleyn family moved to Hever Castle, in Kent. After her educational spell in the Netherlands as a young girl in the court of Margaret of Austria, she became very popular. Anne was beloved of her guardian, for her exceedingly good manners and studiousness. Her father Thomas Boleyn, then arranged for her to attend the French court of King Louis XII, as maid-of-honour to his wife Queen Mary, Henry VIII's sister. There she lived and grew up into a very accomplished young woman, learning a vast amount over the next seven years, which would put her in good stead in the future.

Character synchronicities

As in her past life as the rambunctious and adventurous pilgrim, Margery Kempe, Anne also became a well-rounded character, learning many skills in her privileged position in France. She came to be known for her striking looks. Teal likewise had always stood out with her long, thick dark hair, tanned skin and a very attractive face with lively large eyes. Personality-wise, she too was very charming, driven, forthright, opinionated and passionate. She was vivacious and loved to flirt, having a great and intelligent sense of humour. She enjoyed masculine company and sports such as pool, carrying the guns for hunting royals at Sandringham Estate, racing cars, helping with wild animals in a game park and hitch-hiking her way across West Africa.

By comparison, here is a description of Anne Boleyn;

> Anne was of average height and had a slender build with long straight and thick black or dark brown hair, dark brown (nearly black) eyes, a strong nose, a definite wide mouth with slim lips, and an olive complexion. She was considered brilliant, charming, driven, elegant, forthright and graceful, with a keen wit and a lively, opinionated and passionate personality. Anne was depicted as "sweet and cheerful" in her youth and enjoyed cards and dice games, drinking wine, French cuisine, flirting, gambling, gossiping and good jokes. She was fond of archery, falconry, hunting and the occasional game of bowls. She also had a sharp tongue and a terrible temper.[62]

Further in the article, it is conjectured that Anne made her acquaintance with King Louis' sister, Marguerite de Navarre and may have thrown over the traces of Catholicism, for a more holistic approach to religion.

---

[62] *https://en.wikipedia.org/wiki/Anne_Boleyn*

Marguerite de Navarre was also an author in her own right, and her works include elements of Christian mysticism and reform that verged on heresy, though she was protected by her status as the French king's beloved sister. She or her circle may have encouraged Anne's interest in religious reform, as well as in poetry and literature. Anne's education in France proved itself in later years, inspiring many new trends among the ladies and courtiers of England. It may have been instrumental in pressing their King toward the culture-shattering contretemps with the Papacy. The latest version of Ives's biography considers whether Anne had evangelistic conviction and a strong spiritual inner life. William Forrest, author of a contemporary poem about Catherine of Aragon, complimented Anne's "passing excellent" skill as a dancer. "Here", he wrote, "was [a] fresh young damsel, that could trip and go. - Wikipedia, Anne Boleyn, see footnote

Likewise, Teal had been raised in fear of her mother's strict Catholic beliefs and overbearing rules, but kicking over the traces and throwing all cares to the wind, she set off alone at eighteen to travel the world and discover her own set of beliefs and values. Teal found her way to the mystical by visiting many spiritualist mediums over the years, for psychic readings. She had been personally acquainted with malevolent spirits early in her life when she experienced shewings of ghosts in her bedroom, from the age of three onwards. Her mother, despite also having the psychic gift, would most certainly have viewed her beliefs as heretical as a Catholic, and had given little Teal no emotional support with regard to the frequent hauntings, and their traumatic effect! She developed a strong spiritual inner life as a result, just as Anne had.

Just as her sister Mary Boleyn had been, Anne was eventually recalled from France to marry her Irish cousin James Butler, at the English court. This did not transpire, but she made her debut in royal society on 4 March 1522 and became very popular amongst the gentlemen for her charm, wit and french style. Other matches did not materialise, so she spent some time at Hever Castle again, with her family. They then secured her the famous position as **lady-in-waiting** to Catharine of Aragon and this was how King Henry VIII eventually came to be entranced with her in 1526. During this time he wrote her many love letters, spanning the seven years preceding their marriage. Whilst she was living at Hever Castle, Henry would visit to court her, when he was hunting at the **manor house** that Karen had listed, a lodge not too far away. Having set the scene, I will remind you of the further keys Karen had given Rose, revealing the many synchronicities between Anne and Teal's lives.

Understanding key clues from psychics and shamans

If you remember, in the previous chapters Karen had given Rose a list of names, on 6 January 2018. In this chapter we will look again at the key clues pertaining to Mary Boleyn's younger sister, **Anne** Boleyn:

> **Catharine of Aragon**, a Tudor lady
> **Anne**
> **Thomas**
> **John**
> **Manor House**
> **Castle with a moat**
> **Belgian/French connection**
> **I was a Lady in Waiting** (a most senior position in the Privy to the Queen)
> **Cardinal Pope**
> **Canterbury**

As we have seen, Anne had also been educated in King Louis XIII's **French court,** which was the **French** connection Karen had listed. She also became a **lady-in-waiting** to Margaret in the Netherlands, Queen Mary in France and finally, Queen **Catharine** of Aragon, in the English Court. We will now find out how the **Cardinal Pope** became involved, and how the reference to **Canterbury** also played a key role in Anne's life, as the story unfolds further.

Once the already married Henry VIII had set his cap at Anne Boleyn, there was no deterring him. It is thought that his long courtship with Anne was not consummated, at least not until right at the very end. Seemingly, this was because she was determined not to suffer being a caste aside lover, as her sister Mary had been! He was desperate when Lord Chancellor **Thomas** Wolsey failed to obtain the **Pope's** assent. Anne became pregnant in 1532 and the situation came to a head. **Thomas** Cranmer, the Archbishop of **Canterbury** was employed in much research with other learned ones, and finally granted the annulment of the marriage. Henry divorced **Catharine of Aragon** and married Anne in 1533 (3.33). Pope Clement VII excommunicated King Henry for marrying her. Anne was hated by the people and called a "witch" and a "whore" as the commoners still loved their beloved Queen Catharine. When Anne gave birth court astrologers had predicted a boy, but she gave birth to a surviving girl, Elizabeth.

As for Anne's daughter, who became Elizabeth I, here was yet further soul connection in Rose's current spiritual circle of friends. Linda from Suffolk, with whom she had become acquainted over the last couple of years, through her writing group. The spiritual seeds Rose later unearthed in 2021 connecting their past lives together, will come to fruition in Chapter 8.

Rose was also to discover as late as April 2022, heretofore hidden clues as to **Thomas** Cranmer's significance and connection to her current-day soul counterpart, Clare. She had become one of her long-standing friends, when Rose had moved to Trowse Newton some years previously. We will see more of this wily character emerging in Chapter 9.

Returning to 2018, and to recap the story, three days after Karen had channelled the above list of words, Teal had come to visit Rose. The two started talking about narcissists and then Teal described a date that had let her down and was trying to dictate when they would meet. She decided she would put her foot down and say no to him. The friends discussed how they were both learning their lessons about loving themselves enough not to get hurt and how to put firm boundaries in place.

As the conversation developed, Rose mentioned that she thought she was connected in some way to the historical figures of Anne Boleyn and King Henry VIII. She related that she had been reading about the way Anne had kept him waiting for seven years as she wouldn't sleep with him unless he married her. As they talked Rose suddenly realised that she may have been Mary Boleyn (who was red-blonde and more mild-mannered, like Rose) and that Teal perhaps could have been Anne Boleyn (a feisty brunette). At the moment she uttered these words, the two women felt goosebumps go up and all the hairs stood up on their bodies. This was the second time this had happened simultaneously to them both and they knew at once that this was another experiential bodily sign of confirmation, that they were on the right track.

With heightened awareness, they then discussed King Henry VIII and his character, concluding that he was probably a narcissist and suddenly they had more truth bumps and angel tingles all over their bodies. Rose felt that this was confirmation that Teal was still learning the lessons of becoming entangled with narcissists. As soon as Anne Boleyn had capitulated and married Henry after he had manipulated his divorce from Catharine of Aragon, he started to fall slowly out of love with Anne, because she hadn't borne him a living son. Henry's narcissism had come to the fore, he was insecure and felt less of a man because he couldn't produce a son and heir. He displayed that narcissistic trait of getting one's own way at all costs. With the political instability of the War of the Roses in the not-too-distant past and with present threats to the kingdom, he felt he needed a man to rule as his successor. But within three years of her marriage to the King, Anne was dead and beheaded.

This was a sobering lesson for Rose and Teal, to learn to be very wary of getting involved with narcissists! The fallout could be huge! Even though Anne had kept him waiting all those years, he still betrayed her. It seems he had no empathy, ruthlessly setting her up and accusing her of adultery with several different young men, who literally all got the chop on her account! In this lifetime, Teal had married a narcissist with whom she had her son. The father snatched him off the street and took him away from her when he was only seven, and she had been fighting in the courts to get him back ever since.

Location synchronicity

The lesson for Teal, as they saw it, was to walk away from this controlling man, and to value herself. Also, there was a piece of release and healing work to be done around unjust passings Rose decided. She and Teal further discussed how the lake at Blickling Hall is said to be haunted by the ghost of Anne, amongst many other places. King Henry VIII's ghost is also seen regularly to this day, passing by the lake. Of note is that

Teal was born and raised in Fakenham, only thirty minutes drive from Blickling Estate, so here was another location synchronicity to a past life. Therefore the friends decided to visit Blickling Hall and conduct a clearing ceremony in situ, in order to lay the souls of their spiritual ancestors to rest. Unbeknown to them, there would be more such soul-release work to do, but this was a good start. It was all a part of their process of waking up, remembering and choosing the path to forgiveness, therefore paving the way on their 'yellow brick road', the spiritual path of ascension.

Birthday synchronicity

Wikipedia lists the dates of the Boleyn siblings as[63]
Mary Boleyn, mistress of Henry VIII of England (c. 1499 – 19 July 1543)
George Boleyn, Viscount Rochford (c. 1503 – 17 May 1536) Anne Boleyn, Queen consort of Henry VIII of England (c. 1507 – 19 May 1536)

Looking at the dates of their executions, Rose noted that Mary's sister's tenure as Queen Anne lasted until **17 May** 1536. Teal's birthday is on **17 May** and it is to be noted that her brother George was executed on **17 May**, another date synchronicity. Let us look at the events that led up to this tragic end.

Anne Boleyn had become pregnant but miscarried three times. The last death had definitely been a boy and Henry had begun to think she was cursed and not the right wife for him. He became more and more paranoid that he would never sire a legitimate son and he felt a sense of urgency to produce one. Gradually Queen Anne's men at court disappeared one by one and were arrested. Finally, she was captured and tried on trumped-up charges of adultery, treason and even incest with her innocent brother George and they were all taken to the Tower of London. She was executed in 1536 at Henry's command (here was another raft of unjust passings which the shaman Peter had alluded to in his reading for Rose two years earlier).

The friends undertook some more research and realised that five young men were executed because of Anne, on Teal's birthday, **17 May**. Anne lost her tenure that day too and was herself executed two days later on 19 May.

---

[63] https://en.wikipedia.org/wiki/Elizabeth_Boleyn,_Countess_of_Wiltshire

The delay to her beheading may have been a holdup awaiting the arrival of the specially hired expert French swordsman on his journey there. This was her husband's one merciful concession to his fallen Queen. At any rate, 19 May is when the present-day hauntings occur at Blickling Hall every year, on the anniversary of her death. This is when Anne's ghost is observed by soothsayers, sweeping into the Blickling Estate in a carriage with horses. Here, she is reported to have been 'seen' many times over the years, roaming the halls mournfully with her head under her arm!

One summer's day Teal and Rose visited the lake next to Blickling Hall and amongst the gardens, chose a nice grassy spot to conduct the spiritual clearing. They took with them a large selenite crystal wand belonging to Teal, which is especially good for clearing negative entities. Rose practised Reiki and crystal healing and laid the long crystal over her friend's heart chakra, whilst chanting incantations. These were intentions to free the troubled souls of two of the most infamous characters in English royal history. As she prayed, a huge flock of geese rose from the water and flew overhead, confirming that the release work had indeed been done.

Loss of child synchronicities

Anne died with grace, probably to protect her young daughter Elizabeth. She did not renounce the King (although historians are fairly convinced that she was totally innocent of the charges against her) and she remained respectful throughout. It must have been the most harrowing experience. Here Rose discovered another energetic link to Teal, who had said she felt as if she was going to the gallows every time she climbed the steps to the courts, to fight for custody of her only son, Lee. Anne of course was leaving behind her only daughter, Elizabeth, at the tender age of two years and eight months old. Fear for her child's future would probably have superseded the fright at her impending doom.

Here I quote from Anne's execution speech:

> Good Christian people, I am come hither to die, for according to the law, and by the law I am judged to die, and therefore I will speak nothing against it. I am come hither to accuse no man, nor to speak anything of that, whereof I am accused and condemned

to die, but I pray God save the king and send him long to reign over you, for a gentler nor a more merciful prince was there never: and to me he was ever a good, a gentle and sovereign lord. And if any person will meddle of my cause, I require them to judge the best. And thus I take my leave of the world and of you all, and I heartily desire you all to pray for me. O Lord have mercy on me, to God I commend my soul. - English History[64]

Teal's pattern, over the several past lifetimes that Rose had been inspired to uncover, seemed to be the bitter heartache of losing young children, in particular young sons, but in this instance a daughter. We now know of course that she need not have worried as her daughter eventually became the revered Queen Elizabeth I, who ruled England graciously for forty-five years! This would have been Anne's reward if she had been aware of it. Elizabeth was also discovered to be one of Rose's soul family. We discover this later the book, in Chapter 8.

Body pain related to a past life trauma

As we discussed in Chapter 4, Teal had been for some spiritual hands-on healing with a nearby group. A man had given her non-contact energy healing with one hand at the front and one at the back of her body. He said he felt it was as if a thick spear had run through her. As the healing progressed, he said that he was pulling it out through her back and healing the wound.

She mentioned that she had been discussing past lives with Rose the day before and that she may have had a past life as Anne Boleyn. He agreed that when there is such a death as this symbolised by the spear, it could often mean the person had died by hanging, were pierced or beheaded. Anne Boleyn was beheaded of course. Teal felt that this healing could have now broken the cords of this traumatic past-life death, and she may be able to move forward now.

Rose thought about this experience and realised that this is the reason they were discovering these past lives and why it is so important

---

[64] https://englishhistory.net/tudor/anne-boleyn-speech-at-her-execution/

to acknowledge them. In understanding the experiences and deep lessons around these woundings, one learns how to release and heal, to clear the ancestral spiritual lines and patterns of suffering. Also Teal said that she always had constant problems with her throat since she was a child, with tonsillitis, Glandular Fever and swollen glands still troubling her to this day.

Rose decided to do a quantum timeline healing on her throat as Teal had connected it to the beheading. This was a combination of Reiki and intention to clear both her past and future lifelines. Imagining a domino effect in her mind's eye, they were all placed standing on end near each other. With one push, each domino falls into the next and eventually, the whole set falls in a line. Clients had previously fed back to her that they see the faces of their dead ancestors, starting with parents, grandparents and great-grandparents, materialising over Rose's face. These would recede in time to the point where the suffering began, in which case this would be a bloodline or ancestral clearing.

The spiritual line clearings are based on the soul choices made by the individual, to materialise as chosen characters in history in order to learn certain lessons. These could be cleared, by calling on a strong protector such as Arch Angel Michael, requesting him to bring his sword of the violet flame and to cut through the cords connecting the person to these experiences. Then they would visualise together the transmuting of these scrolls and contracts into the elements, to be cleansed and healed for all time. He would be asked to hoover out any stubborn hooks, torture or death implements and dissolve them into the violet flame too, cutting all ties to these lifetimes energetically. Spiritual contracts can be very stubborn to release sometimes and this may need to be done more than once if the client is finding it hard to let go. We all have attachments to pain and sometimes the ego can prevent change, so we have to work at different levels to clear it through in a conscious manner.

Background to Anne Boleyn's remains and hauntings

There were burial folk rumours concerning the remains of Queen Anne Boleyn at the Chapel of St. Peter Ad Vincula. As Rose read more about the un-ceremonial burial of Queen Anne Boleyn in the Chapel which was near the Tower of London, she noticed that renovations had taken place during Queen Victoria's time in the 19th Century. Great pains were taken to ensure that any remains discovered were kept and re-interred once the foundations had been renewed and then new paving slabs were to be laid to restore the church to its original purpose for worship. The strange thing is that there seemed to be some controversy about the alleged remains of Queen Anne and after examining all the evidence found and references to both her figure and appearance and that of Katherine Howard, it would seem that the bones laid in the spot marked on the map may not have been Anne's.

> Alison Weir believes that the bones identified as belonging to Anne Boleyn might in fact be those of Katherine Howard who was aged between 16 and 23 years in 1542 and 'miniatures of whom by Holbein show her with what could be a jutting square jaw' (Weir, pg. 326). - The Tudor Trail[65]

Could this tie in with the story that her father's family were responsible for stealing her exhumed body away in the night and taking it back to Norfolk? It was rumoured that she was buried in the graveyard at Salle Church, in an unmarked spot. Rose and Teal decided to do a field trip and see if they could pick up on any energies around Anne there. Rose had researched some more beforehand and discovered that there were a lot of rumours about her re-burial:

> Other Possible Burial Sites - Thomas Wyatt - Did he know a secret? There are a few legends regarding the resting place of Anne Boleyn, with some people believing that her body is not in the Tower of London at all:-
>
> **Salle Church, Norfolk** - Agnes Strickland writes of the "curious tradition" from Anne Boleyn's "native Norfolk" which tells of how Anne's remains were secretly removed from the Tower of London at night, taken to Salle Church, "the ancient burial place of the

---

[65] http://onthetudortrail.com/Blog/anne-boleyn/anne-boleyns-remains-the-restoration-of-the-chapel-of-st-peter-ad-vincula/

Boleyns, and there interred at midnight, with the holy rites that were denied to her by her royal husband" under an unmarked slab of black marble. Although Strickland states that there is no evidence to support this legend, she does quote Sir Thomas Wyatt: "God provided for her corpse sacred burial, even in a place as it were consecrate to innocence", saying that this could suggest that Wyatt was in on the secret and had something to do with the removal of Anne's remains."

In her book "Anne Boleyn", Norah Lofts writes of how she visited Salle Church and was shown the black marble slab by the sexton. She asked if it had ever been lifted and was told that the patron of the church was not in favour of having it lifted for investigation. The sexton also told her that Anne was said to "walk" the church every year on the night of the anniversary of her execution and that one year on the 19th May he had been keeping vigil when "a great hare" appeared in the church and led him "a fine chase." Lofts explained to the man that a hare was one of the forms that a witch was supposed to be able to turn into at will and Anne "was supposed to have been a witch."

Alison Weir writes of how the Salle Church myth was debunked when the slab at the church was lifted and nothing was found underneath it but an article entitled "Where was Anne Boleyn Buried?" on the Reepham Benefice website (the benefice of Salle Church) makes no mention of the slab ever being lifted."

Horndon-on-the-Hill, Essex– Agnes Strickland also tells of this legend, saying that "in the ancient church of Horndon-on-the-Hill in Essex, a nameless black marble monument is also pointed out by village antiquaries as the veritable monument of this queen." Strickland thinks that this legend and the Salle Church legend grew out of "rumours of the murdered queen's removal from the Tower chapel" which "were at one time in circulation among the tenants and dependents of her paternal house, and were by them orally transmitted to their descendants as matter of fact."

St Mary's Church, Erwarton, Suffolk – According to legend, Henry VIII and Anne Boleyn often stayed at Erwarton Hall in Suffolk and Anne loved the place so much that she gave instructions that her heart should be buried in the local church. During renovations at the local St Mary's Church in 1838, a heart-shaped casket was found set into an alcove in the north aisle and legend has it that Sir Philip Parker of Erwarton Hall, Anne's uncle, was the one who buried Anne's heart there. The casket was then reburied beneath the organ and a plaque states that Anne Boleyn's heart is buried there. Alison Weir writes of how this legend is unlikely because heart burial was only fashionable until the end of the 14th century (yet it is said that Henry VIII buried Jane Seymour's heart in the Chapel Royal at Hampton Court Palace), and the uncle's name is wrong. Anne's aunt, Amata Boleyn was married to Sir Philip Calthorpe. Whatever the truth of the matter, the village pub is called The Queen's Head! What do you think? Do you think that Anne Boleyn is beneath that memorial tile or do you think she lies beneath that of Lady Rochford? Or, is she somewhere else entirely? - The Anne Boleyn Files[66]

It seems it is still a mystery!

Experiential synchronicity

It was in the summer of 2019 that Rose suggested she and Teal test out the rumours experientially and they visited Salle Church in Norfolk and walked around the graveyard to see if either of them could pick up any energies or find any clue of Anne being buried there.

It was a beautiful hot sunny day and Rose and Teal had taken a blanket and picnic. Teal can sense with her body if the energies change when she walks around, so they decided they would test if there were any cold spots or if she got energy tingles anywhere. Then they would sit and have their picnic on that spot and do a clearing. They hadn't walked very far when Teal sensed an energy spot, walking on past it they went all the

---

[66] https://www.theanneboleynfiles.com/anne-boleyn%e2%80%99s-body-found/

way around the church and came back through that spot to test if it would happen again. Sure enough, it resonated again in the very same spot, so they sat down and ate their snacks. Rose took her crystals and rattle out and conducted a mindful healing and intentional blessing ceremony. As they drove back home, Teal remarked that she was feeling totally drained and tired.

Later that evening as Teal was dropping off to sleep exhausted, she sensed the presence of a man in her doorway, despite being on her own in the flat. She felt he was a large man, quite broad, and he had on a flat wide hat. He seemed genuinely perplexed as to why he was there, looked at her sternly and then left again. As Teal was explaining this to Rose the next day, she said "oh that is exactly the kind of outfit and Tudor hat that King Henry VIII wore!" The next time Rose spoke to her psychic friend Karen about it, she was told by her guides that he had to come back and needed to be forgiven by Anne or her soul incarnation, in order for him to move forward in the spirit world. Another friend of theirs said she was also aware that Anne's spirit needed to forgive and release the wrongdoing done by Henry to a long line of women, unknowns, who were not ever written about, who had also suffered at his hands.

Past life clearing and forgiveness

Further discussions arose around Anne's execution and the five young men, including her brother George, who were all beheaded on Teal's birthday **17** May, on trumped-up charges of adultery and incest with Anne. In another session with Karen, she was shown the room where a young woman was kept locked up. It was at the top of a spiral staircase, in a dark room with nothing but a bare bench of wood or stone. Karen sensed she felt great fear hanging in the atmosphere and a deep sadness in the room, which would be because of the terror of impending death, experienced by those being held therein. This is where Anne was kept from early in May whilst awaiting her trial on the 15th and then her subsequent beheading on the 19th of May 1536.

Rose wanted to understand why King Henry had appeared to Teal in her flat that evening. Why was he standing at the bedroom door on the day that they had visited the church? They knew it was the alleged place, where

Anne's remains had been moved to in secret by her family, stolen away in the night from their resting place in the church near the Tower of London. Karen connected to her guides and channelled that he was bewildered and didn't understand why he was there or why Teal had gone to Anne's 'grave' that day. Karen advised Teal to do a ceremony of forgiveness so that a part of her soul could be released and go with Henry's lost soul, to the light. She said that he has been given the command from spirit to come back to all the women to whom he had shown hate, greed and had secretly murdered, due to their not producing him a son and heir. She said that it was very important for him to understand his part and admit his wrongdoing. Once the wronged women could forgive him, then he could move on. Karen also heard her guides say that he had murdered many more women than were recorded in history books, because of his greed and manipulative ways and that this would eventually become known, in the future.

As confirmation, she described in her mind's eye, Henry's appearance. She clearly saw an image of his longish hair in a bob under his cap and said that it matched his boots and was of a golden autumnal shading with a tapestry coat. She said he carried a hessian sack bag containing lots of gold pieces which he would use to get his own way i.e. manipulate and bribe people to do his bidding.

Karen was then given the vision of an old stone castle with a moat and a broken-down drawbridge. There were slits at the windows and it was made of flint stone. There was a flag flying that had the colours orange and black on it as well as a coat of arms. There were gargoyles on the castle turrets and inside, something under glass, some artefacts. She was then shown two sets of stairs, one leading up a spiral staircase to a room so dark that it was pitch black and had only a wooden or stone bench and was very cold and uninviting. I guessed that this was the room that Anne would have been taken to in the Tower of London before her public beheading.

Karen said that the feeling inside the room was terrible and people had died there. She was shown a woman with her arms chained above her head by the elbows and her feet were in stocks too. She felt this was a woman that was used as an example to others. She wore rough garments of a deep purple and her head was hanging down when she was taken out. On his journey in spirit, it was explained that it would take Henry hundreds of years to find forgiveness, but that he would return gradually once the women he killed were reincarnated, in order to set the laws of the universe straight and acknowledge his part in the bloody drama his life became.

The reason it is taking him so long, she continued, is that many women are not spiritually awake enough to acknowledge his spirit in their future incarnations, but by appearing to Teal that evening it showed he had acknowledged the atrocity of his actions towards Anne. Now that Teal had become aware of him, her part was to forgive him on behalf of Anne and allow a part of her soul to ascend with his. It seemed that what was needed was to do a soul rescue ceremony where these spirit attachments were addressed, so that she could surrender and forgive, releasing these tortured ones for good.

Another scene Karen was then shown, was of a church where there is a stone or metal plaque either on the floor or on the wall with King Henry's name on it. She said it could have been sandstone or some kind of copper as it was very dark and had turned green but there were glints where it shone underneath. In this church, there is a huge stained-glass window and the light shines through beautifully into what seems to be an old monastery. She then 'heard' the name Iona connected to King Henry in some way. The only connection that Rose could make here was the reference mentioned earlier to the black stone where Anne's exhumed body was said to have been buried at Salle Church.

Clearing the "unjust death" of Anne Boleyn

On 29 October 2019, the friends found a suitable spot outside the boundary of Blickling Estate. In the nearby woods, Teal lay down on the rug that Rose had brought, which covered the golden hued carpet of leaves. As the sun shone through the trees and ferns surrounding them, it felt like a perfectly idyllic setting for this piece of work and they both felt very relaxed. Rose began to pray for protection and insight and then called to the spirit of King Henry VIII. As she did this, she felt a surge of bright energy come into her, as if the sun was shining extra strongly on her upturned face. It felt like it was the right time to explain to his spirit that they were there to acknowledge what had happened all those centuries ago.

They prayed their forgiveness of him and Anne's part in the drama and said the Ho-oponopono – the Hawaiian reconciliation and forgiveness release prayer, acknowledging collective responsibility for all that happens in all lives and timelines. They offered love and forgiveness to themselves and all beings. Here is some more information about this ancient prayer, the words of which are very simple and powerfully effective:

I'm sorry, please forgive me, thank you, I love you

I quote an explanation of the background to this ancient prayer from Wikipedia, as follows:

> The Hawaiian word translates into English simply as "correction", with the synonyms "manage" or "supervise", and the antonym "careless". Today it is sometimes used with juvenile and adult offenders where they work with an elder who conducts ho'oponopono for their families, as a form of alternative dispute resolution. Much research has been conducted in the spiritism movement around the powerful healing effects of saying this mantra on a regular basis. Interestingly one example where it was met with huge success on mental health inmates, was in a ward for the criminally insane, in Brazil.

> The concept of ho'oponopono is that are all collectively responsible for the insanity experienced by some (just as we are all one as a human family). Often psychotic breakdowns are misdiagnosed as they could very possibly be "spiritual breakthroughs" instead. Signs of this could be hearing voices and seeing visions just as a mystic would. In modern medicine these outbreaks are quickly attributed to mental health issues and medicated. This does not help the sufferer to see the connection to possible trauma in past lives as well as their current one and to release these patterns for the greater collective good.

> In 1976 Norrnah Simeona, regarded as a healing priest or Kahuna Lapa'au, adapted the traditional prayer of mutual forgiveness to the social realities of the modern day. For this she extended it both to a general problem solving process outside the family and to a psycho-spiritual self-help rather than group process. As with the

Hawaiian tradition she emphasizes prayer, confession, repentance and mutual restitution and forgiveness. Unlike Hawaiian tradition, she describes problems only as the effects of negative karma, saying that "you have to experience by yourself what you have done to others.

That you are the creator of your life circumstances was common knowledge for the people of old, as things we had brought with us from other lifetimes". Any wrongdoing is memorized within oneself and mirrored in every entity and object which was present when the cause happened. As the Law of Cause and Effect predominates in all of life and lifetimes, the purpose of her version is mainly "to release unhappy, negative experiences in past reincarnations, and to resolve and remove traumas from the "memory banks". Karmic bondages hinder the evolution of mind, so that "(karmic) cleaning is a requisite for the expansion of awareness" Using her 14-step-process would dissolve those bondages. She did not use mantras or conditioning exercises.

Wikipedia explains further that:

Different from egoistic prayers, "altruistic prayers like ho'oponopono, where you also pray for the release of other entities and objects, reach the Divine plane or Cosmos because of their high vibrations. From that plane the Divine energy or "mana" would come, which would transform the painful part of the memory of the wrong actions in all participants to "Pure Light" on whatever plane they are existing; "all are set free". Through this transmutation in the mind the problems will lose their energy for physical effects, and healing or balancing is begun.... After Simeona's death in 1992, her former student and administrator, Ihaleakala Hew Len, co-authored a book with Joe Vitale called "Zero Limits" referring to Simeona's Ho'oponopono teachings.

Len makes no claim to be a kahuna. In contrast to Simeona's teachings, the book brings the new idea that the main objective of the prayer is getting to the "zero state – its where we have zero limits. No memories. No identity. Nothing but the Divine." To reach this state, which Len called "Self-I-Dentity through Ho'oponopono", includes using the mantra "I love you. I'm sorry. Please forgive me. Thank you". It is based on Len's idea of 100% responsibility, taking responsibility for everyone's actions, not only for one's own. If one would take complete responsibility for one's life, then everything one sees, hears, tastes, touches, or in any way experiences would be one's responsibility because it is in one's life. The problem would not be with our external reality, it would be with ourselves. Total self-responsibility, according to Hew Len, advocates that everything exists as a projection from inside the human being. - Ho-opono pono, Wikipedia [67]

With all this in mind, Rose intended that Teal would be released from the continuing trauma in this and past lifetimes, which could be traced back to medieval times. It is also a conscious healing of those of her soul tribe who would benefit from the clearing work as well, but she had to first understand it and then create the intention to heal for herself before it could ripple out to heal the lives of others.

A further birthday synchronicity

Henry VIII had four of Anne's alleged 'lovers' beheaded on **17 May** 1536 as previously discussed (on Teal's birthday). Eight years later, King Henry signed the secret Treaty of Interest with Scot Earl Matthew Lennox on **17 May** 1544. Elizabeth 1 was moved from the Tower to house arrest for a year on 22 May.

As an aside, Anne's nickname, given to her by the people, was Nan Bullen. Rose had discovered a rare family shield in a medieval Norfolk church named St. Margaret's in Tivetshall, which still bore the image of three bulls' heads on a white background. Despite the ravages of the Protestants who tore every Catholic vestige from the churches in Henry VIIIs time, it survived and is still attached to the rood screen in the centre

---

[67] https://en.wikipedia.org/wiki/Ho'oponopono

of the church. The name Bullen, clearly associated with the bull images, changed to Boleyn over time.

As another interesting aside, Julia, another of Rose's soul family was independently drawn to visit Blickling Estate in 2017, where she did a tree healing on the grounds. Afterwards, she was told by a psychic that this had healed the bloodline of a soldier. What she didn't know until her psychic friend enlightened her afterwards, was that this bloodline went back on her husband's Italian side of the family and healed a timeline. This could be something for Rose to investigate further in the future. Blickling Hall is reputed to be Britain's most haunted building, so any healing may need to be repeated more than a few times![68]

Another legend linked with Teal's birthday:

On 28 September 2019, Rose received her usual email subscription newsletter from The Tudor Travel Guide. As she was reading about Ockwells Manor in Berkshire, a paragraph jumped out at her, because of the date:

Ockwells Manor and the Legend of the Severed Head

History is full of legends. One such story revolves around the tale of what happened to Sir Henry Norris' (sometimes called 'Norreys') severed head after he was executed on Tower Hill on **17 May** 1536. The story goes that his family managed to retrieve it, and while Sir Henry's body was buried in the grounds of the Tower, close to the Chapel of St Peter ad Vincula, his head was spirited away to the family home of Ockwells Manor in Berkshire, where it was buried beneath the floor of the chapel. - The Tudor Travel Guide[69]

This was, of course, one of the five young men that were beheaded on the **17 May**, on the trumped up charges to get rid of Anne Boleyn! Also

---

[68] http://www.ghost-story.co.uk/index.php/haunted-houses/168-blickling-hall-norfolk-england

[69] https://thetudortravelguide.com/2019/09/28/ockwells-manor/

on the 19 May her brother, George Boleyn known as Lord Rochford, has been sighted by 'sensitives' being dragged across the countryside by four headless horses. His headless ghost has also been seen wandering the grounds of the estate, searching for peace and justice. Blickling Hall is also said to be haunted by their father, Sir Thomas Boleyn. Some say he is the driver of the coach that delivers Anne to Blickling Hall on the anniversary of her execution. After dropping Anne off at the front doors at midnight, Sir Thomas continues on, pursued by hoards of screaming demons cursing him for his betrayal of his family. He is forced to drive his spectral coach over twelve bridges that lie between Wroxham and Blickling for 1,000 years as penance. [70]

If we are to believe it, Anne Boleyn's ghost haunts the most sites of anywhere in the UK and as ghosts go, must be the most travelled in Britain – if not in the whole world! When researching Anne's afterlife, Rose found at least seven locations where her spirit is said to walk:

1. Hever Castle, her childhood home
2. Blickling Hall, her alleged birthplace
3. The Tower of London, where she was executed
4. Hampton Court Palace and,
5. Windsor Castle, where Anne and Henry resided during their marriage
6. Salle Church in Norfolk, where according to folklore, Anne's body was allegedly moved to
7. Marwell Hall in Hampshire, a residence of the Seymours between 1530-1638

When Rose read further about others that had lost their lives at The Tower of London, she came across a mystic, who was once revered for her visions, but came into mortal danger when such forecasts painted King Henry VIII in a bad light.

These are turbulent times in Tudor England. King Henry VIII has decided to divorce his Queen, Katherine of Aragon, and marry Anne Boleyn. Elizabeth Barton claims visions from God,

---

[70] https://www.theanneboleynfiles.com/the-ghost-of-anne-boleyn/

threatening divine punishment. But to threaten the king is treason, and soon she finds herself a prisoner in the Tower. Is everything as it seems? Is she being used by powerful enemies of the King? Elizabeth Barton, the Holy Maid of Kent and Alice Wolfe, accused of piracy, have been imprisoned at the Tower in 1533. If convicted, they face execution. Meanwhile (criminal) life goes on. Alice Wolfe and her husband John have been imprisoned for luring rich merchants onto their boat on the Thames, murdering them and stealing their money. Maybe the King will be lenient if Alice can uncover any incriminating evidence on the Holy Maid. But Alice has plans for a daring escape. - Historic Royal Palaces

As with these poor souls, apparently Henry VIII did not show any remorse towards Anne, even observing her death by wearing yellow, along with his new bride-to-be, who he married very shortly afterwards. To give him his due, yellow was worn by the Spanish at funerals in those days, which could have been a nod to Catharine of Aragon, but seems a strange thing to do. Who knows what was going on in his head. The man moved Anne to another tower to watch the executions of her brother George and others, all accused of sleeping with her, so we are not talking about a compassionate person.

Now for the next instalment, in which we look at the lives of the three half-brothers and half-sisters born to King Henry VIII by his various wives, and how they also came to life again as part of Rose's soul family.

CHAPTER 8

Tudor past life, Elizabeth I

Queen Elizabeth I (7 September 1533 – 24 March 1603) was Queen of England and Ireland from **17 November** 1558 until her death. Sometimes called The Virgin Queen, Gloriana or Good Queen Bess, Elizabeth was the last of the five monarchs in the House of Tudor. She was eventually succeeded by her first cousin twice removed, James VI of Scotland. She had earlier been responsible for the imprisonment and execution of James's mother, Mary, Queen of Scots.

Linda (author, poet, prophetess, healer) b.**1 July**

Rose met her friend Linda a couple of years ago when she joined her writers' group. She had needed some tuition around sales, marketing and self-publishing. As they were talking about their writing, Linda said she felt that she and Rose had a past life connection of some kind. She was writing about the Tudor family, and Linda admitted that she had sensed several past lives of her own already, one of whom she felt was Elizabeth I. Rose was fascinated and wondered if this discovery would link them as soul family.

I smiled from my vantage point in heaven, as I had scattered some more fairy dust on the trail and Rose picked it up beautifully, just as a bloodhound would pick up the fresh scent of blood on the track.

Disinheritance synchronicity

One of Linda's friends, a good astrologer, once explained that Linda's date of birth, **1 July,** symbolises loss of the mother. Linda herself was adopted and of course Elizabeth became an orphan at the tender age of two years and eight months old. That was when her mother Anne Boleyn, Queen Consort, was beheaded on the 19 May 1535.

Linda said she can relate to a feeling of 'not quite belonging' or having a solid place in the family, having also experienced losing her mother herself. With Elizabeth, the feeling of unconditional love from a parent had been swept away, not only due to the loss of her mother, which a child under three would only comprehend as abandonment, but also being disinherited shortly afterwards, by her own father King Henry VIII and his Parliament on **1 July** 1536. Here the date linked not only to Linda's birthday, but also to the pattern of abandonment they both shared. Elizabeth was then moved from pillar to post and felt like an outsider.

Birthday synchronicities

Having discovered this first important date synchronicity Linda's birthday, I will explain a little about its significance. Elizabeth was now declared illegitimate by Parliament. This was when the Second Succession Act or Marriage Act came into force, following the death of Anne Boleyn. The First Succession Act had declared Mary illegitimate when her mother Catharine of Aragon was divorced from King Henry VIII, and her daughter was then demoted from Princess to Lady Mary.

A further date synchronicity that Rose was excited to find, was that of Queen Elizabeth's coronation on **17 November** 1558. This is Rose's mother's birthday, **17 November**. We will see how Constance **Mary** ties in with Elizabeth's half-sister **Mary I** in Chapter 11. The secret keys were beginning to unlock the links between them as a soul family. As we will find out in Chapter 10. both Elizabeth and Mary were further disinherited from succession to the throne by their half-brother Edward VI. To tie in the number **17** again, in the previous chapter we found this number linked to Teal's birthdate, **17 May**, and her past life as Anne Boleyn. In fact **17 November** has special significance as it is not only the birthday of Rose's mother and the day of death of her past life, Mary I. It is also the birthday of her late best friend Jasmine. Rose was already writing a sequel to this book, to include links to other soul group members and Jasmine was to feature within. Suffice it to say, **17 November** was a very emotive date in Rose's heart and one which she could never forget.

Character synchronicity

Linda feels she is usually diplomatic in her dealings with others, just as Elizabeth would have learnt to be around her step family and siblings. To slip up could have cost her life! This strategy was to develop into one of her greater character strengths, during her forty-five year reign. She diplomatically managed to tread the middle path between the Catholics and Protestants, which was no easy feat.

Writing and poetry synchronicity

Elizabeth I was a profuse writer, having copied whole books, one of which she gifted her father Henry VIII. She is recorded as being very talented and also spoke many languages. Linda reflects some of these aspects in her present life, because she has also written many books and poems. Her mother also wrote very many books. Linda recalled that her younger son, who is very good at history, remarked on the similarity of timbre with one of her poems called 'Windows" to one written by Elizabeth I. Linda is also very good at holding court, joining the conversations around poetry, creative and artist projects, such as her private 'Writer's Hollow' group[71] and @naturalcocreatorscommunity - both on Facebook.

Location synchronicity

Linda's birth mother's partner used to work at **Hampton Court** and he took her on a personalised tour of it not so long ago. The young Elizabeth spent quite some time at **Hampton Court.** Although it was one of King Henry VIII's favoured palaces, it was reported to have been one of her least favourite:

---

[71] https://www.facebook.com/groups/2472594799444709/ and https://www.facebook.com/naturalcocreatorscommunity

Queen Elizabeth I's court was often at Hampton Court Palace, but it was one of the Queen's least favourite residences. She fell ill of smallpox twice at the palace and, a story goes, she saw the ghost of Edward VI's governess there. - Elizabeth R[72]

Hampton Court Palace also ties in as a location where others of Rose's Tudor soul family would have lived or visited.

Scottish name and roots connection

Linda told Rose how she remembers clearly, that she used to draw sketches of King Henry VIII all the time, when she was young. She would give these pictures to the children she knew at school. She also admitted that she 'felt' some guilt associated with Mary Queen of Scots in that lifetime. This would tie in with Elizabeth I having Queen Mary (known as **Mary Stuart**) beheaded on 8 February 1587. She had been a house prisoner for nineteen years in England, but Elizabeth I became aware of Mary's plots against her. She prevaricated for some time about the execution but eventually had to make the difficult decision to preserve the throne. Another link here to Rose's mother, Constance **Mary**, are her paternal Scottish roots, and can be traced back to the **Stuart** family. Linda's son's name is **James** which links him to **James VI** of Scotland, whose mother was Mary Stuart. Rose's soulmate's name was **Robert Stuart. James VI** of Scotland succeeded Elizabeth upon her death.

Spirit apparition synchronicity

Linda spoke to Rose about a past life workshop she had attended with some others, years ago. She hadn't been able to go deep into the regression herself, being too busy with her thoughts. She was a little disappointed but later, when she arrived home and was looking at herself in the mirror, she was astounded to see a reflection of Queen Elizabeth I looking back at her! Her face was white with makeup, and she wore the same garb as The Queen. It was unsettlingly clear, as if she were standing in the room with

---

[72] https://www.elizabethi.org/contents/palaces/hamptoncourtpalace.html

her, and is something that she rarely talks about. The vivid and personal memory still haunts her, so to speak. Rose was delighted with this new piece of experiential evidence and noted it all down, to be included in her musings on soul family.

As an aside, Rose regaled Linda with a story of her own. She remembered with amusement, that when she was working at Universal Pictures in London fifteen years ago, they distributed the movie 'Elizabeth -The Golden Age' about Elizabeth I. It starred Cate Blanchett. Rose and her sister had literally 'bumped into her' at the film premiere in London. Cate was coming out of the powder room, as they were walking in, which was rather a strange place to have such a jaw-dropping, star-bedazzled moment.

The success of this movie was closely followed by another historical blockbuster in 2008, 'The Other Boleyn Girl.' It was distributed in 2008, starring Scarlett Johansen, Natalie Portman and Eric Bana. It tells of the love triangle, which historians have documented between Anne, Mary and Henry VIII, and which third-party situation is reflected in Rose's present soul group. If you remember, we discussed trickster energy at the beginning of this book.

Rose and Linda discussed this topic further, in April 2022. Linda said that she was given the name Lady Jane Grey by her spirit guides, as a connection to her Tudor past life, Elizabeth I. Rose did a little research and soon found out that Jane was the first cousin once removed, from the young King Edward VI. This now linked in with her half-brother, Terry and his past life as Edward VI. The jigsaw pieces where becoming a true picture now. Upon Edward's deathbed, his first cousin, Lady Jane Grey, became Elizabeth and Mary's arch rival to the throne. This was due to the further disinheritance from their half-brother contained in his last will and testament:

> In June 1553, Edward VI wrote his will, nominating Jane and her male heirs as successors to the Crown, in part because his half-sister Mary was Catholic, while Jane was a committed Protestant and would support the reformed Church of England, whose foundation Edward laid....The will removed his half-sisters, Mary and Elizabeth, from the line of succession on account of their

illegitimacy, subverting their claims under the Third Succession Act. - Wikipedia, Lady Jane Grey[73]

We will see further on, how this situation impacted Rose's soul group even further.

Date Synchronicity

Elizabeth I was born in Greenwich (this links her further with Rose's soul family because she had lived there for some years with her sister. Annabel and her boyfriend Stephen are still based there. In fact they live fifteen minutes drive away from where the palace was situated. It is of course, where Stephen's past life, King Henry VIII, was born and raised. Elizabeth was moved to Chelsea, also in the City of London, when she was a teenager. Without her mother Anne Boleyn to protect her, she was later accosted by her brother's uncle **Thomas** Seymour at the age of fourteen, (here we find the name **Thomas** that Karen was given, yet again, this man had married Elizabeth's step-mother Katharine Parr). The sexually tinged games and frolics the couple engaged in with her, is thought to have affected her emotionally for the rest of her life. Elizabeth was clearly traumatised, as she got up extra early to hide and instruct her ladies-in-waiting to put him off the scent.

> Thomas's marriage to Katherine brought him into close contact with Elizabeth who was blossoming into an attractive young woman. He began making advances towards the princess and the ensuing scandal thrust Elizabeth abruptly into the harsh adult world. - Royal Museums Greenwich[74]

Accusation of treason synchronicity

> When Katherine died in 1548, shortly after giving birth, Seymour decided he could further his political ambitions by marrying Elizabeth and seizing control of the Kingdom. He was arrested

---

[73] https://en.wikipedia.org/wiki/Lady_Jane_Grey
[74] https://www.rmg.co.uk/stories/topics/young-elizabeth-seymour-scandal

in January 1549 and executed for treason by his brother, the Lord Protector, in March **1549.** Elizabeth was interrogated about her part in the plans but skilfully denied the charges of treason and was eventually exonerated. - Royal Museums Greenwich

Dear readers, make a mental note if you will, of the date **1549**, as there is a key event which took place in Norfolk in the summer of that same year, for which Robert Kett became famous. All will be revealed in Chapter 12, but suffice it to say, it was the historical Peasants' Revolt and the Kett brothers were also tried for treason over that summer, by Edward VI. As you will see, these events will tie Linda in with those of Rose's soul family who had moved to Norfolk with her, Julia and Simon. This then linked them all together, with her half-brother Terry, whose past life I will tell you more about in Chapter 10.

Surname synchronicities

Young Elizabeth was sent away somewhere else, after the Seymour scandal. As history tells us, she never married and became known as The **Virgin Queen**. Oddly enough, Annabel's married surname was **Virgin** and her current boyfriend's surname is **Kingley** which fits to his royal past life as Henry too, at Greenwich Palace!

> Elizabeth's unmarried status inspired a cult of virginity related to that of the **Virgin** Mary. In poetry and portraiture, she was depicted as a virgin, a goddess, or both, not as a normal woman. - Wikipedia, Elizabeth I[75]

The comparison to The Virgin **Mary**, also linked Rose's mother's second name **Mary** with her past live as Elizabeth's half-sister **Mary** Tudor. The intricate threads of the tapestry were all weaving together rather nicely now.

When the monastery was dissolved at the Reformation, Henry VIII granted the Ashridge estate to Princess Elizabeth, later

---

[75] https://en.wikipedia.org/wiki/Elizabeth_I

Elizabeth I. Elizabeth spent 8 years living at Ashridge, and it was here that she was arrested by her half-sister Mary in 1554 and taken to the Tower of London. She had every right to fear for her life, but Elizabeth survived the ordeal to become queen on her sister's death. The Ashridge estate remained in Crown hands until Elizabeth's death in 1603. - Britain Express[76]

Date Synchronicity

Here we find another date synchronicity linking Princess Elizabeth to her mother Anne Boleyn, **19 May** 1554. By strange coincidence, Elizabeth was released from the Tower of London to go to Woodstock on the very same date, **19 May**. This was eighteen years after her mother Queen Anne Boleyn had been executed there on **19 May** 1536. Rose wondered if Mary I chose that day or whether she was unaware of its significance. Rose mused that she wouldn't put it past her. This date would of course link Linda's past life to that of Teal's, as Anne Boleyn. The soul family had grown, yet again.

Later on, the half-sisters Mary and Elizabeth were disinherited by their half-brother Edward VI, which must have been a very traumatic experience for them both. It may also have led to another possible reason for Elizabeth remaining single during her reign. Being on the throne as a woman, was a position of power and emancipation that she used wisely and was very keen to hold on to! Of course this led to her not having an heir to the throne, but the rewards for the people were, that she ruled competently and fairly over England for forty-five years! She was able to keep the people more or less happy and smoothed out the religious tensions by keeping her stance between the Catholics and Protestants neutral. A trait that Linda shares with Elizabeth.

Of course the Spanish Armada were also defeated with her beloved Dudley at the helm, which, although it was in fact a storm that decided the fate of the Spanish fleet, all due reverence was given to Elizabeth I. As the legend goes, she rode out bravely to rally the troops at Tilbury dressed in white velvet. There are three versions of the rousing speech she gave and

---

[76] https://www.britainexpress.com/best/8-Historic-Houses-asociated-with-Elizabeth-I.htm

she was aware that morale had been low and that image is everything. It certainly paid off and she has gone down in the annuls of history as an icon.

The Queen's tapestry shoes, the lost dress and letter mysteries

Further mysteries to be explored, emerged from another conversation between Rose and Linda. She told Rose that she had her first reading with a psychic medium at the age of fifteen. This lady told her that she would find a pair of Dutch tapestry slippers one day, which would be flat and have a pointed toe. When Linda wore wear them, she said it would release things for her and she would feel complete. Later in her life, Linda had a dream that she was Elizabeth 1. In this vision, she saw the Queen receiving a devastating letter. She remembered in her dream state that she had looked down at her feet and she had the Dutch tapestry slippers on. Rose searched the internet for something to jog Linda's memory, but they didn't find anything that quite fitted, so to speak.

Rose postulated that the letter Linda had seen in her dream, would have been one from her beloved, Robert Dudley. This would have been either when he finally married his second wife (which made her madly jealous), or, it could have been written by him, saved and sent to her, upon the sad news of his death. Elizabeth was, of course, beside herself with grief and kept the letter hidden on her person for the rest of her life. It was only discovered upon her death, tucked in with her most personal possessions.

The Lost Dress of Elizabeth I

During Rose's discussions with Linda she mentioned that she had seen an article about a dress that had belonged to Queen Elizabeth I and showed it to her friend. Immediately, Linda recognised the fabric flowers and colours because she had 'seen' the pattern only recently, although she had pictured the images on it as wallpaper. The fabric had covered an altar for centuries, but had been discovered only in 2016 by expert Eleri Lynn, to be that of one of Elizabeth's dresses, cut into rectangular strips. These beautiful pieces of cloth were adorned with stunning embroidered flowers and you can read more in the given link below:

> A rare piece of cloth dating from the reign of Elizabeth I that has covered the altar of a rural English church for centuries is now thought to have originated as part of a dress worn by the monarch and will go on view in an exhibition on 12 October 2019 at Hampton Court Palace. Accompanying the altar cloth in the exhibition, titled The Lost Dress of Elizabeth I, will be the so-called Rainbow Portrait of the queen dating from around 1600-02, in which she wears a dress with strikingly similar embroidered flora and fauna.
>
> Eleri Lynn, a collections curator for the independent charity, Historic Royal Palaces who specialises in Tudor fashions, discovered the connection between the two pieces in 2016 when she came upon a photograph of the altar cloth at St Faith's Church in the village of Bacton in Herefordshire. The church is closely associated with Blanche Parry, a Bacton native who was a member of Elizabeth's inner circle and served as her first lady of the bedchamber. - The Art Newspaper[77]

Location synchronicities

Linda was born in Hampshire but was moved to York by her parents when just one year old. She grew up there and said that she spent a lot of time in the seaside town of **Whitby** (where Annabel was born). This means that she would have been there at the same time as the two little sisters, Rose and Annabel, for a couple of years, before they moved down to Sussex in the South of England. Of course, this would also tie in Elizabeth's half-sister Mary I, as the sisters' mother Constance Mary, lived in **Whitby** with their father too. Another location synchronicity connecting the four women, tying into their past Tudor lives. Annabel's past life as Catharine

---

[77] https://www.theartnewspaper.com/2019/10/10/expert-finds-lost-dress-of-queen-elizabeth-i-in-english-village-church

of Aragon would have linked in with her mother's here, as Princess Mary was her daughter.

Sudeley Castle, in Gloucester which the baby Elizabeth visited with Queen Anne and Henry VIII in 1535, was also a connection to Rose's previous past life as Lady Eleanor Talbot, detailed in Chapter 5. This was during The War of The Roses, when King Edward IV seized the castle and his brother Richard III took ownership. The connection to Eleanor was that Ralph Butler, **Lord Sudeley,** was her father-in-law, when she married Sir Thomas Butler. A further connection to her following incarnation, as Mary Boleyn (Chapter 6).

Thomas Howard, the 2nd Duke of Norfolk, (father to Elizabeth Howard, Anne Boleyn's mother) is thought to have undertaken much of the Tudor refurbishment of **Framingham castle. Framlingham Church** is in Suffolk, which is the county where Linda lives. As they talked about Framlingham, Linda recalled the heart healing she received there at start of her early spiritual journey. This was when she was living and meeting up in a spiritual development group which took place next to Framlingham Church. Perhaps she was sensing her past-life roots there.

Other little known royal links to sites connected to Elizabeth I and the Boleyn Family, are mentioned by The Tudor Travel Guide in a new video released in June 2022 – 'In the footsteps of Elizabeth I: The 1578 Progress to Norwich'[78]. Rose made a note to visit these sites herself and wrote down the following information to form part of her research for you, dear readers.

St. Margaret's Church in Tivetshall, Norfolk

This little-known gem of a church, right out in the middle of nowhere, contains a very rare and beautiful architectural artefact. A rood screen, which divided the knave or main church from what would have been the chancel or high altar in Catholic times. The fact that the tympanum and rood screen used to keep the sections separate still survives, is noteworthy. Please find a link to an image of it inside the church. - Geograph[79]

---

[78] https://youtu.be/rB4R7Wf9i0M
[79] https://www.geograph.org.uk/photo/1366654

The Protestants all but destroyed these vestiges of the Catholic faith, along with the crucifix of Jesus Christ which would have hung on it. No doubt due to Norfolk folk allegiance to the famous Boleyn family, it survived. On the screen, there are still various shields and images containing Tudor symbolism, including the rose and crown of Henry VIII and the pomegranate of Mary I. The royal Coat of Arms now had the initials E.R. emblazoned on it, on either side of the shield. Amazingly, Anne Boleyn's badge with the white falcon and red and white roses remains, a legacy from the Houses of Lancaster and York. See a further description on the Anne Boleyn Files website.[80] Rose thought about her special connection to the energy vibration of the rose, smiled and thought of the Magdalene.

On the badge, the eagle symbolised Christ, which holds a gold sceptre in its talons, wearing a golden crown on its head. Anne was depicting her honourable roots as there were connections to the noble lineage of the Butlers in her family line (which Lady Eleanor Talbot had also married into). Interestingly, Linda only recently moved to a location just twenty minutes drive from this location and Rose was equidistant. It seems to be a repeating pattern to be drawn to live or visit within a certain radius of their past lives and their locations. There always seems to be a certain mysterious 'feel' to the visitor with past life energies, which if developed, acts as another way to prompt them to access their akashic records.

Could St. Margaret's have been one of the churches Elizabeth I passed by on her eleven-week royal Progress in 1578? It set out from Greenwich Palace in London and travelled up to East Anglia through Suffolk and Norfolk, during which time she ostensibly honoured the Boleyns. It is fascinating to read about the splendour and great inconvenience these processions brought with them, as everyone had to pay the burden of the lavish royal visits, out of their own pockets. Zillah Dovey wrote about this in a book entitled 'An Elizabethan Progress - The Queen's journey into East Anglia, 1578.'[81]

Elizabeth's not so covert aim apart from being highly visible as a monarch, was to save money over the summer months and to bring areas in her kingdom that were tardy, back in line. Her agenda was to stamp out

---

[80] https://www.theanneboleynfiles.com/anne-boleyns-badge/
[81] https://books.google.co.uk/books/about/An_Elizabethan_Progress.html?id=0S5hRUfyv6AC&redir_esc=y

any last traces of allegiance to the Catholic faith or of witchcraft, in areas where there had not been a physical royal presence. We will look at one of the lives lost as a so-called witch in The Cage of St. Osywiths Abbey near the coast of Essex, in the next book.

Progress from London to Norwich Anglican Cathedral

Elizabeth 1 would have arrived at the main gate into Norwich city centre via what is now known as Newmarket Road or the A11. With all due pomp and ceremony she was welcomed at St. Stephens Gate. As Rose was researching this subject, it also happened to be the same time as Linda was celebrating her birthday, on 1 July, so it seemed an appropriate and festive 'coincidence.' The podcast is a great description of the succession of pageants Elizabeth enjoyed as she travelled at a snail's pace through to the marketplace. It still thrives to this day, open seven days a week. Her entourage then processed through the marketplace, where it concluded at the Protestant Cathedral.

Elizabeth had her throne strategically placed facing the Boleyn chantry chapel. This would have been a high honour to their family indeed and a sign of her deep regard for her mother Anne and the Boleyns. The Boleyn coat of arms is displayed, showing the crest of Anne's great-grandfather and grandfather, depicting the three bull heads. She had also been called Anne Bullen for this reason, as we discussed earlier. Her great grandmother Anne Hoo was buried here when she died at the approximate age of sixty and there is a faint tracing of the original brass dedicated to her, etched faintly on a flagstone in the passageway behind the altar. See the blog on Elizabeth Norton's website entitled "The First Anne Boleyn.[82] She also wrote a book entitled 'The Boleyn Women."

125-127 King Street, Norwich

There is a surviving Tudor-style house and gallery in King Street, which was originally owned by William Boleyn, Anne Boleyn's great-grandfather, who was originally the mayor of London, at the beginning of

---

[82] http://elizabethnortonhistorian.blogspot.com/2013/06/the-first-anne-boleyn.html

the fifteenth century. He also bought Blickling Hall at this time, where Mary and her siblings were later born. The Tudor building with a gallery in King Street was subsequently given to his son, Sir Thomas Boleyn, her grandfather. In his time this street would have been a bustling hive of activity with the quay just behind it. The river Wensum served the roaring wool and cloth trade, but today it is derelict and has lain empty for many years. You will find a video about it by The Tudor Travel Guide, starting at approximately thirteen minutes, linked in footnote 80. It is, amazingly, yet another location synchronicity for Rose.

As we read at the beginning of this book, Rose had lived close to King Street not too far from the shrine of Julian of Norwich, but here was another link to her third past life, as Mary Boleyn. It is further down the road from where she lived at the old mill, but she walked past this medieval building many times into town, without being the slightest bit aware of its significance to her distant past. This was also another link to The Wensum River which ran alongside King Street. The Wensum also connected Rose to the second of her past lives, Lady Eleanor Talbot, a fifteen-minute walk past Norwich Cathedral, to Whitefriars. Here was a sacred river indeed and Rose was glad that she had blessed the water as a healing to all three of these back-to-back medieval lives she had led. More of this in Chapter 13.

It was strange to think that so many of Rose's and friends' past life dramas were concentrated in such a small but significant area over the centuries, but now I would like to take you back in time to when she alighted in Seal and how this linked into other's of her soul group past life connections, in The Garden of Kent.

CHAPTER 9

Tudor Past Life, Archbishop Thomas Cranmer

Archbishop **Thomas** Cranmer (b. 2 July 1489 – 21 March 1556)
Clare, b. **28 May**, Essex

> A leader of the English Reformation and Archbishop of Canterbury during the reigns of Henry VIII, Edward VI and, for a short time, Mary I. He helped build the case for the annulment of Henry's marriage to Catherine of Aragon, which was one of the causes of the separation of the English Church from union with the Holy See. Along with Thomas Cromwell, he supported the principle of royal supremacy, in which the king was considered sovereign over the Church within his realm. - Wikipedia, Thomas Cranmer[83]

We remain in Tudor times with its themes of political turmoil, religious conflict, and the threat of severe punishment and death. Rose accidentally uncovered yet another story that needed to be told. She discovered another member of her soul family, which manifested itself just as I was assisting with the completion of the first draft of this book, in the spring of 2022. It felt right that it should include this important last-minute realisation, as a further example of persecution and heresy patterns in past lives, still needing to be addressed in the present.

---

[83] https://en.wikipedia.org/wiki/Thomas_Cranmer

Key psychic seer synchronicities

Over four years ago, on 6 January 2018, Karen the seer had given Rose clues detailed from Chapter 6 onwards. Karen had thrown her hands up and admitted she was never good at history and she didn't have any idea how these names were woven into the tapestry of her lives. Rose would just have to figure it out for herself. As a reminder, here is the information that she 'heard' in a clairaudient form, from her guides in a 'download':

> **Catharine of Aragon**, a Tudor lady
> **Anne**
> **Thomas**
> **John**
> **Manor House**
> **Castle with a moat**
> **Belgian/French connection**
> **Rose was a lady-in-waiting** (a most senior position in the Privy to the Queen)
> **Cardinal Pope**
> **Canterbury**
> **James**

I will summarise events, before we look deeper at the details Rose spun from amongst the threads, as she stitched together her time mantle. Here again, was another repeated name, that of **Thomas**, apparently it was a very popular name. This time it was the Lord Chancellor, **Thomas** Wolsey. He had failed to obtain the **Pope's** assent for Henry VIII to divorce **Catharine** of Aragon. Karen had also listed the city location of **Canterbury** in Kent, which you will now find fits in with the further unfolding of this story perfectly! **Anne** Boleyn became pregnant by Henry VIII in 1532 and the situation with their years-long courtship came to a head. **Thomas** Cranmer, the Archbishop of **Canterbury** eventually granted the annulment of the first marriage himself and Henry divorced Catharine of Aragon and married Anne in 1533.

Pope Clement VII excommunicated King Henry VIII for his defiance of the mandates from the Holy Roman Empire and marrying her in defiance of the very head of the Catholic Church. Rose was to discover that this was a huge piece of the puzzle linking her to Clare. Not only was it as a friend but as another soul connection, with a shared timeline. Also, their experiences and religious circumstances seemed to reflect each other today in some aspects, as we will see.

Birthday, name, and numerological synchronicities

Clare's birthday is on the **28 May,** which is the historically crucial day that Henry VIII was married by Archbishop **Thomas** Cranmer to **Anne** Boleyn, on the **28 May 1533** (3.33 in numerology). The name **Thomas,** if you remember, was another on the list of Karen's names. A little background dig on this particular **Pope** Clement VII, unveiled yet another numerological link to Clare's date of birth on the **28 May,** as follows:

> **Pope Clement VII** - Latin: Clemens VII; Italian: Clemente VII; born Giulio de' Medici; **26 May** 1478 – 25 September 1534. - Wikipedia, Pope Clement VII[84]

Although his birthday was two days before Clare's, the year of birth contained an **8** which ties the whole date in for numerological purposes. We find more information about the fateful day they were married as follows:

In another date synchronicity, we see this article posted By Claire Ridgeway on **May 28,** 2018 as follows:

> **28 May** 1533 – Archbishop Cranmer proclaims that the king's marriage to Anne Boleyn is valid:

> On this crucial day in history, just four days before the coronation of Queen Anne Boleyn, and just the day before the coronation celebrations kicked off, Thomas Cranmer, the recently appointed

---

[84] https://en.wikipedia.org/wiki/Pope_Clement_VII

Archbishop of Canterbury, proclaimed the validity of the marriage of Henry VIII and Anne Boleyn.- The Anne Boleyn Files:[85]

To enrich the tapestry further and, as we are discussing birthdate synchronicities, in July 2022 and at the ninth hour, Rose unveiled a hugely significant festival, which took place at Thomas Cranmer's **Canterbury** Palace and the Cathedral. Taking us back in time by some years, Henry VIII had arranged the biggest party of the century, The Field of Cloth of Gold, when Catharine of Aragon was his Queen. The entourage left London and stayed at Otford Palace and Leeds Castle, but they also visited Canterbury Palace in order for him to meet Charles V. There they received a blessing from none other than The Archbishop of Canterbury, Thomas Cranmer! It just so happened to take place on Clare's day of birth, **28 May** but five hundred or so years earlier, in 1520 as described by The Tudor Travel Guide:

> In late May 1520, the English royal household began to make its way from Greenwich toward the Pale of Calais to enjoy what would become one of the most lavish and celebrated parties of the Tudor age: The Field of Cloth of Gold. This would be the celebrated meeting between King Henry VIII of England and his French counterpart and rival, King Francois I of France. But before all that drama could unfold, there was a last-minute meeting held at Canterbury Cathedral and its adjacent Archbishop's Palace.
>
> Charles V, the Holy Roman Emperor at the time, wanted to gently remind Henry of England of the power of the Hapsburg Empire before the English king had a chance to meet with his French rival. As ever, when it came to the three dominant Princes of Europe, there was a fair degree of one-upmanship on display. The outcome? One enormous, glittering party that dazzles even at a distance of 500 years! - Canterbury Cathedral: Dover, Pomp and one amazing Tudor party[86]

---

[85] https://www.theanneboleynfiles.com/28-may-1533-archbishop-cranmer-proclaims-that-the-kings-marriage-to-anne-boleyn-is-valid/

[86] https://thetudortravelguide.com/2022/06/10/canterbury-cathedral-power-pomp-and-one-amazing-tudor-party/

Charles V almost didn't make it to England in time for this sumptuous event, due to the inclement weather when he was setting sail from Spain. Eventually, it was reported that he landed on British soil and on the 26 May travelled up from Dover Castle to Canterbury on 27 May, just in time for the two-day event from the **28 May!**

This royal extravaganza would now tie Clare to Rose's sister, Annabel, who was Catharine of Aragon in a past life. This event took place thirteen years before The Archbishop of Canterbury presided over the marriage of the king to Anne Boleyn. The hard work he had put into this behind the scenes, would have catapulted Cranmer to fame and good standing with Henry VIII at the time. At any rate, it was another key location, which Rose had visited a few times when she lived in Seal. Once with two of her soul family from Tudor times, her fiance Robert and her good friend Channel.

In the distant future, Anne Boleyn would give birth to the baby Elizabeth and Cranmer would be named as one of her godparents. This was another piece of the jigsaw, as it linked Clare to another of Rose's soul family, Linda. We looked at her past life as Elizabeth in Chapter 8. Rose resolved to introduce her friends as soon as possible, and she had a feeling the conversation would be intriguing.

By now, Rose's soul tribe had grown to nine and counting! She made a list of these for future reference, as it was getting complicated to hold everything in her head. She remembered that James Redfield had written about the subject of the higher self and spirit-based soul groups. She had read his book The Celestine Prophesy. It was published in 1993, many years previously, when she lived in Seal nineteen years ago. He conjectures that there is a core hub of a small group of souls with whom we plot the next physical life each member will take when reincarnating into a future physical body. Challenges for our growth, along with the next roles played together, are decided upon for each member, beforehand. From my standpoint, in the heavens, I can tell you that all that he said is true.

The intention of the Source of All That Is, would be for each of our lives to bring the us greatest learning opportunity, for the highest good of all. A process of alchemy develops over the timelines, which we have the calling to remember in these current significant times of change on earth. The effect of our remembering and clearing any trauma picked up, mushrooms from an individual healing journey into a collective one. It can confirm to you that the celestial hosts are looking on and supporting us in any way that they can, to refine our energy body now.

When you, beloved ones, in conjunction with Mother Gaia, raise the energy vibration of all things on your planet, this is what is meant by the term 'the ascension path.' Together you can achieve enlightenment. This would protect the world as you know it from the darkness and destruction that has been witnessed over the centuries. Finally, by learning from these experiences, you can retrain your steps to walk the pilgrimage of light, in harmony with all that is. Where the formal religions of the world have failed or distorted these truths, by using your instinct and honing your memories, the process of alchemy will heal any trauma patterns. Instead of carrying these over into countless lives, a true sense of compassion can develop in you and lead to forgiveness, for yourselves and all others. The subsequent opening of your hearts will lead to peace and understanding of what unconditional love is, for all beings. You all will be able to change the timelines because you actually have more power, as beings of the eternal flame, than you realise. Then you will be living the dream, if you can only imagine you can intend it now.

Religious manipulation synchronicity

To zip forward again from 1520 to 1532, we are at the scene of a very tumultuous time in history. Henry VIII had shown his manipulative side in the way that he appointed Archbishop **Thomas** Cranmer and **Thomas** Boleyn to pull all the strings for him. He had to find a way to make the desired marriage to Anne Boleyn happen. To this end, he had employed Cranmer.

The Archbishop's consecration had been sneaky too, regarding his falsely spoken 'allegiance' to The Pope in Rome. This was in contrast to his own underlying religious beliefs, which were that he was secretly loyal to the protestant Luther. - The Tudor Chronicles[87]

It seemed Clare had been manipulated all her life by her Catholic

---

[87] https://thetudorchronicles.wordpress.com/2015/03/30/on-this-day-in-1533-thomas-cranmer-was-consecrated-as-archbishop/

mother's beliefs and this would have been the feeling Cranmer had experienced earlier in his life regarding the strictures of celibacy in the Catholic Church. Previously, he had married and subsequently been defrocked because he broke his religious vows. Clare likewise had experienced a fear of standing in her truth publicly. Later on, in the employ of the wily King Henry VIII, the task thrust upon Thomas could also have seemed life-threatening for Cranmer, when he was researching for a reason or solution for an annulment of Henry's marriage to Catharine of Aragon! A tremendous amount hung on this outcome and did indeed shape the course of history.

Heresy synchronicity

Archbishop Cranmer brought about a lot of religious changes as he openly became a staunch Protestant. Likewise, my friend Clare had come away from the mainstream Catholic religious upbringing bestowed upon her by her mother. She had discovered her own form of spirituality, one not recognised or supported by her primary carer and was bold enough to talk about it with her family, although it fell on deaf ears. In this way, Rose and Clare's lives had been very similar.

The fate of Archbishop Thomas Cranmer was to change like the wind and eventually he was executed due to the rapid throning of Mary I. Remember that her Spanish mother, Catharine of Aragon was a staunch Catholic and her daughter, Mary Tudor, had been highly included to follow in her footsteps. She even became known as the infamous Bloody Mary, for the number of Protestants she went on to have executed! Her half-brother Edward VI had desperately tried to hold to his late father Henry VIII's wishes, to prevent a swing away from Protestantism. To this end, he had disowned his half-sisters Mary I and Elizabeth I, by disinheriting them. He had instead unusually, stipulated that his first cousin once removed, Lady Jane Grey, become Queen in the event of his death. He died young at the age of fifteen, but her resulting sudden rise to the throne had only lasted just over a week. She became known throughout history as The Nine Day Queen! Let us recap the events that took place twenty years after Henry's marriage to Anne here:

In February 1553, at age 15, Edward fell ill. When his sickness was discovered to be terminal, he and his council drew up a "Devise for the Succession" to prevent the country's return to Catholicism. Edward named his first cousin once removed, Lady Jane **Grey**, as his heir, excluding his half-sisters, Mary and Elizabeth. This decision was disputed following Edward's death, and Jane was deposed by Mary nine days after becoming queen. Mary, a Catholic, reversed Edward's Protestant reforms during her reign, but Elizabeth restored them in 1559. - Wikipedia, Edward VI[88]

Rose surmised that Clare had already broken the spell of tribal disapproval, as she had refused to back down with her family on both her physical identity and her religious and health principles. In contrast, Cranmer, unfortunately, should have stood his ground and only did so at the eleventh hour, which looked a bit lame. He was already bound and about to be burnt at the stake by Mary I, when Cranmer reverted and proclaimed out loud his original staunch belief in Protestantism. Earlier, his overwhelming fear had led to the betrayal of his principles, when confronted by the teeth of the ferocious Catholic machine.

This seemed to be the tragic pattern that Clare had to confront and heal from, in her lifetime. To choose to be authentic in the face of opposition in her family took a lot of courage, but she could be proud, knowing that she had taken this hero's path. Her final steps in this process were to release the past now. Clare had been tirelessly working her way through such similar feelings of fear of rejection over the years of her awakening path, being regarded as a heretic of sorts.

Even in the present day, another such challenge presented itself, because she riled against the health system recommendations during the pandemic. She had enjoyed a life-long career as a nurse, with the much-lauded NHS (the UK's National Health Service). Much to the consternation of her family, she would not comply with the pandemic health mandates, along with approximately twenty per cent of their staff! These rebels were threatened with the sack by the Government in 2021, who used bullying tactics in a cult-like way to exclude and threaten those not complying with losing their employment. The pressure was intense and

---

[88] https://en.wikipedia.org/wiki/Edward_VI

worldwide, but eventually, the powers that be had to make an about turn, due to the less dangerous nature of the mutating virus and the exposure of the increasing injuries resulting from the medications they prescribed, over time.

Experiential body confirmation and readings

As the friends exchanged these thoughts, they simultaneously experienced 'truth bumps' or body tingles, which they had come to know were experiential body confirmations that they were on the right track. Clare then related to Rose that she had received a spiritual healing in Spain many years ago and the psychic reader had 'seen' a vision of her as a male, being crowned or ordained in a past life and wearing long, rich robes. The message she concluded with was that one day, Clare would come to know who she was. Clare had felt the 'energy' of a male in that lifetime. Perhaps now was the moment for this information to be revealed, as Clare experienced the death-throes of her long struggle for autonomy in her current life. It seemed as if this could be the time to release this particular wounding once and for all eternity.

With Clare's permission, Rose grounded down the energies in sacred ceremony with Reiki healing and used rose oil on rose petals, invoking the Magdalene energy and bringing in calm and peace to the traumatic events now being released. The energies were felt strongly by both of them and it felt complete.

Location synchronicity

Westminster Cathedral - at the end of the healing ceremony with Rose, Clare then remembered she had experienced a strong sense of foreboding when she had visited Westminster Cathedral some years previously but had not known why. This could have been the energetic link to her past life when Cranmer may have known that he was going to have to betray his oath to the papacy. There at Westminster Cathedral, is indeed a plaque with his name scribed on a pulpit, where he had once preached.

Marriage synchronicity

A month later, the friends discovered yet another synchronicity. Just as Cranmer had only been married to his wife for a short while before she died in childbirth, Clare had only been very briefly married for a year, when she was much younger. Britannica.com rounds this out nicely.[89]

Further Location Synchronicities

The Dolphin Inn - of Cranmer, it is quoted:

> He went on to Cambridge in 1503. In 1510 or 1511 he was elected to a fellowship at Jesus College but was soon compelled to vacate because he married a relative of the landlady of the **Dolphin Inn**. During this time he earned his living by teaching at Buckingham (later Magdalene) College, leaving his wife to lodge at the **Dolphin**; out of this arrangement grew a later story that he had started out in life as a hostler.....His wife died in childbirth soon after their marriage, however, and Jesus College restored Cranmer to his fellowship. - Capturing Cambridge[90]

The location synchronicity they then discovered is amazing. It transpired that all of Clare's maternal side of the family including her aunt live around St. Ives, Cambridge, which is just five minutes drive from the very same **Dolphin Inn** of Cranmer's time!

Merton Hall - King Edward VI's appointed heir, his first cousin once removed, Lady Jane **Grey,** had featured in Cranmer's scenario. Clare had investigated the ancestry of the current owner of the manor, Lord Walsingham and found a connection to Lady Jane Grey. Rose was fascinated and took a look further back in time. What she discovered was that the name **Grey** stretched back even further in time before the Tudor period and into Rose's past life as Lady Eleanor Talbot, during the period of The War of The Roses. This was during Julia's lifetime as the avatar

---

[89] https://www.britannica.com/biography/Thomas-Cranmer-archbishop-of-Canterbury

[90] https://capturingcambridge.org/centre/sidney-street/the-dolphin-inn/

Elizabeth Woodville (The White Queen), as discussed in Chapter 5. We find that the revealing key was through her first husband, who died at twenty-nine:

> Thomas **Grey** was born in 1455 close to the Palace of Westminster near the City of London. He was the elder son of John **Grey** (c.1432-1461) of Groby in Leicestershire, by his wife Elizabeth Woodville, who later became queen consort to King Edward IV. - Wikipedia.[91]

Originally from France, it is the **De Grey** family, on Lord Walsingham's maternal side of the family, who inherited **Merton Hall** a couple of centuries later. This property is now converted into rental flats and **Merton Hall** is the exact location Clare had been drawn to move to and make her home recently. What are the chances of finding this clue and her being drawn there, the friends wondered? Clare had been unaware of this ancestral link until they started to discuss her past life, as Thomas Cranmer, in April 2022. She remarked that upon her arrival at the premises just before Christmas, she immediately felt that something heavy had to be cleared, energetically.

As she is a healer, Clare used her Reiki Master experience, coupled with tools such as smudging with white sage, rattling, crystals and intentional incantations to clear the property and the surrounding lands of any residual darkness and past life traumas. At the time she was unaware that this was for her own timeline and she agreed that she could continue the healing intention, armed with the new information they had garnered.

During late July 2022, Rose visited Merton Hall and they did a ceremonial healing on the land and all on it. They sang the Ho-opono pono prayer under a beautiful pine tree in the forests of the huge estate. There were small stocky ponies roaming through the fields of corn, with border strips of wild flowers surrounding them. The mix of yellow dandelions, blue cornflowers and red poppies took their imagination back to the days when wild flowers would have been a natural site, not a seldom one. The sprawling red brick buildings built in 1846 have stone dressings with eagles

---

[91] https://en.wikipedia.org/wiki/Thomas_Grey,_1st_Marquess_of_Dorset

atop them. It all looked beautiful, framed by towering hollyhocks in all shades of pink.

Waltham Abbey - Once Clare had read through the description of Thomas Cranmer's life, her eye caught the words 'Waltham Holy Cross', which is also known as **Waltham Abbey** in **Epping Forest,** the county of Essex. Clare recalled that her father had lived near **Waltham Abbey** in his childhood, but only for six months. Here were yet more location links, albeit a very brief stay for both of these men. **Waltham Holy Cross** was where Thomas had been confined and had written up the crucial research papers for the proposed divorce of King Henry VIII and Catharine of Aragon's marriage. Rose often found that there were location synchronicities to several places she and her soul family or their relatives had lived, or worked, which were acting as flags, like the one below:

> In mid-1529, Cranmer stayed with relatives in **Waltham Holy Cross** to avoid an outbreak of the plague in Cambridge....two of his Cambridge associates, Stephen Gardiner and Edward Foxe, joined him. The three discussed the annulment issue and Cranmer suggested putting aside the legal case in Rome in favour of a general canvassing of opinions from university theologians throughout Europe. - Wikipedia;[92]

Otford Palace and **Knole House,** Kent - non coincidentally, it further transpired that Rose had lived ten minutes drive from both of Archbishop Cranmer's properties, which he had owned in his heyday. That was until Henry VIII 'persuaded' him to give them over to him as a 'gift'. In other words, he appropriated them. Princess Mary, who was perfunctorily demoted to the lesser title, Lady Mary when her mother **Catharine** of Aragon was divorced from Henry VIII, was then forced to live a life of semi-banishment at **Knole House.**

---

[92] https://en.wikipedia.org/wiki/Thomas_Cranmer

'Entrance to Knole House, Sevenoaks'

Rose planned to do another clearing ceremony at both of these sites when she visited her friends there at the end of **July 2022**. It was all coming together nicely before the submission of her book, the loose threads of the tapestry were being finished off for the beautification of the piece of cloth. These locations will be examined further in Chapter 11 about Mary I, but suffice it to say Rose visited **Knole Park** often over the five years she lived there when she returned from Bavaria. In Chapter 10 we will now take a look at the soul connection to another member of Rose's family, her half-brother Terry.

CHAPTER 10

Tudor past life, King Edward VI

Edward VI (b. 12 October 1537 – 6 July 1553). Edward was the King of England and Ireland, reigning for six years from **28 January** 1547 until his death in 1553. His father, Henry VIII died, on **28 January** and Edward's succession was announced to all on 31 January. He was then officially crowned on 20 February 1547 at the age of nine but died from a lung infection, possibly tuberculosis, when he was only fifteen.

Terry (b. **28 January,** half-brother to Rose and Annabel, who also shared the same mother, Constance Mary.

Birthday synchronicities

In the spring of 2022, Rose was finalising her research for this book and combing the internet for any last- minute date synchronicities before she completed her writing. Idly she thought of her half-brother with whom they shared the same birth mother, Constance Mary. He is twelve years younger than her and ten years younger than her full-blood sister, Annabel. Rose decided to type in Terry's date of birth to see if there were any major events connected to it. Imagine how surprised she was to find that **28 January** is one of the Tudor period's most significant dates! Her heart started to beat a little faster, Terry's birthday is **28 January**. Now that her curiosity was piqued, she followed the breadcrumb trail and began to see the familiar connections to their past life family and circumstances. Here are the key figures that make this date stand out in history:

It was on the **28 January** 565 years ago, in **1457,** that Henry VII - whose victory over Richard III at Bosworth in 1485 heralded the dawn of the Tudor Dynasty - was born. The Anne Boleyn Files[93]

In Rose's previous life as Lady Eleanor Talbot, which we covered in Chapter 5, she developed connections to her soul family Julia, as The White Queen and Simon, as Richard III. The crowning of Richard III had also taken place on 28 June **1461,** which had tied in with Rose's year of birth, **1961.** Now, Terry's date of birth on **28 January** was to act as a bridge. It linked him not only to just after that past generation in the same soul group, but also to another important era, which was to usher in more dramatic stories to be examined.

Exactly 90 years later, in **1547,** his son Henry VIII - arguably the most infamous monarch in history - died after a turbulent reign at the age of 55; exactly **475** years ago at the time of writing this in 2022. As a result, **28 January** is also the date that Henry VIII's only legitimate male heir, Edward VI, became King of England. Tragically, his would be a far shorter reign than that of his father and grandfather.

As Annabel's boyfriend Stephen was discovered to be an archetype of Henry VIII, there was a strong link with Terry, who was the only surviving legitimate son of Henry's to rule, when he died.

Numerology synchronicity

For those interested in numerology, I will re-cap and expand on this subject. A significant Tudor date in the family's past was that of Edward's grandfather. On the day his ancestor Henry VII (known as Henry Tudor) died, not only was it Edward VI's ascension to the throne on Terry's date of birth, the **28 January,** but his grandfather Henry VII had ascended the throne on the 22 August 1485, aged **28 years.** The 28 January 1457, was to be found another key. The digits **1457** are interchangeable with Edward's year of ascension to the throne, in **1547** when his father Henry VIII, died. This was **475** years ago this year, 2022! Also as we saw in the previous chapter, one of Rose's soul group, Clare, has her birthday on the **28** May,

---

[93] https://www.theanneboleynfiles.com/28-january-1457-birth-henry-vii/

linking two people within her group, to the same day of the month. We saw this occur with the number **17** too. Rose searched for the angel number meaning of **28** and found the following:

> This makes **28** a number of receptivity, partnerships, duality and attainment; as well as a number of wealth, authority, finances and leadership. - Sacred Scribes Angel Numbers[94]

This number certainly seemed to fit the key dates of three Tudor kings!

Disinheritance and family shunning synchronicities

To serve as background to the fickle nature of wills and inheritances, we know from previous chapters what transpired in the royal Tudor household regarding the half-sisters Mary and Elizabeth and how their fate hung in the balance with each family drama that unfolded. Now another character would step into our spotlight. I quote:

> The Third Succession Act of 1544 had previously restored Henry VIII's daughters, Mary and Elizabeth, to the line of succession, although they were still regarded as illegitimate. Furthermore, this Act authorised Henry VIII to alter the succession by his will. Henry's will reinforced the succession of his three children, and then declared that, should none of them leave descendants, the throne would pass to heirs of his younger sister, Mary, which included Jane. For reasons unknown, Henry excluded Jane's mother, Frances Grey, from the succession and also bypassed the claims of the descendants of his elder sister, Margaret, who had married into the Scottish royal house and nobility.
>
> Both Mary and Elizabeth had been named illegitimate by statute during the reign of Henry VIII after his marriages to Catharine of Aragon and Anne Boleyn had been declared void. When the 15-year-old Edward VI lay dying in early summer 1553, his Catholic half-sister Mary was still his heir presumptive. Edward,

[94] http://sacredscribesangelnumbers.blogspot.com/2011/06/angel-number-28.html

in a draft will ("My devise for the Succession") composed earlier in 1553, had first restricted the succession to (non-existent) male descendants of Frances Brandon and her daughters, before he named his Protestant cousin "Lady Jane and her heirs male" as his successors, probably in June 1553; the intent was to ensure his Protestant legacy, thereby bypassing Mary, a Roman Catholic. Edward's decision to name Jane Grey herself was possibly instigated by Northumberland. - Wikipedia[95]

Things were also not good when young Edward succeeded the throne on 28 January 1547 at the age of nine. From the moment he was crowned on 20 February 1547 till his death in 1553 at the age of thirteen, his reign was marked by economic problems and social unrest. In 1549 this eventually erupted into riot and rebellion. It was when the now famous Kett Brothers (Robert and William) led the well-known Peasants' Revolt, sacking the city of Norwich in the name of justice for the commoners and met a sorry end. After a bloody battle and a huge loss of life, the brothers were found guilty of treason in the Tower of London. You will find out more about this traumatic tale in Chapter 11, as here were further connections to Rose's soul family. Everything was tied in nicely with the extended tribe!

This is a brief synopsis of Edward VI's short life and the key clue to the situation that was playing itself out again in the current timeline, in Terry's life. At the age of thirteen, Edward VI unhappily contracted a life-threatening sickness. He attempted to make his first cousin once removed, Lady Jane Grey, regent (to protect the Protestant faith). She though was expelled from this position in just over a week (being famously named the Nine Day Queen). Then supported by her loyal followers, Mary I, became regent. Just like her mother Catherine of Aragon, Mary was a staunch Catholic. Then when Bloody Mary died, Elizabeth I took the throne.

Some interesting parallels can be found here, to the way that Terry behaved in his current incarnation. Initially, when Annabel had also left the JW's, there had been a joyful reconciliation between them all.

It was at the time that Rose had moved from her **Tudor** flat in Seal to **Tudor** Drive, close to the ruins of the King's Otford Palace, in Kent.

---

[95] https://en.wikipedia.org/wiki/Lady_Jane_Grey

She and her fiance Robert had thrown a big party for her long-lost sister Annabel. It was a surprise gathering because she had invited her half-brother, Terry, with whom she now had contact again.

They had both left the family religion around the same time, three years earlier. Annabel had only recently made her bid for freedom and Rose wanted to get the family together again, at long last. The siblings could be reunited even though they were still shunned by their parents, who remain in the religion to this day. It was so exciting to see Annabel race towards her brother as she hopped out of the car, in her haste to get to him. She couldn't believe the size he had grown to, as he had become a powerlifter in the interim years and was now built like a 6'1" brick wall. Delighted he swung her off her feet and spun her around, whilst those watching cheered and laughed with glee.

Present there to welcome her, were their other long-lost childhood friends Julia and Simon, who she invited especially for the occasion. They all hugged and embraced until they had practically winded themselves. The throng, which also included Terry's cousins from his father's side, bustled happily indoors into the large lounge and raised a glass as a toast to reunited friends and family. Afterwards, the serious partying began until they could dance no more. Tired but very, very happy they all left one by one and finally, it seemed as if Rose had found her peace and joy again. She reflected on this happily in the quiet of the night and as she recalled, it was one of the happiest days of her life.

In a cruel twist of fate, a couple of years later, Terry had a turn of heart and began to turn inwards. He was obviously still damaged by the shunning treatment meted out by their parents. He closed down again like a portcullis and shunned his two half-sisters Rose and Annabel for the next nineteen years. It was not until Rose reached out to him in 2018, that they mended the long-term rift between them all. Although they enjoyed a couple of years of blissful reunion as siblings, he again cut off all contact with them in 2021 and til the current day, had sadly failed to respond to any messages and calls from either of them.

Unfortunately, the practice of shunning had created deeper negative roots than it seemed, where a brother can turn away from his sisters, not even out of religious grounds or a personal grievance and cut them off. Psychological damage inflicted in childhood, coupled with a lack of deep work in mending these wounded aspects using ancestral healing, or conscious release of our shadow side, means that we cannot flee our trauma wounds. We cannot truly move forward in a state of unconditional love. This was a huge motivating factor in Julia's training and the launch of her business page on Facebook: 'Peaceful Minds & Souls,'[96] which offers a combination of counselling and hypnotherapy techniques to her clients in search of healing.

As she sadly pondered over the rift, wondering what had caused it again, Rose thought about how Terry himself had been shunned by his mother for the last twenty-eight years, for religious reasons. This, she realised, was a reflection of the role he played as Edward VI, disowning his half-sister Mary. In turn, her role had seemingly been reversed in this lifetime, by his mother Constance Mary. He had been disinherited by his parents in this timeline and now he was disinheriting his siblings too. This often happens with past life cycles, so that one can experience the same repeating circumstances from a different perspective, wake up and learn a lesson from them!

These past life woundings had engendered a feeling of lack of safety, trust and a sense of betrayal within one's family circle. Either from being disowned or being cut out of a will or inheritance. History had repeated itself yet again when, a few years after their initial estrangement, all three siblings were cut out of their grandfather's will. Their step-father and mother kept back the money promised to all his grandchildren, and rather than honouring a dead man's wishes, had spent it on buying themselves a second home. This felt like the ultimate betrayal. When would these painful cycles ever end?

For Rose, another nuance to her soul learnings had been that of learning to be honest and authentic about who she is and what principles she holds dear. She had learnt how important it was to openly share her garnered knowledge and wisdom with others, it had always felt slightly dangerous beforehand. She had been in fear of publishing her first book as she perceived retribution from her parents. This had held her back for many years, but she finally summoned up the courage to talk openly about it. Since then, she felt the relief of standing in her power and had been more determined not to sabotage the project she was working on.

---

[96] https://www.facebook.com/PeacefulMindsandSouls111

In Rose's songwriting and singing was a keen desire to be seen and heard. Yet she had held back from pursuing a career in music over the years, burying her desire to be on the stage. She asked herself, "What is the worst that can happen? They can't burn me at the stake or ostracise me, well maybe on social media, but why should I take any notice?" As the bible says to those early believers being persecuted for following Jesus, "take courage in both hands". So she decided she would follow suit and perform as if her life depended on it!

Rose was prepared to sacrifice not only her familial relationships and disapproval from the community she grew up with, but she also knew that any future financial support may be in jeopardy. These material outcomes had to play second fiddle to maintaining her freedom of thought, speech and action. This, she realised during the pandemic from 2020, is why she could so readily spot a pattern with the mind-controlling and shaming narrative around the lockdowns and mandates. It seemed to be directed at those that would not comply. No, she would trust in her gut instincts, rather than lose her freedom of choice again. This was the similarity that she shared with her soul friend Clare's life stance, which was detailed in the last chapter.

Family heir synchronicity

Just as Edward had been Henry VIII's first male heir to the throne, Terry's father, Andrew, had married twice but not produced any children of his own. Here was a similar setting to that of Edward, who was the first surviving and legitimate son of Henry VIII and Jane Seymour, his beloved third wife, who died in childbirth.

After being married for a couple of years to Rose's mother, her step-father Andrew began to desire his own child, and she had agreed to add to the family, conceiving successfully. Rose actually remembered her mother exclaiming drolly upon Terry's birth, that "he is Andrew's son and heir, to carry on the family name." Similarly, the people were described as being very excited to witness King Henry VIII begat a male heir at long last, for "whom we hungered for so long, with joy and relief." It has to be said that Terry's parents are not so proud of their only son, now that he had been banished from their presence at the young age of twenty-one.

Religious change of belief synchronicity

Edward VI was the first English monarch to be raised as a Protestant. Further to the dramatic religious swings and changes in Tudor times, here was another synchronicity that Rose noticed. Her step-father had met Constance Mary at the event where she had converted from the Church of England and was baptised into their new religion. It was noteworthy, as not many people change their religious convictions in adulthood.

Now I turn to another piece of the puzzle, Terry's mother Constance Mary, and look at which role she plays in this present day and in their past life soul group.

CHAPTER 11

Tudor past life, Mary I

Queen Mary I of England and Ireland (b.18 February 1516 – **17 November** 1558). Mary I was also known as **Mary** Tudor, and as "Bloody **Mary**" by her Protestant opponents. She reigned for five years from **July** 1553 until her death, **17 November** 1558.

Constance Mary, b. **17 November.** Mother of Rose, Annabel and Terry.

Mary I was married to Prince Phillip of Spain on **25 July** 1554, which ties her to Rose's sister Annabel whose birthday is **25 July.** Annabel was Catharine of Aragon in her past life and this meant that in that time the roles were switched as she was the mother of **Mary** Tudor. So the roles are reversed in this lifetime. Rather than being shunned by her mother Constance **Mary** as in the present timeline, Catharine taught and nurtured her daughter, until the sad day that she was sent into semi-banishment by Henry VIII. There was still the trauma of separation rippling down through the fabric of time, between these two.

Name and birthdate synchronicity

Rose's mother, Constance **Mary**, not only held the same name as her past life counterpart **Mary I**, but Constance's birthdate, **17 November** is the very same day that Mary I, daughter of Catharine of Aragon left this mortal coil in 1558. Automatically this meant that **17 November** was the date that Elizabeth I, half-sister to Mary I, would have ascended the throne. As we saw in Chapter 8, this linked Linda in her past life as Elizabeth I, to Rose's soul family. By now Rose had realised that the number **17** was significant. In Chapter 7 we saw that the number **17** had linked to Anne's brother, George Boleyn, and his execution on **17** May. It was reflected in Teal's birthday on **17** May. This led Rose to examine if there were yet other elements of all of their intertwining lives, which reflected each other's experiences, in real-time today.

In July 1553, Lady Mary learnt that she had been accepted as rightful queen, following the death of her younger brother, Edward VI, some two weeks previously. Another link between Rose's soul family was that Henry VIII died on **28 January** 1548, which meant that his **only son,** became King Edward VI. As we read in Chapter 10, **28 January** was the birthdate of Constance Mary's **only son** Terry, another member of Rose's soul family.

With her succession to the throne, Mary's long road of rejection and struggle appeared to be finally at an end. Lady Jane Grey had only reigned for just over a week and had been nicknamed The Nine Day Queen. Mary's triumph in securing the crown so quickly had been due to her faithful council and followers. This would of course have been yet another swift countermove on the chessboard of her sister Elizabeth's life. It seemed that she was in checkmate once again. One woman's loss was another woman's gain! This win for Mary I would now ensure that Elizabeth would not succeed the throne. Yet again, there must have been feelings of displacement within the royal family. As Mary's half-sister, and holding opposing religious leanings, what would Elizabeth's fate now be, with Mary I at the helm?

Location synchronicities

Mary I inherited estates in **Norfolk, Suffolk** and **Essex** when Henry VIII died. This linked her to other members of Rose's Tudor soul group. In chapter 9 we saw that Thomas Cranmer was connected to **Essex** (where her friend Clare and her family come from). Mary and Anne Boleyn were from **Norfolk,** where we saw in Chapter 6, Rose was born and now lives. Elizabeth I was connected to both **Norfolk** from whence her mother Anne

Boleyn's family originated, and to **Suffolk,** where Rose's soul friend, Linda, lives. This we learnt about in Chapter 8.

Early death of parents synchronicity

Princess **Mary** had a troubled relationship with her father Henry VIII, who was quite cruel to her by sending her away to Wales when she was only nine. Likewise, Constance **Mary** and her sister had been sent away to boarding school. Rose's mother had found it a very difficult transition away from her family. Even worse, when she was **17** and Mary's mother Catherine of Aragon was deposed and no longer Queen, King Henry VIII sent them both away separately and forbade **Mary** to see her mother or even to exchange letters. This was when Mary found herself incarcerated at Knole House in Sevenoaks, with only the vast lonely hall of portraits to keep her company. We see again that the number **17** played a crucial role in the pattern of abandonment. It is noteworthy, that Constance Mary literally lost her father in her mid-teens when he died of lung problems in his fifties, caused by the use of mustard gas in the trenches, when he was serving in the First World War. This caused a terrible upheaval for the little family. Their mother felt that they could no longer stay in their country of birth, Africa, as it was too unsafe for three women on their own. She wished to return to her homeland, where she had relatives in the form of three sisters. Constance Mary was therefore wrenched away from all that was familiar, when they made the long sad trip by ship to rainy England.

Luckily, Catharine's ladies-in-waiting and footmen were loyal to their beloved ex-Queen and made sure to carry **secret letters** between the shamed mother and Lady Mary. Just three years later, when Mary was only twenty, the estranged daughter was inconsolable at her mother Catharine's death at the age of fifty, in 1536. Rose and Annabel were determined that history would not repeat itself and sent their mother the odd **letter** and sometimes, clandestine **texts**, keeping in touch with her, without their step-father's knowledge. They knew though that they would also not be allowed to see their mother in the flesh before her death, due to the religious practice of shunning. The sisters dreaded the day Constance Mary would pass, as there would be so many regrets and tears to be shed, just as Princess Mary had deeply grieved her estranged mother's loss.

Eleven years after her dear mother's death, Lady Mary lost her father, Henry VIII, when she was **thirty-one**. Constance Mary was **thirty-one** when her mother died, in her fifties, from cancer. Although the roles were reversed in this timeline, the painful synchronicities hurt just the same. If we are to believe we reincarnate in order to learn and grow, it seemed that Constance Mary had not consciously remembered her woundings and unbeknown to her, her life was playing out as it had hundreds of years ago. It seemed to Rose to be too late for her mother, now eighty-three, to wake up and remember that the bond of family love should triumph above all, including your religious incarnations. Jesus and Mother Mary were after all, proponents of a deep unconditional love for all beings, no matter what their standing in life. Rose breathed a sigh of relief that she had at least woken up in time to break the pattern of emotional abandonment for her own daughter. Although separated by land and sea, they were in constant contact and visited each other regularly. On the day she graduated with a Bachelor in Microbiology, she felt a mother's pride bursting from her heart and a sense of relief that she had the means to support herself financially now.

Religious conflict synchronicity

Both of Constance Mary's parents would have turned in their graves had they known what converting to a fundamentalist cult would mean for her and her daughters. The battle between Catholicism and Protestantism has reflected again in Rose's mother's life. Raised strictly Church of England and Protestant origins, she had converted when Rose was ten.

The Great Harlot and The Beast of Revelation

As with the Catholic church, the new cult Constance Mary had joined, believes that they belong to the only true Christian religion and that all other organisations in Christendom are likened to The Great Harlot in the last book of the Bible, Revelation. Therein, she is depicted as having committed prostitution by making a pact with the Wild Beast, who they believe to be the United Nations, with its seven head and ten horns depicting the major influential nations of the world. I quote to you dear ones from the New Testament of the Bible, from Revelation, Chapter 17:

> One of the seven angels who had the seven bowls came and talked with me, saying to me, "Come, I will show you the judgment of the great prostitute who sits on many waters, with whom the kings of the earth committed adultery, and the inhabitants of the earth were made drunk with the wine of her sexual immorality...Then he carried me away in the Spirit into the wilderness. I saw a woman sitting on a scarlet beast which was full of blasphemous names, having seven heads and ten horns....The woman was arrayed in purple and scarlet, and adorned with gold and precious stones and pearls, having in her hand a golden cup full of abominations and the filth of her sexual immorality....On her forehead a name was written:

> MYSTERY,
> BABYLON THE GREAT,
> THE MOTHER OF PROSTITUTES
> AND OF THE ABOMINATIONS OF THE EARTH.

> ...I saw the woman, drunk with the blood of the saints and with the blood of the martyrs of Jesus. - TheBibleGateway.com[97]

The Bible contains other examples of the importance of numerology, with 777 denoting God's perfection. These scriptures in Revelation though, are the texts where people today draw the modern idea of the "Mark of the Wild Beast" on which the number **666** is emblazoned. The awakened ones apply it not to Satan, as is its common association, but to possible future government control or a One World Order, which could use inserted electronic chips in people's wrists, stamped with numbers or codes, to identify people.

Already there were whisperings on social media of coming mandatory medical procedures being monitored by the state using a luminescent gel ingested in the body of the clients. They were already boasting that such

---

[97] https://www.biblegateway.com/passage/?search=Revelation%2017&version=MEV

a system could be alert to the number of pills one took. The same chip could also easily be linked to all their personal funds, in a government-controlled digital bank account. In the event of engineered war, inflation and an impending economic crash, there would be food poverty. The chip could force rationing of all goods consumed and even travel could then be controlled by digital means. Eventually, there would also be an AI (Artificial Intelligence) take-over, controlling even the human mind, as it was blended using DNA manipulation. Not hard to believe when looking at virtual reality gaming today. The elites could then control human thoughts from inside their brains and devise a God of their own making, taking away the ability to use one's own instinct and retain their self-sovereignty. This could be the futuristic "Mark of the Wild Beast" that so many were talking about.

Strangely, after completing this paragraph, Rose remembered she had seen a car number plate the evening before on her drive back from work which contained the number 666 and she then began thinking about the biblical application. Later on, she went downstairs to make herself a hot drink and her flatmate began to talk about a receipt she had received from shopping at the market the previous day. The total on the bill had come to £6.66! She mentioned it to the vendor, referencing the book of Revelation and he replied that if one adds all the numbers up on the wheel used for Roulette, it totals 666. This was a bit freaky, even for Rose who was used to seeing triple or multiples of 111, 11.11, 222, 14.44, 22.22, 333 or even 555 quite often! It seemed strange for this rare number synchronicity, 666, to appear in this way, within such a short space of time.

Teaching synchronicities

Catherine of Aragon's religious dedication to the Catholic faith had grown as she became older, as did her interest in academics. She continued to broaden her knowledge and provide training for her daughter, Princess Mary. Education among women became fashionable, partly because of Catherine's influence, and she donated large sums of money to several colleges. Here Rose could draw another parallel with her maternal grandmother, who became a teacher and led the example for her two daughters who also became teachers. Unfortunately, despite their education and the authority they had exercised over the children in the classroom, both Constance Mary and her sister Sarah, felt that the male was still viewed as the more important member, in their own families. This was especially true for Rose's mother when she joined the patriarchal religion and her new husband became an Elder (similar to a priest), in the congregation. In their view, the male is the head of the household, with the woman subject to him in decision-making. The woman is also viewed as subservient in the congregation, not being able to give a sermon or counsel directly to the congregation at their meetings.

Location synchronicity

As we saw earlier, Rose had realised that the very place that the previously Princess Mary had been sent away to by Henry VIII, when he divorced her mother, was **Knole House**. We know that when Rose first returned from Bavaria, having left her marriage and the cult, she went to live in Seal. In her **Tudor** flat on the main road, she was no further than ten minutes drive from **Knole Park.** Today there is still a beautiful deer park spanning acres, the legacy of Archbishop Cranmer's hard work and the envious Henry VIII's royal hunting days.

Rose had always felt a magical connection to this estate, now partly a golf course. She spent much time walking there and even wrote a song called "This New Way" sitting in the grass. The track was about finding a new family life with her birth father, in the absence of her mother. Now she knew why! There, her mother the avatar of the demoted Lady Mary had been trapped by her father Henry VIII. She was now also estranged from her mother, Catharine of Aragon, leading to a very unhappy period in that past life. Of course, location-wise, Mary and Anne Boleyn had grown up approximately seven or eight miles away, at Hever Castle, and would no doubt have spent time at this beautiful estate and park in Kent. Here is a little history of the place:

> Knole was extended by the Archbishops of Canterbury in the 15th and 16th centuries. In 1538 Henry VIII was so impressed that he forced Thomas Cranmer to hand Knole over to him. It remained in royal hands until 1561 when Elizabeth I gave it to her favourite

courtier, Robert Dudley. In 1566 the house passed to Thomas Sackville whose descendants still own Knole today. - The National Trust website:[98]

Rose found herself writing about Knole Park, once again, in the spring of 2022, after the healing session with her friend Clare. The release work she had performed using the power of rose oil and petals, had been regarding Clare's past life avatar as Thomas Cranmer, Archbishop of Canterbury. As often happened when she allowed her mind to relax and wander, Rose had started connecting the dots. Suddenly she remembered that she had lived in **Tudor** Drive, when she had moved from her **Tudor** flat with its low hanging wooden beams, to an apartment in **Shoreham** village.

There, next to the roundabout, which doubles as a famous duck pond in the village centre, lie the scant remains of the **Tudor** and once resplendent, **Otford Palace.** It had once been vaster than Hampton Court. Rose still had good friends who live five minutes' walk away from the ruins and she had wandered around it many a time, in curiosity. Sadly there is not much of it left to see, just one of the front towers, the Gatehouse, where you would have had your credentials checked before entering. It is described thus:[99]

> Originally a moated manor house, Otford was part of a circuit of residences visited frequently by the Archbishops of Canterbury and their households. It was closer to London than the Archbishop's Palace at Canterbury and this made it more convenient for travelling to attend court and other business in London. During the period when it was in the possession of the church, it was also occasionally visited by the reigning monarch, who would reside there as the archbishop's guest. That was until 1537 when Henry VIII's covetous eyes alighted upon the palace. In short order, Henry managed to wrest its ownership from the then Archbishop of Canterbury, Thomas Cranmer. Cranmer gave the palace up

---

[98] https://www.nationaltrust.org.uk/features/tudor-links-in-london-and-the-south-east
[99] https://thetudortravelguide.com/2021/08/14/otford-palace/

reluctantly and from this point forward, Otford Palace belonged again to the Crown. - The Tudor Travel Guide[100]

This was a second majestic property wrested from the grasp of the ambitious Archbishop by Henry, in addition to Knole House! Rose was curious to see if there were any clues to her past life soul connections at Otford Palace and was delighted to find the following:

> So, just who can we associate with Otford? Well, Warham's episcopal mansion played host to royalty on a number of occasions; Henry VIII visited in August 1519 and again on 21-22 May 1520. Alongside him was his first wife, Katherine of Aragon. The royal couple and their vast entourage of around 4,000 people were on their way to France to meet Francis I, a gathering that would later become known for its magnificence as 'The Field of Cloth of Gold.' Clearly impressed by Warham's newly built palace, Henry returned in May 1522 and again in September 1527. In 1532, after the archbishop's death, the eleven-year-old Princess Mary spent two summers at Otford. - The Tudor Travel Guide

The stamp of the Tudor family had been all over Kent. Rose realised that some years later, **Otford Palace** and Sissinghurst Castle, would likely have been where the royal entourage stayed over on their later journey to Calais to present Anne Boleyn to Francis I of France. This was the glittering event from October to November 1532, where Mary Boleyn would probably have solidified her friendship with one of the soldiers to the King, William Stafford. The National Trust highlights the key mansions in Kent. As Rose read through, she felt drawn to find out more about one in particular. A key Tudor residence is **Ightham Mote,** which we read about in Chapter 6. It is in relation to Rose's friend Channel and her past life avatar as Sir Richard Clement, the Knight.

---

[100] https://www.nationaltrust.org.uk/features/tudor-links-in-london-and-the-south-east

Disinheritance and religious synchronicities

As we already saw in the previous chapter, Lady Mary's royal half-brother Edward VI, behaved in a ruthless fashion towards her. In this lifetime it was Constance Mary's only son, Terry that experienced betrayal.

> When Edward became mortally ill in 1553, he attempted to remove Mary from the line of succession because he supposed, correctly, that she would reverse the Protestant reforms that had taken place during his reign. - Wikipedia, Mary I of England[101]

Mary had already been plagued by uncertainties around her future, brought about by her father Henry VIII's, untoward actions towards her mother and herself. We learnt that she had been deemed illegitimate after he divorced Catharine of Aragon.

> Henry insisted that Mary recognise him as head of the Church of England, repudiate papal authority, acknowledge that the marriage between her parents was unlawful, and accept her own illegitimacy. She attempted to reconcile with Henry by submitting to his authority as far as "God and my conscience" permitted, but was eventually bullied into signing a document agreeing to all of Henry's demands.- Wikipedia

Although Henry VIII then reviewed the succession to bring Mary and Elizabeth back into the royal line, this changed again after her father's death. Insult was added to injury when his now reigning son Edward VI, re-drafted his will on his deathbed. He cut his half-sisters out of the succession to the throne once again. Upon his death, nominating his first cousin once removed, Lady Jane Grey. Although she took to the throne so quickly, she had not reckoned with how popular Lady Mary was with the people. This was now her chance to regain control of her life and circumstances, at long last.

Rose thought about her mother's life and how she was now estranged from her son Terry due to her religion, for the last twenty-eight years. To

---

[101] https://en.wikipedia.org/wiki/Mary_I_of_England

re-cap, as a young woman, her mother had lost her father when she was only fifteen. Her mother Sarah had then moved her two daughters to the country of her birth, where they would be safer after his death. This was not a happy move for her teenage daughters, who were complete strangers to England. Although she followed her mother's allegiance to the Church of England, in her early thirties Constance Mary was to convert to a radical new religion that, although Christian fundamentalist, was very different from the Protestant church. All these upheavals in family and belief systems seemed to reflect this past life of hers, as Mary I.

Character synchronicity

Mary I, also known as Mary Tudor and "Bloody Mary" by her Protestant opponents, was Queen of England and Ireland for five years from July 1553 until her death on **17 November** 1558 (Rose's mother's date of birth). The young Princess is described as a precocious child, entertaining her father Henry VIII's foreign visitors. This she did with confidence and aplomb, even as a very young girl. Likewise, Constance Mary was quite a handful all through her childhood and was very good at 'holding court' when she was an adult. She had been extremely glamorous as a teenager and became a keen young member of the local Operatic Society. She starred in various plays and looked like a movie star. She had kept all of her glossy dance gowns and long silken gloves, which her daughters Rose and Annabel, loved to play 'dressing up' with. They really enjoyed clacking around their home in their mother's glitzy high heels and jewellery, fit for a Princess.

Constance Mary had also learnt Latin at school and it appears that Mary I was talented in this and other languages from a young age:

> Mary was a precocious child. In July 1520, when scarcely four and a half years old, she entertained a visiting French delegation with a performance on the virginals (a type of harpsichord. A great part of her early education came from her mother, who consulted the Spanish humanist Juan Luis Vives for advice and commissioned him to write De Institutione Feminae Christianae, a treatise on the education of girls. By the age of nine, Mary could read and write

Latin. She studied French, Spanish, music, dance, and perhaps Greek -Wikipedia.[102]

Likewise, Constance Mary had been taught by her mother Sarah, who was an English teacher and had given her daughters good elocution lessons and sound table manners in her colonial home in Africa. In fact, they had black maids, which would have been another parallel with Princess Mary. She would have been attended by servants and ladies-in-waiting at the Palace de Placentia in Greenwich, London. Rose smiled when she thought about her mother. There was always an air of superiority around her, she groomed herself elegantly and was always perfectly coiffed, with attractive makeup and nails. She did seem to have rather a queenly presence.

Mary I's religious zeal, coupled with the buried anger she had been unable to express towards Henry, had built up over the years and when she finally came to power, she was a terrible force to be reckoned with:

> She is best known for her vigorous attempt to reverse the English Reformation, which had begun during the reign of her father, Henry VIII. Her attempt to restore to the Church the property confiscated in the previous two reigns was largely thwarted by Parliament, but during her five-year reign, Mary had over 280 religious dissenters burned at the stake in the Marian persecutions.- Wikipedia

Likewise, Constance Mary seemed to carry a huge amount of anger towards men. Rose had always thought it was due to the untimely death of her father but she had learnt from her Aunt how her younger sister was also disciplined by him with a belt, in her younger years. This bullying reminded Rose of King Henry's behaviour towards Mary, she must have been ashamed and raging inside, when forced to pacify him by signing the agreement that her parent's marriage was illegitimate. Likewise, Constance Mary's treatment by her father may have precipitated the rage that she then unleashed on the future men in her life.

Constance Mary was also an incorrigible, religious zealot, preaching regularly in the door-to-door ministry, assigned to all members. As a

---

[102] https://en.wikipedia.org/wiki/Mary_I_of_England

new convert, she relentlessly called back to people in their homes, leaving magazines and pushing them to study the bible with her. It was her way or the highway and she was convinced that she was right and that she had found The Truth. Nothing and nobody would get in her way now! This led to the manipulation of her first husband's visiting rights and the prevention of all contact with his daughters and their paternal grandparents.

It seemed that revenge was sweet to her and that the new family with her second husband would be protected by her new God. Unfortunately, this back-fired on her severely when all three of her grown children eventually left her religion. Now she was forced to shun them if she wanted to maintain her standing with her God. As with Mary, she had also experienced seismic shifts in her life and had an overwhelming need to feel as if she was now firmly back in control.

This situation felt karmic to Rose and is something that she worked hard to heal over the decades since her estrangement from her mother. Although it looked likely that her mother would stick to her guns till her death, Rose had to find peace and forgiveness in her own heart, in order to heal these repeating wounds of religious oppression, shunning and abandonment. She became aware of a type of therapy that dealt with such unresolved and ambiguous loss and decided she owed it to herself to face her shadows head-on and confront her buried feelings. She wanted some kind of resolution to the unfounded fears she experienced in later life, which were still interfering with her relationships and were in need of healing.

Therefore, Rose undertook a course in therapeutic letter writing. The process was that she should first pen a letter from little Rose to her adult self, explaining in her naïve way, the earliest traumatic event she could remember as a young child. She needed to re-live these memories as far back into her early childhood as possible. She experienced again, the passionate convictions her parents had thrust upon her and how disempowered she had felt. It wasn't easy at all, but she felt compelled to continue with the treatment.

The next stage of the therapy was to write a return letter as the grown Rose, assuring the young Rose that she had done no wrong. She was to tell her that she was deeply loved, unconditionally, and despite the traumatic circumstances she had experienced, she was always protected. This back-and-forth letter-writing process really seemed to help Rose. It resolved some of the inner suppressed trauma that had been dogging her for years. She wished that her mother had been able to do this too.

Family separation synchronicity

As we know, Lady Mary had lost her dear mother when they were cruelly separated and she had been banished to the countryside, far away from all her family. Her demotion from Princess to Lady and being sent away to Knole House in Kent is well documented as causing her deep distress. Her father's shameful break from Rome and the Catholic church must have mortified her deeply. Henry VIII was aware of her feelings and forbade her any contact with her mother, who was now banished from court and went to live out her years in devotion in a monastery.

Likewise, Constance Mary had felt abandoned by her father, who died when she was only fifteen. Her own religious choices also created distance from her mother who remained staunch Church of England. It had caused a breach between them, that was never really healed before her mother's early death. To add insult to injury, Constance Mary was now estranged from all three of her children, when they left her religion. History seemed to be repeating itself in twists and turns.

Location synchronicity

I discussed in Chapter 9, Thomas Cranmer, the Archbishop of Canterbury and the properties of his that King Henry VII had appropriated. Thomas had owned the mansion in Sevenoaks, Knole House, which is yet another breadcrumb in the past life trail. We know that Princess Mary had spent a couple of summers there when she was eleven, but now she had been obliged to live there since her mother's divorce from Henry VIII. It is recorded that Lady Mary spent many lonely and unhappy hours, wandering the courtyards and halls, gazing up at the vast array of stern royal portraits, probably hating every minute of it. Rose could imagine that her mother unconsciously felt the same, being trapped in an unhappy marriage and a controlling religion for over fifty years.

'Knole House courtyard clock tower'

To this day, a huge collection of these royal paintings survives, including a more unflattering, small portrait of Anne Boleyn! There is also an enormous amount of Tudor furniture which has been very well preserved, with extensive renovations to the Knole Estate taking place in very recent years. This location had now connected Rose to two additional members of her soul family, Clare (Thomas Cranmer) and her mother Constance Mary (Mary I). Rose lived in **Tudor Drive** close to the **Otford Palace** ruins and had previously lived for five years very near to **Knole House** in Seal! The manor was a mere ten-minute drive from her home and she often walked there amongst the rolling hillocks and oak trees. The park is still full of deer and she had enjoyed many a picnic there, in the summer months.

Looking back at the preceding conclusions Rose had drawn from all these reflections on her past lives and those of the people she had shared them with, she knew it was something she needed to write about. For some reason, she felt that it was an important message to those on their spiritual ascension path. She came to see it as a prerequisite for herself, before becoming a healer or beacon of light. The phrase "physician heal thyself" came to mind as many wounded healers were unwittingly projecting their own past trauma onto others, disassociated from their pain and the need to expunge it.

In more recent years with the cataclysmic events on the world scene, it felt like a more urgent requirement to look into the mirror of one's own murky past. Now is the time to brush away the cobwebs in the manors and seek out the hidden skeletons in the cupboards of the castles, in order to lift the portcullis guarding the heart and to build new bridges to a higher consciousness of love.

With these thoughts in mind, Rose sent her mother a couple of messages as a way of waving the white flag of peace. To her great surprise, she sent her back a photograph of the most stunning red rose from her garden, which had orange underlining the petals. It was a beautiful sign of connection to the Tudor rose, a symbol of their past lives together. Before that it had also represented The War of The Roses, which was laid to rest in Tudor times. To Rose, the red rose also symbolised Mary Magdalene's energy. It felt as if she was giving Rose her assistance in healing the wounds between mother and daughter. Rose uttered a prayer of thanks, in gratitude for this kind gesture of love and sent up a prayer of deep thanks.

Returning to the subject of castles, there was one more past life that needed to be included in these tales, as it is tied together with the very first clues that Rose had been given by Peter the shaman. It was the historic events surrounding The Kett Brothers, leading up to the battle in 1549 and ending at Norwich Castle in Norfolk. In the next chapter you will come to see just why Robert Kett became a key example and is still honoured as a brave champion for justice for us today!

CHAPTER 12

Robert Kett, The Peoples' Hero

Robert Kett (c. **1492** – 7 December 1549), the leader of Kett's Rebellion. Died at the age of fifty-seven.

Julia (b. 26 March). Married to Simon. Previous life as Elizabeth Woodville, The White Queen.

This chapter is dedicated to Rose's soul friend Julia, with whom she had made an important spiritual discovery some years previously. Recently they had pilgrimaged to Glastonbury if you remember, to invoke a healing release regarding an earlier past life connection between them, as Lady Eleanor Talbot and Elizabeth Woodville. As we saw, The White Queen lived out the last five years of her life at Bermondsey Abbey in London and passed over on 8 June **1492** at the age of fifty-five. Her great-grandchildren amongst others were King Henry VIII and Mary I. Julia did not seem to figure in King Henry VIII's court, as others in Rose's other soul circle had done, but was re-born in the county of Norfolk, during the reign of Henry VIII's young son, Edward VI.

As you can see, Robert Kett was born in the same year that Elizabeth Woodville had died, circa **1492.** In this next incarnation, Julia was to take on a very different character, as the hero, Robert Kett. Her husband Simon will also feature in this timeline as Robert's older brother;

William Kett (b. 1485- 7 **December** 1549) (brother of Robert Kett (1492 – 7 Dec 1549). He would have been sixty-four when he died.

Simon (b. **14 December** (Julia's husband).

Birthdate number synchronicity

Rose had deduced that Julia and Simon had various previous life scenarios together over the last six years of writing. His previous life was covered in Chapter 5 regarding King Richard III who died in **1492.** In the same year, Rose's instinct told her that he was brought back immediately as William Kett, the older brother by seven years, of Robert. Simon's birthdate contains the number **14** and is the month of **December** when William Kett was executed. The timings also fitted for his transition from one life straight into the next, just as Julia had done.

If you remember in Chapter 4, some of the visual keys garnered from Peter the shaman's visions, was the wooden pole, with the metal basket containing a skeleton. Later on he had seen a tree being planted and watered and beautiful glowing light, symbolising healing for unjust passings. Rose had seen a photo of the lookout beacon on Kett's Heights a week later and then began reading about The Kett Brothers. She had been delighted to find out that there was an open-air play about Robert Kett in the summer of 2016 which was held under the trees at the historic location of Kett's Heights Gardens. The Mayor's procession featured actors, who had turned the play into a comedy and very amusing it was too. The story needed lightning up! Now we will begin to see how this past life tale unravelled, as we learn more about the people's hero, Robert Kett.[103] [104]

The more Rose researched the more she understood that Robert Kett, although a relatively well-off tanner and businessman, had taken the part of the common people. Collectively all over England, they were becoming increasingly disgruntled, then extremely angry over the injustices heaped on them by the greedy feudal and tax system. In 1381, there had been a long period of unrest spanning two hundred years, the first of which came to a head in London and was famously named The Peasants' Revolt, Wat Tyler's Rebellion or the Great Rising. This was precipitated by the Black Death, which we touched upon in Chapter 1, in Julian of Norwich's time. In addition, The Hundred Year's War with France had put a strain on

---

[103] http://www.kettsociety.org.uk/
[104] http://www.britainexpress.com/History/tudor/ketts-rebellion.htm

London's coffers and their pursestrings were tightening as a result of sky-high inflation and higher taxes for everyone.

We have reflected on the similarities to our recent times with the pandemic, a new war in Ukraine and subsequent rocketing prices of fuel and food due to the sanctions imposed on Russia, by the US President et al. All this brought unwanted suffering to the rest of the world and threatened a global financial crash, followed by the predicted recession.

Fast forward from 1381 two centuries to the year 1549 and we find that in addition to the aforementioned repression of the lower classes, the wealthy had been stealthily enclosing areas of the public lands. These Landlords' fields were reserved for grazing the commoners' livestock or growing food. By moving the property boundaries, such open pastures were gradually being appropriated by the landed gentry causing an agricultural crisis and leading to starvation. Five hundred years later, we find ourselves facing a similar fate, with looming food poverty to come in the years ahead, due to systematic breakdown of the supply chain of liquid fertilizers and food to Europe and beyond.

When Robert Kett volunteered himself as the people's captain, he is quoted as giving a rousing speech before they set off from Wymondham to ambush the rich landlords and noblemen of Norwich.

Lara Eakins, Tudorhistory.org:

> Then **Robert Ket** went on to commit himself body and soul to the movement, resolved that the peasants should not be left unaided in the struggle they had begun and willing to take upon himself the burden an responsibility of leadership...."You shall have me, if you will, not only as a companion, but as a captain; and in the doing of the so great a work before us, not only as a fellow, but for a leader, author and principal." It is plain from **Ket**'s speeches to his men, and from The Rebels' Complaint, which he published at this time, that to **Robert Ket** the rising was not only to put down enclosures, its aim was rather to strike at the root of the evil and to put an end to the ascendancy of the landlord class, and make England a free common wealth.

> Either the people must put down landlords, or very soon the landlords would have the whole land in their possession, and

the people would be in hopeless and helpless subjection. Had an act of parliament been actually passed making "slaves" of the landless men, dispossessed by enclosures? When parliament was establishing slavery it was time for honest men to be up and doing, rousing the people to action.

Ket's speech at Eaton Wood is a fierce attack on the landlords, and a reminder that having ventured so far, the peasants must advance yet further: Now are ye overtopped and trodden down by gentlemen, and put out of possibility ever to recover foot. Rivers of riches ran into the coffers of your landlords, while you are pair'd to the quick, and fed upon pease and oats like beasts. You are fleeced by these landlords for their private benefit, and as well kept under by the public burdens of State wherein while the richer sort favour themselves, ye are gnawn to the very bones. You tyrannous masters often implead, arrest, and cast you into prison, so that they may the more terrify and torture you in your minds, and wind our necks more surely under their arms. And then they palliate these pillories with the fair pretence of law and authority! Fine workmen, I warrant you, are this law and authority, who can do their dealings so closely that men can only discover them for your undoing. Harmless counsels are fit for tame fools; for you who have already stirred there is no hope but in adventuring boldly. In 'The Revels' Complaint," the same note is struck. Only by taking up arms, and mixing Heaven and earth together, can the intolerable oppression of the landlords be ended. - Tudor Palace[105]

Unbelievably, the need for Common Land to be recognised and not poached by the ruling classes is still occurring today! Here is the current website of a Landrights Campaign for Britain, and I quote their strap-line:

---

[105] http://www.tudorplace.com.ar/Documents/robert_ket_and_the_norfolk_risin.htm
Lara Eakins: https://www.tudorhistory.org

It campaigns peacefully for access to the land, its resources, and the decision-making processes affecting them, for everyone, irrespective of age, race or gender. - The Land Is Ours[106]

The Kett brothers became known as heroes and leaders for justice for the common folk, but not, unfortunately, until many centuries thereafter. This was to be one of the unjust passings the shaman had been directed to and now we will find out how Rose followed the breadcrumb trail, eventually coming to understand the soul link to her close childhood married friends Julia and Simon. Also, we will come to understand the significance this had for your current times and the unsure future that lies ahead.

Location synchronicity

Although the friends were raised and lived in West Sussex, Rose had not known that Julia's paternal ancestors originated in **Wymondham**. This is the first key synchronicity she pieced together with Julia's past life because Robert Kett and his brother William were born and raised in **Wymondham**. As Rose probed further, Julia exclaimed that she also had some relatives that lived in nearby Dereham and also in **Hethersett!**

This was an exciting nugget of information because it just so happens to be near to one of the most famous trees in Norfolk Tudor history, **Kett's Oak**. This majestic tree, one of fifty great British trees, still survives and is now over five hundred years old. It is located at the side of the B1172 road between **Wymondham** and **Hethersett.** Kett's Oak has been propped up with a huge wooden joist and filled with concrete. Huge bands of iron have been affixed around its trunk to keep it from splitting off. In 2020 the Norfolk County Council took another step to save it by applying biochar to the roots to keep it healthy. It has a little metal railing around it with a metal plaque bearing the name 'Kett's Oak, 1549.'

---

[106] https://tlio.org.uk/?fbclid=IwAR2_s0ZsM3k3hhSEbPe9Fw5TLFQOeCVG58 GYpplb4uy9oSMou5YPeZFFzzU

'Kett's Oak, propped up'

The reason this tree has become so famous is that it marks the very spot where the businessman Robert Kett was persuaded to meet and rally with the peasants and farmers known as the Commoners. They were the equivalent of labourers in the working classes of today. They were desperate for help and convinced the fifty-seven-year-old into the role of army leader. He had previously helped them save their parish church. Upon listening to their sad story about the arable land, his conscience had driven him to tear down his enclosure fences, in solidarity. Thus he became a force to be reckoned with.

Once he had marshalled the mob together and planned their strategic attack, they mustered at Kett's Oak. From here they famously and heroically set off for Norwich, gathering other supporters along the way, until their numbers reached 16,000 men. Armed with their sharpest farming tools and any offensive weapons they could find, The Kett brothers led the angry peasants on their first march to set up camp near the city on 8 July 1549. They were moved on from a couple of sites initially, being challenged by the sheriff the first day and the Mayor the next. As there was no negotiation between the two factions, the rabble stood their ground and law enforcement retreated in haste, to the safety of the city, or so they hoped.

Further location synchronicities

As Kett's army was refused permission to march through Norwich, they continued on over the **River Wensum** at **Hellesdon**, where they overnighted in **Drayton**. Here is another location connection to Julia and Simon. They first lived in King Street next to the **River Wensum** upon moving to Norwich and in latter years had chosen a home in the **Drayton** area, setting up their business in nearby **Hellesdon**. So here were more synchronicities. Now the rebels had a straight run to take over Mousehold Heath, which boasts a high vantage point over the city. Here Kett chose the ruins of St. Michael's Chapel as his war room which is why it was later dubbed Kett's Castle. They also appropriated the deserted Mount Surrey to hold their prisoners and prepared for the ensuing battle. There is a street named after these 'commotion times' called **Kett's Hill** and is a road that always stood out to Simon for some reason. Sometimes our past life locations stir faint subliminal awareness in us of times gone by. It seems that only those on the holy grail of awareness, will become fully conscious of the need to remember what happened there and heal the land.

Once settled on the heath, Kett chose another oak to set up the court. Here is where he is famed to have meted out justice beneath the 'Oak of Reformation.' In 2021 Julia gifted Rose a beautiful silver bracelet which has three oak trees filigreed and studded with Swaroski diamond chips, which sparkle in the sun. When Rose thanked her for the beautiful piece, she remarked that it pictured the Tree of Life, but then realised the symbolism of The Oak of Reformation and Kett's Oak and how they stood for justice. Julia admitted she had bought it without realising its significance, but that it made sense now that she would be drawn to giving it as a present. There is an emblem of the tree carved into the stone of Norwich Castle, giving recent honour to Robert Kett as a man of the people and a freedom fighter.

On 29 July 1549, the Peasants' Revolt began in earnest and they thundered down the hill towards The Wensum River. This is close to Lollard's Pit where the witches were executed over the centuries. They mounted the cannons, finally breaking the city wall and defences at the fortressed toll, built on Bishops Bridge. This was operated by the monks from Whitefriars, which as we know, is just a ten minute walk along the river. This key trade gate was protected by the lookout, Cow Tower, on the city side of The Wensum and is another location synchronicity.

It is now a beauty spot near where Rose had worked on the site of the Carmelite monastery in Whitefriars. It is a magical place and somewhere she was drawn to eat her lunch in the summer months. If you visit and walk along this beautifully restored pathway today, look closely at the top of Cow Tower and you will see small chunks of masonry missing from the top turret. These were taken out with cannon fire by Kett's men. Despite this attack, it is known to be one of the best preserved look-out towers in England.

The ire of the commoners spurred them on to a brave victory and they successfully broke in and sacked the city. Their triumph was followed by a series of open courts, where those landlords and gentry guilty of stealing land were dragged to Mousehold Heath. The Oak of Reformation no longer survives, but you will come to see why Kett's Oak near Wymondham, with its iron bands, was another significant clue on the trail of the grail.

Unfortunately, this huge unruly protest had to be suppressed at all costs and the young King Edward VI, who we read about in Chapter 10, ordered in cavalry and troops from Northamptonshire, to quell it. The peasants' army was no match against these fierce royal soldiers on horseback and they were well and truly beaten and captured.

> After skirmishes in and around the city the rebel army was drawn eastward into the Battle of Dussindale (near Boundary Lane, Thorpe St Peters) where they were defeated by a superior army of 14,000 reinforced by German mercenaries. Nine of Kett's men were hanged from the Oak of Reformation; Kett himself was hanged in chains from the walls of Norwich Castle but the same walls now bear a plaque declaring him a local hero.

Rose was now fully aware that she needed to do a series of clearings along the Wensum River. Beginning at the monastery connected to Lady Eleanor Talbot, taking in the Magistrates Courts and all the trauma that had been experienced there over the years, along to Cow Tower and of course including Bishops Bridge next to The Red Lion and Lollard's Pit. She took this clearing further along the river which runs onto King Street where the ancient Boleyn family had owned property, past Julian of Norwich's shrine, right up to the mill where Julia, Simon and Rose had found their first home in Trowse Newton eight years ago. Healing takes time! There was more to come!

Robert Kett died one of the most gruesome deaths, which meant being left to die for a couple of weeks, bound and standing in a metal gibbet cage. This was the awful practice in those times who had really crossed the line and were to be made an example of. The protest against this from the locals was so loud after his death, that the Mayor had him taken down earlier than was typical.

His brother William Kett suffered the same fate but was hung in chains on the tower of Wymondham Cathedral, in order that they might be held up as a bad influence on the people in both towns. Their deaths were commemorated each year over the centuries, but as a warning rather than as feted heroes. Unaware of this history, Julia and Simon had visited Wymondham Cathedral in the summer of 2019 whilst on a work day out, a car treasure hunt. They climbed the tower looking for clues and stumbled across the statue depicting William Kett being hung over the wall, commemorating his death. Again, another subliminal experience. Julia was horrified when she found out how he had died afterwards.

As Rose gradually drew her conclusions over time, she discussed her ideas with Julia one evening over the phone. She immediately experienced the body shivers when Rose suggested that perhaps she had been Robert Kett as he was hung in chains on Norwich Castle walls and that maybe Simon had been William Kett. Over the two years since Rose had begun researching Robert Kett, she had not been able to make a connection to a past life for herself. Now she seemed to be hot on the trail. Spurred on by this information, Julia told her how she and Simon had visited Norwich Castle not long before and had descended into the basement where there is a huge collection of torture instruments in the chamber. She had been staring at the gibbet cage with its iron bands from top to toe and had an overwhelming feeling that she couldn't pull herself away from it. Simon had snapped her out of her reverie because she had been lost in thoughts of how horrific such a death must have been.

Experiential body synchronicity

On 11 February 2018, two years after the shaman's reading, Rose felt sure she was onto something huge that needed releasing in this past life scenario. She invited Julia to visit for a quantum timeline healing. She explained where she felt a tight uncomfortable band around her chest and her tummy. She also mentioned that her ankles had been stinging all the time too. Rose focused on these areas and the Reiki energy that flowed through, caused Julia to convulse or shake it out through her body. This was something the friends had learnt about during their forensic healing workshop three years previously. Now they were putting their training into practice in their own lives. It was dawning on them that time doesn't heal, but that healing takes time!

During the healing, Rose sensed that the discomfort Julia felt was partly due to a past life as a captive in chains or metal bands and Julia confirmed she had also been told about this some time ago, by a psychic friend of hers. Rose had a vision during the healing, of Julia being hung in chains just like the scene Peter the Shaman had described in his reading, where the person was left to die in the basket on a pole or gibbet cage. The iron bindings kept the person in an upright position so that they couldn't move. This extreme trauma is what can be bound to the soul as it passes over, becoming an imprint in future lives.

Rose wondered if perhaps the chafing of the metal cuffs around her ankles was a metaphorical representation in Julia causing her ankles to sting, reflecting on how the skin would have been rubbed raw. Rose asked if she thought these could be physical signposts in order to flag up what she needed to do to step into her life path fully, to assist others with injustices. Julia felt this could be birthed through her Reiki healing, coupled with hypnotherapy and the counselling training that she is currently finishing. Rose agreed that often we can be held back by overlapping timelines and the fear and trauma waves could cause us to hold ourselves in check, sabotaging our progress.

It is interesting to note that in the shamanic reading Peter had seen a large tree being planted in a church courtyard next to a grave. The tree was watered with a white crystalline fluid and as it turned to darkness, the tree absorbed the white energy and started to glow. He said it was very beautiful and a representation of much-needed healing. Rose concluded that through 'remembering' comes awareness of the trauma, and intention to release. This cuts away any residual victim mentality and can be followed by deep feelings of peace and gratitude. The end of a karmic cycle and the beginning of fresh new things.

Later in the summer of September 2019, Rose arranged for Karen the psychic medium, Hatti, an expert in soul life clearings and Julia to come together to do some healing work around their past lives. When they met together they immediately felt a connection as a group and the energies started to rise. As they discussed the spiritual work at hand and issues that were holding them back. It seemed that Julia still had a lot of past life trauma to clear. Rose had been practising a new aura healing modality that Karen had been guided to develop so they arranged with Julia to be their first "client".

As Karen and Rose worked with her they became aware of the way she was still holding various traumas in her body which seemed to be from different lives and timelines. There still seemed to be a slight tightness where the physically felt bands were previously and also the stinging of the ankles was still present. Rose was really enjoying flexing her healing abilities in this way. In the fourth healing session with Julia they also picked up on metal plates to which she was chained in a medieval past life! Karen could sense a bolt at the back of her neck attached to a metal plate and the shackles around her ankles. Also, she 'heard' the constant dripping of water and said it continued for so long that it was like Chinese water torture. They worked as a team to clear energies around this as well.

Location Synchronicity

Rose realised that she had been in the **dungeons** of Norwich Castle two weeks earlier with her brother Terry when he had come to stay for the weekend. They were the only ones there and the tour guide apologised that the torture instruments had been put away during the ongoing repairs to the basements. Instead, he gave them a much more detailed historical account and had been explaining to them how the rainwater would have leaked down through the layers of the old stone building and would sometimes have dripped constantly in this fashion in the dungeons. The amount of water would sometimes reach a few inches and any prisoners chained to the wall would have been sitting in the water for long periods, in the cold and dark!

The Kett brothers had been captured in August but not executed until 7 December 1549 and would have spent four months in captivity starting in The Tower of London, then being transferred at some point to Norfolk. Robert would have been incarcerated in the **dungeon** beneath Norwich Castle before he met his sorry end. No doubt he would have experienced the dripping water as the late autumn rains began.

Although the pair had already been doing some healing work on this with Julia, the water torture was something new. They thought it would be good to see if they could finally release this with Julia. First of all, using methods of working with her guides, they requested that all those participating be protected from any negative or dense energies that may arise. They then started the work of requesting that any past life contracts, agreements, cords, hooks and bindings connected to that lifetime as Robert Kett, be loosened and brought up and out of the body.

Karen and Rose asked Julia to do the following;

1. Visualise these scrolls and objects coming up through her energy chakras from the red base chakra to the purple or indigo head chakra and then up and out through her crown.
2. Imagine a deep well into which anything that she saw leaving the body would be thrown.
3. They inspired her to see a central flame of indigo and violet light and visualise the contracts, any torture instruments, cords and bindings being burnt in the purple flame, then taken up to the universal light and transmuted for the good of all.
4. Command a golden, white light to descend and fill any gaps and voids that were left when the cords and hooks were taken out of her energy field and body.
5. Pray for Arch Angel Michael to continue to hoover out any last vestiges of contracts. Julia was to continue to visualise going into

the central flame and being burnt until absolutely nothing was left to release.

6. Invoke protection, now it was processed and ask that the purest light from Source, be brought in to seal it shut, with a blessing.

7. Give thanks and gratitude to the guides and all loving ancestors or spirit animal totems, that had assisted with the clearing.

Only at the conclusion of the writing of this book, had Rose realised that her half-brother Terry, who had taken the part of the young King Edward VI, had been intrinsically linked to this very castle. It was he, that had the Kett Brothers indicted at The Tower of London. He then arranged for them to be brought back to Norwich and executed in front of all their loved ones. Unknown to Terry at the time, his very presence here now, was an opportunity to acknowledge the cruelty and suffering he had been responsible for inflicting on his soul group, in that past life scene. Rose felt that here was another piece of work that she could undertake with Julia on behalf of Terry, to release and cut pain ties. When he was in his teens he had been close to Simon's younger brother, but they were prevented from developing their friendship when Terry left the Witnesses. There was so much to heal. Rose hoped that if they worked on this remotely it could heal the rift between them currently, as she dearly missed her brother.

After the quantum timeline healings with Julia and the very next day, Hatti was guided to go to Kett's Heights with her colleague, a medium by the name of Ron Kett. Bizarrely, he had traced his family line and his ancestry back to the ancient Kett family alive in 1549! Hatti told them how she suddenly became aware of thousands of lost souls up there on the heath that needed to be released to the light. As they walked around Mousehold Common, the spirit of a very bolshy and quite angry man appeared to her and did not seem happy about her being there. He challenged her presence there and she explained that she does soul clearings and rescues to assist those that have passed over, but who have not found the light to return to their soul home in spirit. Eventually, Hatti was able to persuade him that this work was for the greater good of all and with his permission, she started to feel many many of the lost souls ascend upwards to the light.

As they were discussing this in their development circle a week later, Rose understood that her friend must have been communicating with the spirit of Robert Kett. He seemed to be the Gatekeeper of that land now, so it was no wonder that he was angry when his ghost had appeared to her. Hatti knew that Kett's Heights had been the mustering point for the civilian army that he was leading. Although initially very successful in their mission, eventually they were overcome by mounted troops from Northamptonshire. This led to the unjust and early death of thousands of farmers and workers and could well have been the reason that their souls had not been properly laid to rest.

Hatti explained to Rose that there was still a lot of dark energy up there and that she would like her to return there in order to confirm that the entire site was fully cleared and lifted to a higher vibration in the light. Rose found herself driving up and parking opposite the old prison, where there is a bench directly overlooking the common, with the picturesque city skyline in the background. Once at dusk, she sat there meditating on the various forms of healing that had taken place, individually and collectively for those fallen to be remembered and their souls laid to rest.

As she pondered, she observed a stunning sunset behind the Cathedral whilst she uttered some final blessings and prayers for peace. She remember a quote she had read and knew these people had not died in vain, that their strength was remembered;

> If the ambition which clutches at sovereignty and rule is despicable, even more despicable is the weakness which refuses to take command at times of peril. - www.Tudorplace.com

The second sentence of this quote reminded Rose of the human struggles in her times. The spread of the viral pandemic and the subsequent lockdowns and mandates to take the new inoculations. Many bravely protested the mandates in those lands and they were being sacked for not having the poorly tested injections. Doctors were being threatened with having their medical licence revoked if they spoke against the narrative or used early treatments and out of patent alternatives. In particular, she noticed that the 80,000 British NHS staff who refused to conform, were being threatened with dismissal by 4 April 2022. Luckily this didn't happen as the virus mutated into a less dangerous variant.

In a great show of solidarity, they all took to the streets on 22 January

2022. They were joined in spirit by their awakened colleagues up and down the cities of England. There were photos taken of the hospital rebels in London, throwing down their scrubs or uniforms in various key places. This was a clear sign of their non-compliance and bid for freedom of choice and bodily autonomy. They showed strength against the tyrannical Government and were even prepared to lose medical careers of thirty years, in some cases.

It seems that we collectively need to wake up to what was quoted centuries ago:

> Even more despicable is the weakness which refuses to take command at times of peril.- Robert Kett

The amended Human Rights Act was passing through the Commons and a new Bill of Rights was awaiting the approval process. Rose had signed the protest to have this stopped as there were aspects of the changes that insinuated even more rights to sovereignty were being taken away.

It was interesting that Rose had been working for criminal justice a couple of years previously and that The Magistrates courts are now just across the river from her office at Carmelite House. The Tarot card 'Justice' had come up for her in several psychic readings with her favourite angel card reader, Debbie Divine (see her website Divine Rays in the footnote below)[107] - Julia confirmed it had also come up for her with Debbie. With regards to justice, it is notable that the current Magistrates Courts were built over the ancient Norman ruins which have been restored and Rose was able to go on a tour of the courts and actually visit the ancient basement. The stones have been beautifully restored and lit for visiting tourists to observe.

In the footnote, is an article about this restoration work, with a wonderful image of the preserved ruins.

Quoting from the website:

> In 1981, just prior to the building of the new Magistrates and Crown Courts complex between Bishopgate and the River Wensum, an extensive archaeological dig uncovered the remains

---

[107] www.divinemessenger.co.uk and Www.divineraysspiritualhub.com

of a stone house dating back to the twelfth century. The ruins, immediately adjacent to the river and with walls still present to a height in excess of two metres, were the remains of the undercroft, or cellar, of what was once a substantial house probably built for a wealthy Norman family. - Norwich 360[108]

Here Rose had also found the connection to her past life across the Wensum as Lady Eleanor Talbot in the form of the ancient Whitefriars monastery, Arminghall Arch. It is similar to the one that commemorates her outside Carmelite House. Again quoting from the link above:

Also in the Magistrates Courts building is the Arminghall Arch, an elaborately carved fourteenth century stone archway which was originally part of the Carmelite Friary, a short distance across the river from where the court buildings now stand.

Somehow Rose felt that the injustices that have occurred and are still being perpetrated there in the courts on top of this ancient Norman site, still needed permission from the spirit of the land to clear and heal. She arranged with her friend Caroline to do another ceremony on that site. It struck her that perhaps the two arches were acting like a portal and may need clearing of the dense energies brought about by the traumas experienced in their vicinity. Rose then realised that this was the very location that Teal had fought for custody of her kidnapped child, over twenty times, when she had experienced the terror of walking up the steps as if she were going to the gallows. She still has the fire burning in her heart, to bring justice not only for herself as a parent who had her child taken away from her when he was seven but also for all parents who have suffered the injustice of parental alienation and the ensuing failure of the court system to restore the rights of fathers and mothers who have been alienated from their children.

There is a modern-day term for the injustice taking place in some judicial decisions, which is called PAS (Parental Alienation Syndrome). Teal said she intends to challenge those that perpetrate this syndrome at home and take advantage of the justice system, in the future. Her goal is to

---

[108] https://www.norwich360.com/normanhouse.html\

push for a change in the law in order for it not to be possible to trust just one parent, without good cause. Also to fight against the rulings to legally banish one parent from custody, any contact or even visiting rights with their children. It would truly be a significant win in the cause of justice, where it to be changed. Somehow Rose saw this as parallel to the scenes of Robert Kett fighting for justice for the common people in the open courts nearby, over the summer of 1549.

There certainly were many layers of tragedy to be healed in this area, over the centuries! Even in her own life, Rose had the traumatic experience of losing her father at the same young age of seven, as her son Lee had been snatched from her and they knew this was another parallel link between the friends. They knew they were called to be spiritual warriors and stand up for justice now.

Further to these realisations, Rose had also previously written about her soul friendship with Julia, in which her friend's past life came to an end as Elizabeth Woodville. She came to understand slowly, that Julia shared some similar soul woundings to herself. She also struggled with a lack of self-belief or the confidence to stand up and be seen and heard. In her life as Robert Kett, things were certainly turned on their head and she incarnated in an amazing male role, eventually recognised as a hero of the people. I felt that the lesson to be learnt here was that justice needs to be done and those that have this calling are being bidden to overcome their fear. Robert Kett fought to the death for the cause in the end but today, this is manifested as an unfounded fear that Julia carries, as many wounded healers do. It is one that we have to overcome in order to help and inspire others to move forward, beyond their fears.

Rose and Julia had realised from all this hard work that often karmic timelines with members of their soul tribe, could cause cantankerous or challenging relationships in the present day groupings. They had consciously worked on their past life connections realising that it had disrupted their friendship from time to time. Rose was aware of the prolonged rifts this had caused and didn't want this to hold them back anymore. They wanted to work together now, in whichever way spirit saw fit. They felt confident that they had communicated honestly and done the work sufficiently. They were moving forward in peace and grace with each other and their inter-connected friends and families. Just as the message from the card they drew in the Mary Magdalene Oracle pack had reminded them:

My grace lives in you, flowing through you, into the heart of the world.

In the early winter of 2022, another psychic friend Rose was acquainted with, said that she felt that Julia was still feeling entrapped in some way, energetically. Rose explained that although Julia wanted to break away from working full-time with the family business and push forward with her counselling and hypnotherapy business, she constantly got pulled back and probably feels as if she is still in chains. Rose knew that Julia's fear of loss and danger had come over from her past traumatic circumstances as The White Queen and that she would have lived in fear of Richard III. As with her next incarnation, Kett, she was given the opportunity to transmute this pain cycle by emerging as a brave warrior. She had stood for justice against age old atrocities and now she could help those traumatised by their life experiences, through her counselling and hypnotherapy with Peaceful Minds and Souls.

Rose felt there were still more layers of the onion to be peeled. There was more conscious release work to be done around this story and she invited her shamanic friend Caroline on another trip to Kett's Oak on the old Wymondham Road. It was a cold and windy day in February 2022 and they arrived with Caroline's toolkit of natural offerings and crystals. Rose brought her Reiki drum and rattle, with the intention of clearing, as they moved around the little fence guarding the tree. A silver saloon drew up in the narrow lay-by. The road was exceptionally busy for a Sunday and the noise from the traffic was loud. Soon a tall man emerged and walked towards them, calling out "Is this Kett's Oak?" Rose nodded and mouthed in affirmation, so he doubled back and helped a little old lady and another woman out of the car.

By this time the friends realised they were going to have to curtail their healing ceremony. As they gathered up their sacred objects, the strangest, most wonderful thing happened. The older lady was introduced to us by her daughter and husband, as Mrs Kett. Rose's mouth dropped open at the implication of this. They explained that they were on a tour, to see all the sites with a connection to her mother's ancestors. Rose needed no encouragement and being quite the expert by now, suggested some of the key haunts for them to explore, for which they were very grateful.

The gentleman, whose name Rose discovered was Mr Brown, said he had read up on Norwich Council's reparation of Kett's Oak using biochar applied to the roots and Rose's ears pricked up. She made a mental note to include this in her book, and then his wife Karen dropped the bombshell. She told Rose that they had drawn up her mother's family tree and that it went back ten generations, all the way back to Robert Kett himself! Rose felt as light as air, despite the bitter winds, and beamed a warm smile. Here was one of the best synchronicities she had ever experienced since the beginning of this journey. Here in front of her, stood a true blood relative of the very past life she had been writing about. It seemed almost too good to be true that they also took a real interest in what she was writing about. Here was a massive confirmation from The Universe that she was still on track and this story needed to be told!

The little group had chatted away for only ten minutes, but it felt like an eternity to Rose. She had been transported into the flow, where time seems to stand still and all your thoughts cavort. Caroline tugged at her arm and said she wanted to get in the car as it was so cold and noisy, which snapped Rose out of her little trance. As they shook hands and remarked on the amazing coincidence of their meeting, Gill asked for Rose's contact details and promised to send her a link to their Kett family tree. Gill was also keen to read her book when it was finished and asked her to contact her when it was published. Laughing with inner joy, the two bade them all farewell and scuttled off to the car to warm up. This had been a truly magical day they both agreed and a fantastic end to a very interesting story. There are no coincidences.

The friends decided to visit Norwich Castle again with their shamanic offerings of flowers, herbs and stones and Rose read out the sign on the wall near the entrance, by way of recognition of this amazing family.

Plaque on the wall of Norwich Castle

> In 1549 AD Robert Kett yeoman farmer of Wymondham was executed by hanging in this Castle after the defeat of the Norfolk Rebellion of which he was leader. In 1949 AD - four hundred years

later - this Memorial was placed here by the citizens of Norwich in reparation and honour to a notable and courageous leader in the long struggle of the common people of England to escape from a servile life into the freedom of just conditions – Norwich Castle

Having processed and enacted so many healing modalities in this timeline, Rose felt it was high time to finish the book now. But there is still one more thing to unravel. You may have wondered if she managed to solve the mystery of the triangle of light that Peter the shaman had seen over the county of Norfolk. The one that connected the lonely cottage on the coast, with the boggy marshland where Bear, Gandalf and Ankh had taken the gibbet cage. Remember, it was to be dissolved in the body of water. Where was the church in the city, where the mother and child had been buried and honoured? She had figured out that there were past life connections to these locations, but then, she stumbled on another understanding of what was linking these points. It was the last clue on the list that Karen had given her, the name **James.**

CHAPTER 13

Energy Earth Lines & Water Pilgrimages

The Energy Line Triangle

If you remember, during the shaman's journey he described a huge triangle. It appeared to be energy lines, that connected to three locations over the county of Norfolk. In his vision, he saw these as connecting the churchyard (where he saw the graves of the lady and her young child), the lonely cottage on the coast and the pond in the medieval fens or marshland (where Mother Bear, Gandalf and Anke had buried the wooden pole and iron basket). Although she had connected to these sites in one layer of comprehension, could they have a greater spiritual significance?

During Rose's explorations of the countryside and her search for hidden clues, she had a sudden inspiration. It dawned on her that it might depict earth line connections to three churches in three locations in Norfolk all named St. James. The East Anglian county is crisscrossed with all sorts of energy and lay lines and vortexes, but Churches were often strangely located on lay lines. There were sometimes much more ancient sites of interest or worship, such as Druid remains, beneath the churches. In Glastonbury, there is a St. Michael's on each of the barrow mumps.

In one sitting, Karen said she 'heard' the name **James** dating back thousands of years, from her guides. Rose took a look at a current-day map of Norfolk and traced the main thoroughfares in segments. There were several that seemed to take the shape of large triangles, looking at the main roads. She used the St. James churches as a guide, and then she began to see a large triangle forming over the North of Norfolk connecting down to Norwich at the Southernmost point. These she plotted as follows:

1. St. James Church, Southrepps, North East Norfolk

Rose was born in the Cromer area as her father had been posted to the Trimingham RAF site, which is very near to this church. The St. James symbol of pilgrims was scallop shells, as mentioned in the story of Julian and Margery in Chapter 1. When she visited the church in Southrepps with Teal, they noticed there were scallop shells around the base of the 15th-century tower. She also calculated that this church was only half an hour from Blickling Hall where Mary and Anne Boleyn were born, another of their past lives.

2. St. James church, Whitefriars, Norwich

This church is next to where Rose worked, in St. James Close, Whitefriars, Norwich. It was the area where her past life, as Lady Eleanor Talbot, was buried. St. James Church has now been renamed The Puppet Theatre and is used to entertain both young and older folk, hosting many plays and art events.[109]

3. St. James The Great Church, Castle Acre[110]

This church has the orange and black parquet floor that Karen had seen in her vision. Rose had not been able to connect it to anything in particular, at the time she received the message. As she and Teal walked in, she immediately recognised the patterned tiles that Karen had been given by her guides, some time previously. She surmised that this could have been a past life connection for Teal as it is thirty minutes from Walsingham Shrine, Where Henry VIII used to make pilgrimages.

Teal had lived nearby and worked both in the village in her younger life and more lately as an artists' muse at nearby Castle Acre. In this way, she was energetically connected to the land here. When Rose glanced further up the map she saw that King's Lynn was only seventeen minutes away, which of course was where Margery Kempe was born and bred. It all seemed to be tying in nicely and Rose was getting the bigger picture, quite literally a bird's eye view! Excited, she researched further about pilgrims in the area and found a treasure trove of information:

---

[109] http://www.norfolkchurches.co.uk/norwichjamesless/norwichjamesless.htm
[110] http://www.norfolkchurches.co.uk/castleacre/castleacre.htm

Walsingham has been venerated as one of the holiest places in England, and countless people have visited the village to ask Mary to pray to Jesus on their behalf. There is even a Black Madonna there. By the late Middle Ages, it was held to be the duty of every Englishman that at some time during his life he should visit Our Lady at Walsingham. - Walsingham Village [111]

This same article described the pilgrimages and shrine visits that were so popular at the time thus:

Pilgrims travelled to religious sites all over England and routes were well established to help them on their journey. The main route to Walsingham was from London via **Waltham Abbey**, Newmarket, Brandon, Swaffham, **Castle Acre priory,** and East Barsham. From the north, pilgrims crossed the Wash near Long Sutton and came through **King's Lynn** (then called Bishop's Lynn), Flitcham, Rudham and Coxford. From the east the route ran through Norwich and Attlebridge.

Routes were marked by religious houses or wayside chapels to aid the pilgrims with their spiritual and temporal needs. Monasteries and hospices also offered hospitality. Travelling was very hazardous with miles of open or forested countryside, poor tracks, outlaws and wild animals like wolves and boar, so pilgrims were encouraged to travel in groups.

Pilgrims often visited a number of shrines en route to a principal shrine. Pilgrimages to **Walsingham** might include Bromholm Priory to see a relic of the Holy Cross, a visit to the anchorite **Mother Julian** in Norwich or St William's shrine in Norwich Cathedral, St Edmund's Shrine at Bury St. Edmunds in Suffolk.

Rose noted that Teal's past life as Margery Kempe put her on the map of one of the main pilgrimages over The Wash and into **King's Lynn** from

---

[111] https://www.walsinghamvillage.org/about/history-of-pilgrimage/

whence she hailed. From there, she pilgrimaged down to **Mother Julian** in Norwich and then on to Europe, after receiving her blessing.

How could Rose heal not only her own past life traumas, but also the land and water that she had touched by her presence? She had an idea and arranged another field trip with Teal on 19 August 2019. The friends pilgrimaged (albeit by car), to St. James church in Southrepps on the North East coast of Norfolk. Rose had cleansed and programmed one of her healing crystals to use in a spot to which they may feel drawn. After looking around inside and taking a few photos, they wandered out into the sunny graveyard. The sky had grown pregnant with dark clouds and had given birth to a deluge earlier when they were still in Cromer. Here in this quaint village of Southrepps, the ground wasn't even wet.

As they walked along the path gazing at the gravestones, suddenly all the hairs went up on Teal's arms. They stopped in their tracks and looked around. There was a gravestone which was oddly placed against the church wall. As Rose observed it, a butterfly flew over and landed on the wall next to it. She made a mental note of the spot, but they continued to walk around the many gravestones towards the back of the churchyard. After a few minutes they decided to walk back and as they approached the same place, Teal got the shivers again and they stood and looked at the gravestone propped against the wall. As Rose started to speak and say that it must be something to do with that particular headstone, she got full body tingles starting at her feet up, passing up through her legs and then like pins and needles it coursed all around her head.

She knew she was being directed to this spot which needed healing, due to this experiential key clue, so she took the cleansed and re-programmed fluorite skull out of her bag and placed it on the ground nearby. She conducted a little ceremony, praying that all ancestral bloodlines be cleared of any pain and suffering and for any lost souls to be released. She also requested that the crystal activate the new crystalline energy grid and asked for protection for all. The friends felt that they had accomplished what they had set out to do, and walked back to the car, driving happily back home.

Location key synchronicities to shrines and pilgrimages

Pilgrims often visited a number of shrines en route to a principal shrine. Pilgrimages to Walsingham might include Bromholm Priory to see a relic of the Holy Cross. Interestingly, King Henry VIII pilgrimaged to Walsingham and Anne Boleyn, Teal's past life, had planned to visit but never did. What we do know, is that Teal had also worked and lived near Walsingham when she was younger.

Another popular pilgrimage in Norfolk was a visit to the anchorite Mother Julian in Norwich or to St William's shrine in Norwich Cathedral. We also know that Rose lived near this shrine. As it appeared that part of Rose's work was to pray for healing for the souls of the dead in past lives, she was beginning to see the connection for herself and Teal to Saint James as a patron saint and symbol of healing. That they both lived, and were energetically connected to many of these ancient sites, seemed to act as a key to remembering the different aspects of their past lives. Some could be viewed as positive and also some contained pain patterns which were coming to awareness now, for clearing. As we read in the first chapter of this book, both women were linked in several ways, not only as the first women in England leave to write and leave behind religious writings and the other an autobiography, but also because one became a pilgrim and the other was visited by pilgrims. To remind you of her details:

Margery Kemp (1373-1438). A Christian mystic and the first woman in England to write an autobiography, was a pilgrim and travelled to Spain on the St. James Pilgrimage to Santiago de Compostela in 1417 (she would have been forty-four).[112] As an aside, Teal was raised a Catholic and still believes in the Christian faith, albeit developing a strong belief system that supplements, rather than takes away from her spiritual convictions. She loved visiting the churches and shrines with Rose because it seemed to make the connection stronger.

Sometime before this, around 1413, and when she was forty, Kempe visited the female mystic and anchoress Julian of Norwich at her cell in Norwich (this would have been three years before her death (1342-1416) aged seventy-four. According to her account, Kempe visited Julian and stayed for several days; she was especially eager to obtain Julian's approval

---

[112] https://en.wikipedia.org/wiki/Margery_Kempe#Pilgrimage.

for her visions of and conversations with God. The text reports that Julian approved of Kempe's revelations and gave Kempe reassurance that her religiosity was genuine. However, Julian did instruct and caution Kempe to "measure these experiences according to the worship they accrue to God and the profit to her fellow Christians. Julian also confirmed that Kempe's tears are physical evidence of the Holy Spirit in the soul.

Margery also undertook a pilgrimage to Rome to visit the various holy shrines and churches there. In 1438, the year her book is known to have been completed, a "Marguerita Kempe," who may have been Margery Kempe, was admitted to the Trinity Guild of Lynn. It is not known whether this is the same woman, and it is also not known when or where after this date, that Kempe died (probably around sixty five years of age, four years after her book was finished).

Comparisons with other energy lines & elemental pilgrimages

When looking at holy sites as energy lines or triangles, also of interest is that The Way of St. James is a trio of routes that cross Western Europe and arrive at Santiago de Compostela through Northern Spain.[113] Eventually, James became the patron saint of Spain. St. James was of course one of Christ's twelve Apostles. He is associated with pilgrimages, which in turn were connected with the doctrines of purgatory, and prayers for the souls of the dead.

Two versions of the most common myth about the origin of the scallop shell symbol, concern the death of Saint James, who was martyred by beheading in Jerusalem in 44 AD (another unjust passing). According to Spanish legend, he had spent time preaching the gospel in Spain but returned to Judaea upon seeing a vision of the Virgin Mary on the bank of the Ebro River.

'Footsteps of Light' pilgrimages

In conjunction with focused pilgrimages to holy sites and healing of the land along energy or lay lines, there is also a belief system running

---

[113] https://en.wikipedia.org/wiki/Camino_de_Santiago

parallel, concerning the placing of intentional blessed steps on the earth and through the land, a nature pilgrimage of a kind. The thought is that if one is pure in thought, intention and open in heart, the very act of walking in nature is like a set of footsteps of light. This would be done intentionally by requesting permission from the Gatekeeper of that land, whether it be in spirit form or maybe specific birds or animals, these earth pilgrims would consciously tune in and ask if they may respectfully traverse the countryside. Once granted they would be mindful of the way, just as any pilgrim would. There are even those that make these journeys whilst singing or chanting as the very act of sound vibrations assists with clearing and re-energising where they would pass through.

The Gatekeeper Trust, know the value of these footsteps of light on the group pilgrimages they organise in England. They also stress the importance for our wellbeing, of taking solitary pilgrimages in nature as quoted here:

> You recognise a pressing need to seek solitude and beauty in the wilderness of the great outdoors. A few precious hours away from the detritus of modern life. Away from others. You must pilgrimage alone. Nothing else will do. Your focus, the mindful reclamation of your flagging spirits. Your destination, Mother Nature's playground......A world where yesterday's woes fade as you study the pattern on the bark of a tree, where tomorrow's anxieties dissipate as you watch silver water cascading noisily over stones in a sparkling stream. You can linger to watch an interesting beetle, with no fear of holding a group up or being left behind.....Perhaps you find yourself heading for the grey silence of an old churchyard a couple of miles from home, where ancient gravestones with florid inscriptions rise peacefully from wet grass, and the atmosphere wraps you in a comforting cloak of calm....Maybe you have hills and dales, woods, moors, and rivers at your disposal, with far-reaching views that bring home to you your own smallness in this vast universe?....Perhaps a cold, wintry beach is near enough to visit. One where a buffeting wind rearranges your hair as you gaze at the far horizon, the hypnotic sound of the waves brushing

the shingle and cleansing the recesses of your mind as you wander along the shore.- Gatekeeper.org.uk[114]

Rose felt really pleased that she had been able to explore her county of birth in this multi-layered way.

The River Wensum

In the final editing stages of this book, Rose became more deeply aware of how the River Wensum had witnessed the past and present lives of some of her soul group along its banks. Throughout the medieval timelines that we have learnt about, there were key areas next to the river where unjust passings had taken place. Rose considered how she could connect to the spirit of the water, by offering a blessing as she walked alongside it.

She then planned to create a video tour of the river, narrating the relevant parts of her book as she walked. She would begin at the undercroft with the plaque to Lady Eleanor Talbot and acknowledge the Magistrates Courts opposite, where Teal had fought her battles. She would progress past the site of the monastery in St. James Close near the church, explaining where she had worked at Whitefriars, whilst walking past St. James Mill. The narrative would turn to the tale of The Kett Brothers as she followed the swans and ducks along the pathway lined with majestic oaks, till she approached Cow Tower. A little further, there would also be plenty to talk about at Bishops Bridge, where Robert Kett had fought out the battle of justice for the people, linking in with Julia and Simon's past lives.

The next river stop would be at Lollard's Pit across the road from Bishops Bridge, to bless any lost souls that died as witches, or heretics, executed for possessing a modern translation of the bible for example. One such fated soul had been Thomas Bilney. Rose decided to write about him and the anchorite, Katherine Manne, in her next book. These two characters, she had discovered, were yet more of her soul family whose stories needed exploring. Walking further onwards, past the colourful window boxes of the pub along the river, she would trace her way further along to where the river flows past the ancient Boleyn family property at

---

[114] https://gatekeeper.org.uk/2022/01/the-solitary-pilgrim/

125-127 King Street, another link for herself and Teal. This empty Tudor gallery is next door to Dragon Hall, which holds the secrets of yet another aspect of her soul family, and their past lives. Again another tale to be told in the sequel.

Afterwards, she would walk a couple of hundred yards, where she would find herself close by Mother Julian's shrine, tucked up a tiny pathway off King Street. In twenty minutes she would walk past the mill, where she and her soul friends Julia and Simon had first alighted in Trowse Newton, to unwittingly begin their curious past life journey. Her final river destination would be Whitlingham Broad as it wound its way out of the city to the East. It was always her favourite place to walk around the lake. Rose visited several times a week over the years and was inextricably drawn to its beauty, with the wildfowl nature park and teeming birdlife. She had even found the magical spot where there used to be an ancient Druid wood henge, marking the sacred confluence of the rivers, Wensum, Yare and Tas. This very spot was where she had been drawn to do a shamanic blessing in the early spring of 2020 with Julia, a week before the first pandemic lockdown. They had used a tuning fork to raise the energies along with her Reiki drum. Perhaps they had sensed the healing that would be needed, in the forthcoming years.

In May 2022, Rose and Clare attended a healing meditation circle at Swaffham Spiritualist Church. She was delighted to see her friend Jayne again, after two long years of lockdowns and doing everything online. She hugged her and her friends and felt very happy to see everyone in the flesh again. As the meditation proceeded and everyone was relaxed, Jayne began to speak light language. As she began to translate the download that she was receiving, into English, she received messages from her guides about the one thing that spirit needed help with, from this group.

Everyone was curious to know what this might be, usually it felt as if they would be always asking for help or praying for support for themselves or their loved ones, but here was a request to help the unseen ones!

The guides explained that the water needed blessing and that each one of us could be mindful of this and how it would help to raise the vibration of all beings on the earth. They said that together they in heaven and we on the earth, are stronger and we would work as a team. Suddenly there was a sound of water running onto the floor. Everyone had their eyes closed, but Rose was curious and opened hers, looking in the direction of the sound. She couldn't see a glass lying on the floor but could see a wet patch further back, under the chair where a colleague was sitting and feared the worst. Her friend had also started channelling and could not be disturbed, so feeling a little confused and somewhat embarrassed she closed her eyes again and tried to concentrate on the meditation.

Once the session drew to a close, everyone was sharing their experiences and someone piped up about the sound of water. The lady sitting opposite Rose said she hadn't heard anything, but looked behind her to see what happened to her glass of water. She had placed the chair behind her so that she would not knock it over. It was still on the chair, but had fallen over and was empty. It seemed very curious because the glass had been stable for quite some time and the sound of the water pouring out had gone on for longer than it would have taken for the small glass to empty. It had sounded louder than would be expected and everyone had been aware of it they said. Then Rose remembered that during the messages water was mentioned and realised that it was a sign that spirit had given them to reiterate the importance of blessing the water. She put this to the group and they all gasped when they realised the relevance of this sign.

In the following weeks, Rose decided to bless the water when she was at Whitlingham Broad and when she went to her favourite beach, Winterton-on-Sea. On 1 July 2022, Rose sat by the confluence at Whitlingham lake, on a little wooden dock. It was sunny and the planks felt warm to the touch. As she relaxed and breathed in the summer air, she remembered what she had written about the past lives she had lived along the Wensum and decided to do a little ceremony here again.

Praying to the Gatekeeper, for permission to bless the rivers, she intended that the water release any negative energies imbued in it. She thought of all the humans and their experiences, living along its banks from time immemorial to the present day. Uttering the Ho-opono-pono prayer, she acknowledged her contribution to both pain and love energies absorbed over the centuries. She assented to taking personal responsibility for lifting any heavy vibrations up and out of the river and the land. Next, she bade the golden white light from the Source of all that is, to flow down, that it would revitalise and bless the river. Nodding to the Four Directions of North, South, East and West, she called upon them to witness along with the elementals of fire, water, air and earth. It felt like a beautiful conclusion to eight years of remembering and subsequent release healings, leading to the conclusion of these writings.

A couple of days later, Rose attended a healing workshop where she bumped into a friend who also had a deep affinity to Julian of Norwich. She explained what she had been doing at the river confluence and her friend immediately looked relieved. "It's exactly what I was drawn to do, I heard about a group with red cloaks doing a dark ceremony down at The Wensum this week and I wanted to clear the energies afterwards. Now I see that you were drawn to do that, I will consider it done." Rose got the angel shivers as she was talking and confirmed back to her, that it had been accomplished.

The very next day Rose attended the birthday of one of her soul family, Linda. She fell into conversation with a young woman called Tina. She is 'awake' as the spiritual truther community labels it. They realised they had both spent a lot of time sitting near Cow Tower when Tina had lived there. Rose realised that it was the two same years that she had worked there and eaten her sandwiches on the riverbank, close by the relic. She felt curious and asked Amber if she had any medieval recollections and Amber responded that she knew she had been a woman. She remembers sitting on a window seat reading, but more than that she couldn't remember. Rose concluded that she would have been an aristocrat if she had been able to read and promised to sleuth any clues to the possibility that they had been connected in Tudor times. Her forensic searches had been very successful in recent months and she felt excited that there was a new trail to follow. She knew though, that if she uncovered anything it would have to wait till the next book in the series.

Rose felt at peace at this point, knowing that whatever happened to her in these dangerous and unstable times, she had done her best to contribute to the upliftment of all that is. This self-affirmation proved most timely. Unbeknown to Rose, her physical body was to conclude its journey on the earth plane not so long afterwards. Being blissfully unaware of that, she had published this book and become involved in a highly important, but subterfuge mission. It had involved her closest soul tribe and was the reason that she had to discover their connections. I enlisted one of her friends to add the next chapter on her behalf. We will uncover the crucial nature of her forthcoming discovery in the next Chapter, 'My Last Life.'

CHAPTER 14

My Last Life

I did not yet reveal to you how my last incarnation as Rose passed away, but it is the right time to do so now. It was from the thirtieth variant of the original pandemic virus. Although many felt the danger had been over-hyped, the same as with the viruses that came before it over recent years. But she had developed other health issues, one of which was due to handling a secret sample and the new disease got the better of her, very quickly. We all knew that super viruses were being developed in bio-labs to be more deadly than those transmitted in nature, but no one was able to so much as whisper in public, that this was the case.

Sadly, Willow was not yet married and Rose would never get to see her possible future grandchildren. Her daughter was studying cellular regeneration in a high-security microbiology lab in Bavaria. Knowing what she did about the evil origins and purpose for creating the pandemics, she had been conducting her top secret research under the microscope. It was a highly dangerous occupation in these times. Everything was being observed on all levels by The Controllers. This was to prevent any breakthroughs in the field of antidotes, that could not be directed solely by them. She had shared some of what she was working on with her mother, but it was almost impossible to encrypt all the information to send to her. Now she had fallen sick and was fighting for her life, it became crucial that she saw her in person, as soon as possible. She could hardly function from the emotional shock that washed over her in waves. This was the most tragic event in her life, they should have had a decade or more together.

Willow had been delayed when flying to her mother's bedside, due to all of the airline strikes. The Controllers were attempting to stop all unnecessary travel. One had to justify why any travel was essential, but now she had a loophole. Her beloved mother was dying. She had only been able to talk to Rose briefly on the phone, but each time she called, she had the uneasy feeling that they were listening in, so code had to be used, at all times. The crucial moment for her flight was drawing nail-bitingly close. She was distraught, her nerves jangling in anticipation of the grilling she would receive at the airport. Jumping each of the hurdles to get airside, she had queued up for hours to get a cancellation.

At the last hour, she made it onto the evening flight. Once she touched down on English soil, she called her two undercover contacts, Teal and Julia. She used a new satellite phone to call Julia as planned, which she had planted and arranged for her to pick up upon her arrival. These two wonderful women were of course the most trusted of Rose's soul friends, Julia and Teal. Julia was relieved to hear that Willow has arrived safely and was on her way to the hospital, in a self-driving electric car. Although there was no human driver to eavesdrop on her, she was acutely aware that electronic ears would be listening to every word she said. Those spying didn't know or understand spiritual Light Language. Julia had taught and used these new vibrational codes to explain how she and Teal had been able to steal into the hospital under cover. They had been dressed in doctors' uniforms and in full protective garb. She assured Willow that her mother had still been strong enough to hand over the crucial codes and keys for them to keep safe until it was time to act.

The friends had gone to great lengths to obtain a hazmat suit for Willow and Julia explained where she could find it, as she approached the hospital. Now that Willow was briefed about the secret information they held, she just wanted to see her mother's face. She had falsified papers and lied to the reception staff at the high-security clinic. Now she was hurrying along the corridor as fast as her cumbersome PPE would allow her, which was not as speedily as she would have liked. Her breathing was hurried but deep and was causing an annoying amount of condensation on her plastic visor. Beads of sweat trickled down her back, but she raced on regardless. She knew that time was at a premium.

A furtive glance to each side of the double doors assured her that there were no nurses or orderlies to impede her or ask awkward questions.

Luckily it was the night shift, so there were no doctors to be seen anywhere. She burst into the silent empty ward with a bang, in a flurry of blue and white. There was one bed occupied by the window, with its protective tent over it, the flashing lamps, along with occasional bleeping, directed her to her destination. She could have heard a pin drop as she padded silently towards her mother. There was a deep dread overwhelming her every cell, thoughts that she may be too late. Her heart seemed to be beating furiously in her mouth as the adrenaline coursing through her veins, propelling her onwards.

As soon as she rounded the corner of the bed, Rose's eyes fluttered open at the sound of her daughter's soft voice. "Mama, Mama, please don't leave me yet, I love you so much," she sobbed. Willow had risked everything, including the project, to be next to her, holding her hand through her plastic glove. She had thrown caution to the wind, for this last precious moment she could share with her dear mother. A tiny voice whispered back "thank you my darling for risking so much to see me. Now I am at peace," she rasped with a faint smile on her face. She stopped for a few seconds, wincing with pain and struggling to take the next breath. "I will always love you Willow and nothing.... will break the bonds between us....death has no mastery over us....we will be together again. Now you know how vital... the research work is that you are undertaking...I'm so sorry I won't see your children, darling...I would have loved that" she closed her eyes to shield her daughter from her tears, but they erupted over her cheeks and rolled down her neck. Willow gently moped them with a tissue and squeezed her mother's hand, ever so gently. She was deeply saddened by that thought too, but she tried to hide it. She waited with bated breath for her mother to continue.

"You will be in good hands and they will all protect you as much as they possibly can, whilst you work on the results. I know you can do it, my dear child, I trust you." She paused for much longer this time and Willow wept silently awaiting any further words she could muster. "We both know there is no such thing as time, where I am going." She paused again waiting for her daughter's tears to abate. "I am sure I will be with you again in the twinkling of an eye and we can plot our return speedily by the stars, as we have so much more work to do here."

"Yes Mama" she blurted out, "we wrote a pact with Julia and Teal remember, that we would all come back together again in the next life. I know we are to use the keys and codes you have left us to find each other and continue the work." The little team had uncovered deep secrets held frozen in the Arctic. They didn't know if these energy molecules had been kept hidden due to their political and corporate significance, or if they simply hadn't been discovered and tested by anyone. Elements of the ancient ice that had been exposed in Northern Canada, seemed to contain tiny life-giving particles unlike any discovered before. Encouraged but cautious, they had sent an intrepid team further North into the ice caps.

The secret dig had informed them that there was a reservoir of waters in deep caverns below the crust of the icebergs, that had proven regenerative to the whole body when injected. "We just know that it will be the answer to all of our health problems and even survival as a species," she continued and she managed to smile. The light language channellings with their spirit team had become more intense recently. The three friends had been struggling to keep up with their note-taking. They had been receiving multiple downloads about how the testing should take place and where the manufacture and distribution could be kept secret. It was almost as if these light beings knew something crucial was about to happen, well they did.

After falling asleep briefly, Rose felt Willow squeeze her hand again and she tried to rouse herself. "Here I am dying on you before my time, which makes it even more important that you three carry on the work we have started....record as much as you can of your findings so that there is a legacy....in case anything should happen to you. Please be safe and after today, don't take any more risks like this. You are much needed now and in the future". "Willow choked on her words as she assured her, "Oh Mum of course I will, I know how important this is and I will never let you down, I love you so, so much." Hearing those beautiful words, Rose's life force trailed off. Looking her directly in the eyes she managed a tiny squeeze of her daughter's hand, as she closed her eyes for the last time. Willow collapsed over her and wept, knowing this was the last time she would behold her mother in the flesh.

True to her word, early the next day Teal made contact with Willow on her encrypted satellite mobile, as soon as she could secure a connection. She unveiled that there were further secrets they needed to meet and talk about. She said she would send encrypted directions to the secret location she had found, which she had set up with the secret samples and a powerful microscope. There was only one thing on Willow's mind at that moment; "Why didn't my mother tell me about this work earlier?" she sobbed down the phone. "This is invaluable information and will help in the evolution of our immune system. It's priceless and yet you kept it secret from me? Why is that?" "Willow" she replied on the crackling line, "we were worried it would fall into the wrong hands before it was developed as a concept and it wasn't until just very recently we had a breakthrough code channelled to us. Then we knew this was the final key that would unlock the floodgates. You were the only one who knew chromosomes inside out and that we could now trust to carry this crucial work forward."

"We have ensured that you have access to the lab conditions needed to test it. Your mother, God rest her soul, was about to approach you to help us when she was struck down by the intentionally leaked super virus". Teal promptly burst into uncontrollable floods of tears and laments. From my oversoul's vantage point in spirit, she reminded me of per past life as Margery Kempe and her wailing lament. I rolled my eyes if a light being can do such a thing, and drew closer to them all, on their energy vibration. "Oh Willow," Teal sobbed, "I can feel your mother drawing close, I have shivers all over my body which has gone live and all the hairs have stood up on end. I always know someone is close in spirit when this happens."

There was silence on the line and a few muffled sounds that Teal couldn't make out. Eventually, a sob, and then Willow croaked a response through her choking tears. "I am so, so, sorry that I doubted her all these years Teal. I thought she was losing her marbles, talking to Light Counsels and Star Beings in that odd language. It didn't make any sense to me, I'm a science person. She used to tell me about some of the non-coincidences that occurred, but I didn't really think much of it at the time. I know she loved to write about it and was just pleased that she was passionate about something, but if I had known, what I know now…" she fell into grieving silence again. I'm so, so sorry I doubted you all.

"Willow" Teal interrupted "you can't blame yourself, she couldn't have told you about it anyhow. We were warned not to and we loyally stood by each other in solidarity. She didn't need to prove anything to you, she knew that you would be the one to take it forward in the future, and she trusted you one hundred per cent. It had to be the right timing, Divine

Timing, as we call it. We have to try and put our feelings and aching hearts to one side now and be strong. It's crucial that you do what you can with the information we are sharing with you. Are you sure you are willing to take the risks involved, in the lab?"

"Yes, of course, I am" she spluttered. This is priceless information, it could even change the future if I can test it properly. It will be my life mission, in memory of my dear mother. I do wish I could have told her more often how much I loved her, but thank you for making it possible to hold her hand one last time. I will never forget what you risked to make this possible and thank you from the bottom of my heart for chancing your own lives to be there too. I do hope you are right and that she is listening to us now. Oh! I am getting tingles going all the way up my legs, is that what you got?" Teal confirmed she could feel her mother's spirit with them and said she was giving her daughter a message, one of timeless love to seal into her heart forever. Willow and Teal simultaneously broke down and cried some more. I did my best to draw in closer to both these dear souls, beaming as much upliftment and unconditional love down to them as I could. Willow wouldn't always know it, but I would be with her in the lab constantly. I would do my utmost to inspire her to try new things and prompt her to move forward with a plan. All of a sudden, I felt my auric membrane burst into a huge orb of the brightest white light and I disappeared…but I would be back, very, very soon.

Willow stared at the silent phone in a daze. Thoughts were racing through her mind and she couldn't think straight, but one thing she did know. She would double down on this research in her mother's memory, to search for ways in which she could find a solution. It was a major priority to strengthen the human mind, body and spirit with any breakthrough she could find. They were under constant assault from The Controllers and she knew she was a key component to help stop this earthly race from dying out. She was determined to discover a cheap way of doing this. Also, in order for it to be distributed widely, but still under the radar, until it reached the awakened ones first. Once they were protected by an infusion, their bodies would no longer be damaged by the intentional poisoning of society, and the new potion would support key workers to retain their good health, naturally. It had to go under the radar, to avoid dark organisations making any money from it or simply suppressing it altogether, using bullying and censoring, even death threats, as their tools.

One day she was discussing, strictly in code, some of her early positive findings. which she had become quite excited about. There was a new scientist who had started working at the same clinic and she had heard he was open to alternative ideas, having also worked in the same field. As they spoke in general terms, he became more and more interested in her research ideas and they talked animatedly at some length, about it. She was being very cautious not to give away any key information, but she needed a senior scientist's input now before she could take it any further.

There was not enough time that day to cover with him all that she had found. They arranged to meet the next evening and have a more leisurely conversation over a glass of wine and dinner. She discovered that he had been travelling and working in the Arctic for some years and had learnt many things about the mysterious lifeforms and potions the Inuits had introduced him to, whilst he was developing medicine there. He had loved the idea of bringing together his scientific research and practical knowledge as a microbiologist, with their native and instinctual relationship with water. Once they trusted his motives they had revealed long-held medical secrets buried deep in the permafrost of the tundras. Now that the Amazon forests had been depleted this was his only chance. Once he had realised he was onto something, he had taken an expert team further North pushing into Greenland then Alaska.

It was with these ideas in mind and once he had made some exciting discoveries, that he eventually returned to his land of birth. He thought to find a trustworthy research assistant that would be passionate about developing these amazing ideas with him. There was something about Willow that appealed to him. She was a logical and scientific thinker and yet, was not happy with the commercialisation of the pharmaceutical industry which had led to the suppression of natural remedies which could not be patented for financial gain. He got the sense that ultimately her deepest desire was to help people, not harm them. As she listened to this quirky scientist, she could see how much he truly cared for the indigenous people he had been working with and she felt drawn to find out more about how they could work together on this research, to bring these two worlds together for the greater good. She would have to get to know him a lot better she mused before she could risk revealing her key motives for her secret ideas. He may be cautious in order to protect his patent, but she was protecting the world!

Two hours sped past in the twinkling of an eye, and suddenly Jed broke into the conversation, turning to her with a broad smile and a twinkle in his eye. "I had better get you safely home young lady, otherwise neither of us will be fit for work at the lab tomorrow morning". She grinned at him and said "I had no idea it was so late, where did the time go? Yes, we had better go, I really am not a morning person and I need my sleep!" As they walked out of the restaurant laughing and chatting together she had a warm fuzzy feeling inside and she knew it wasn't just the wine.

CHAPTER 15

Conclusion

Are we remembering, learning, releasing & healing?

Rose's step-father, Andrew, who she had only in latter years realised was on the autistic spectrum, used to get exasperated with the three kids. Because of his mindblindness, he couldn't understand why they kept repeating their mistakes. He was very rigid in his thinking and used to hiss "How many times do I have to tell you? I'm always having to repeat myself. I've told you this, time and again. Why can't you learn the first time I say it?" These are the angry sentences we and maybe many of us, may have heard as children from time to time when our parents were annoyed with us. But children learn through repetition, they are not computers, and they need to experience, and make mistakes.

We need to understand that even as adults, we are in a phase of child-like remembering that we are repeating history. We need to question ourselves, just as our parents schooled us to ask ourselves, what are we learning from the past? Peaceful protests are being challenged by the powers that be and our rights slowing being eroded, by subtle changes to the Human Rights Act, now being renamed the Bill of Rights in the UK. Then there is the concerning new medical treaty, which was brought to the table to be drawn up at the annual WHO (World Health Organisation) Conference in Davos, Switzerland, in May 2022. Only the richest, most influential and dubious characters, are invited to this highly secretive event each year.

We have seen down through time that these sociopaths do not have the best interests of the masses at the forefront of their minds. They spread lies about the commoners, who they consider to be useless eaters. They blame them for being responsible for global warming, at the same time suppressing the knowledge of how to make free energy. Their methods paralyse people with guilt and fear, forcing them to spend more and more money on alternative energy projects, which keep the elite rich, whilst those in power skirt around bringing about any meaningful change, as wealthy nations.

True records show that the earth's climate has essentially not changed for the last fifteen years, but this information was kept hidden. Others postulate that our climate is dependent on solar fluctuations. The mainstream media is hijacked as a propaganda machine, with a gun in its back if anyone should dare to report truthfully. Young actors are hired to passionately prove their narrative, in a farcical theatre. Many have almost discovered the secrets to producing free energy solutions and other techniques, which would solve the world's problems. These individual scientists have been deeply suppressed since Nicolas Tesla. Labs have been burnt down, bank accounts blocked and reputations besmirched, in order to force them into silence. This happens in all areas, not just with the green agenda gravy train.

We have seen down through the centuries what happens when the peasants try to rise up and have no recourse to justice. Lessons should have been learnt from the tragic story about The Kett Brothers, for example. Bloody wars have raged with thousands sacrificed, in order to bring back the equilibrium in society. England had experienced not only The War of The Roses, many Peasants' Revolts and The Hundred Year's War with France, but now oppression seemed to be raising its ugly head yet again, but in a more subversive way. Mainstream media had been hijacked by The Controllers behind the scenes of Governments. They were also responsible for the corrupted and biased social media logarithms, leading to subtle brainwashing and control around medical mandates. Anyone uploading any comments exposing injuries was shadow-banned or accounts were threatened with restrictions or even being taken down permanently, as a punishment for speaking out. Freedom of speech had slowly drained away until people were sleepwalking into something worse than a socialist society. Those who were waking up felt it their duty to take action.

We saw that the huge and lengthy Canadian Trucker Convoy for freedom of choice was building resistance, not only in Ottawa but in many countries where the leaders were showing no signs of relaxing the health passport rules for travel. Despite the science showing that these were no longer necessary to protect people, some governments had clung to a controlling narrative. It was becoming obvious to a huge amount of people who were slowly awakening, that the narrative was no longer about the greater good, but much more about suppressing the people and gaining more and more control, over their own ends. Lawsuits were being drawn up for malpractice and direct connections of harm and death related to the forced medications, with the first case in the UK finally awarded, two years after the pandemic began. The Government capped all payments for injuries to £120K and then, you were on your own.

Pharmaceutical giants, exempt from any liability for emergency use drugs, had pushed hard to have these signed off. Due to a court order, that they wished to hold back from release for seventy-five years, the legal team enforced them to start releasing their trial data immediately. Month by month this information began to reveal how much they already knew about the hidden dangers of their products and the tested lack of efficacy, especially in pregnant women, who had not been trialled and of course young children. Gradually the blinkers were coming off and more and more people were waking up to the side effects affecting their health. Joining the dots, they put two and two together and saw that they had been hoodwinked. The medication may have seemed to work in the short term, but cancer, auto-immune disease, heart problems and inflammation, infertility and dementia were beginning to emerge in higher numbers in the second year of the pandemic and would only become worse in time.

As your storyteller, Julian of Norwich, I wish that you have been able to garner something of value from these few examples I have related to you, in these many pages. Tying together all that I have written previously, you can hopefully now see, the correlations throughout time. I would also hope that you find yourself encouraged and therefore empowered, to examine your own journey. To begin to sift through this and other lifetimes, parallel or past, to perceive what type if any, of energy stamp you may have left behind on the land or water. Rather than just pointing our finger at corrupt institutions, I wish to impart to you an understanding of how each individual can negate any heavy past vibrations, which can repeat themselves over and over until they are released and healed. Take your power back and be the light.

May it be known that we can slowly heal before our civilisation collapses. It could be that our own physical lives can heal or harm Gaia and other sentient beings, through conscious intentions and or unconscious actions. Now is the time to awaken to our responsibilities in this regard. To go within and examine what we find lurking there in the shadows and shine a healing light in dark corners. There is a process called retiring into Hermit Mode or even The Dark Night of the Soul. As the terms imply, we withdraw from our usual routine for a period of time and take time for introspection. Shadow work can call to us, as we become more and more aware, or enlightenment can be forced on us through illness, NDEs, death of a loved one or even a sudden accident. All of which Rose laughingly described as "the Universe putting us on our arse!" Time to think, not do.

These previous mysteries can be uncovered by us, and are said to be held in our Akashic records. It has become popular to go to these spiritual inter-dimensional annuls of simultaneous timeline records. Through intentional healing practises and personal meditation, we can consciously defuse them. You, my beloved ones, could also source someone who is able to access them through past life regression or ancestral healing. Perhaps begin by researching pioneers in these fields such as Dolores Cannon, who passed some years ago. She used a method of full hypnosis, just as the gifted Alba Weinman does.[115] The information clues our records contain, pertain to our soul patterns and imprints. Knowledge and understanding are the first steps.

Well, whichever method you choose to come by this information, I hope you have found it inspiring and uplifting to see that each of you dear souls has a critical role to play in the current stream of existence. You are like a wave in the great sea of mankind, joining together as one ocean. Also, know that you are loved beyond measure for your perfect part in each timeline. You personally chose to experience these scenarios for your learning, growth and co-creation with the Source of all that is. If only you could see and sense the myriads of guides and angels that champion you from the sidelines. They are only waiting for your prayer for help and

---

[115] https://albaweinman.com/en/

instructions from you, as to how they can be of assistance. Begin now your pilgrim's progress and choose your guides wisely, asking the right questions.

Eventually, once humans become lucid enough to see their connection to past life energies and loosen the cords that bind them to the perpetuating pain cycles acted out again and again, will they rise. This will be a collective healing for the earth. As they go through this gradually, all sentient beings on the planet will benefit. As the vibration of all creatures rises slowly, more and more creatures can join together in their intention for their thoughts to be purified, cleared and healed in a type of spiritual alchemy. Upliftment of the vibrations emitted in each lifetime and on each piece of land they have touched can lead us all to a greater illumination of the larger puzzle of which one's individual piece, is only a tiny part of the overall picture. Eventually, all the pieces of the jigsaw will be joined and then collectively healed and life can once again thrive in peace and harmony on Gaia.

Several times Rose experienced spontaneous timeline healings with her clients where they had seen the faces of their deceased ancestors appearing over her face during the healing and she imagined these lives like a series of dominos standing end on end. It only takes one well-placed tap on the first brick to knock them over one by one as the momentum of the falling dominos clacks its way to the final one. She called this healing process a type of quantum timeline healing but was also aware that she needed to check with the client in the present moment if they were in agreement. She needed their consensus with guiding them to break their patterns and therefore clear their future timelines too.

Once their intention is granted, the dominos would then fall forward metaphysically, releasing any future incidences around the aspect of suffering that had been handed down. Either as a past life or as a bloodline or ancestral clearing with future benefits for generations to come! There are of course many methods to the same end. Rose knew that singing helped her on this path and although she had not practised Reiki with Tom, painting was his soul's version of this healing practise and a way of mending his broken heart and soul. These were the pivotal points on her healing journey into the magic of the non-reality we call 5D (fifth dimensional existence), sharing a moment of realisation for the client and holding a space in unconditional love, through which the window into the mystery of the universe could open up. Applied knowledge becomes our healing power.[116]

In these precious seconds in time when we are in the flow and the veil is thin between the worlds, one can experience a glimpse of other dimensions normally shrouded from view in our 3D physical world. There are said to be many otherworldly states such as those the shamans experience in the under, middle and upper worlds to which they journey to when conducting healings. To experience a shamanic journey, contact Peter through his website.[117]

With that beautiful thought, Rose drew her writing to a close and determined to publish her strange findings for others to ponder upon. One day she would pick up her pen again, she was sure, but for now it felt that Divine Timing necessitated the release of this hard-won wisdom, to those who have ears to hear and eyes to see the relative meaning behind these words that we all co-created together, for all time and eternity.

Many blessings to you, dear ones
Know that you are loved beyond measure
for all that you already are

---

[116] FB page:@peacefulmindsandsouls111 and FB group @isisiallthingsauthor

[117] https://www.andrewwayfinder.com

INDEX

List of footnote references and internet links

12	'The Divine Feminine Oracle' about Marguerite Porete, by Meggan Watterson	https://www.megganwatterson.com/the-divine-feminine-oracle	1
13	Saint Jerome, 1st Century AD, on the asexuality of mystics	https://en.wikipedia.org/wiki/Jerome	2
14	Anchorites and their rites, 'Anchoritism, Liminality, and the Boundaries of Vocational Withdrawal' by Michelle M. Sauer	https://muse.jhu.edu/article/608444	2
15	'Margery visiting Julian of Norwich' - painting by Norwich artist, Frances Martin	www.francesmartin.co.uk Instagram: @frances.martin.norwich	2
16	Julian of Norwich 'Revelations of Divine Love' by Paula Marvelly, The Culturium	https://www.theculturium.com/julian-of-norwich-revelations-of-divine-love/	2
17	Charles Fernyhough, Episcopal Journal & Cafe about hearing voices, interpreted in more positive ways in the past	https://www.episcopalcafe.com/julian-of-norwich-and-margery-kempe-are-reunited-in-special-exhibition/	2
18	Hesychasm, mystical tradition of the Desert Fathers	https://en.wikipedia.org/wiki/Desert_Fathers	2
19	'Rising from the Ashes of Jehovah's Witnesses' by Isisi Allthings – social media sites	All my social media sites are on Linktree: https://linktr.ee/isisiallthings	3
20	'The Celestine Prophesy' by James Redfield	https://en.wikipedia.org/wiki/The_Celestine_Prophecy	3
21	The Number Witch, numerologist	https://vikkifosdal.wixsite.com/thenumberwitch	4
22	The Trickster archetype	https://en.wikipedia.org/wiki/Trickster	4
23	St. Julian Church, Norwich, Norfolk - Norfolk Churches blog site	http://www.norfolkchurches.co.uk/norwichjulian/norwichjulian.htm	4
24	The Way Finder, shamanic journeys and workshops	https://www.andrewwayfinder.com	4
25	The Shift Network, spiritual and shamanic workshops and information	https://theshiftnetwork.com	4
26	William de Hoo, Friar of the Sack, Norwich by British History Online (BHO)	http://www.british-history.ac.uk/vch/norf/vol2/pp428-433	4
27	Dominican Friary, Golden Dog Lane, Norwich	https://historicengland.org.uk/listing/the-list/list-entry/1220456	4
28	Anne Boleyn's appearance by Elizabethan Era	https://www.elizabethan-era.org.uk/anne-boleyn.htm	4
29	Mary Boleyn's education, Wikipedia	https://en.wikipedia.org/wiki/Mary_Boleyn	4
30	How Lady Eleanor Talbot turned the course of royal history	https://www.thehistorypress.co.uk/articles/eleanor-talbot-the-secret-queen/	5

31	The Rose Oracle-cards by Rebecca Campbell	https://rebeccacampbell.me/category/oracle-cards/	5
32	Discovery, exhumation and re-burial of Richard III	https://en.wikipedia.org/wiki/Exhumation_and_reburial_of_Richard_III_of_England	5
33	Boleyn property, 125-7 King Street, Norwich. The Tudor Travel Guide, YouTube channel	https://youtu.be/KYX8qR-9pYU?t=2	6
34	The Tudor Travel Guide, website	https://thetudortravelguide.com	6
35	The fall of Anne Boleyn 24.4.1536	https://www.thefallofanneboleyn.com/home/24th-april-1536-the-commissions-of-oyer-and-terminer/	6
36	Royal Museum of Greenwich (RMG), Greenwich Palace 2017 archeological discovery	https://www.rmg.co.uk/stories/topics/greenwich-palace-tudors	6
37	Big Picture Question, discuss soul blueprints	http://bigpicturequestions.com/what-is-a-soul-blueprint-or-imprint/	6
38	The Anne Boleyn Files about Henry Fitzroy's marriage to Mary Howard	https://www.theanneboleynfiles.com/henry-fitzroy-marries-mary-howard-2/	6
39	Wikipedia about Henry Fitzroy, Duke of Richmond	https://en.wikipedia.org/wiki/Henry_FitzRoy,_Duke_of_Richmond_and_Somerset	6
40	Wardship of Mary Boleyn's son Henry Carey after the death of her husband	https://englishhistory.net/tudor/citizens/mary-boleyn/	6
41	William Carey left gambling debts on his death	https://en.wikipedia.org/wiki/Mary_Boleyn	6
42	Anne Boleyn acts as her nephew's patron	https://en.wikipedia.org/wiki/Henry_Carey,_1st_Baron_Hunsdon	6
43	William Stafford dies in Switzerland	https://www.findagrave.com/memorial/73929565/william-stafford	6
44	Open Bible Info, explains Matthew 18:15-17 about the treatment of tax collectors	https://www.openbible.info/topics/tax_collectors	6
45	Open Minds Foundation cover ex-Jehovah's Witness appeal against shunning	https://www.openmindsfoundation.org/blog/jw-appeal-shunning-is-a-crime/	6
46	ABC News. When will coercive control become a crime?	https://www.abc.net.au/news/2021-12-03/how-queensland-criminalise-coercive-control-domestic-violence/100670944?fbclid=IwAR00E4v-b9tnk0JRY9VNLn40dvb4mmeM5ywV5rNTJEoc-uaYV8BlnxR8mJI	6
47	Open Minds Foundation article: 'Coercion at its worst: Religious mandated shunning'	https://www.openmindsfoundation.org/blog/coercion-at-its-worst-religious-mandated-shunning/?fbclid=IwAR1xfqZT9O52m2YFXHO6FuwVPhklIfDZzaNEp91ASmo7fsTcRBSuQoQ5dRo	6
48	Supreme Court of Russia pronounces Jehovah's Witnesses as extremists	https://en.wikipedia.org/wiki/Persecution_of_Jehovah%27s_Witnesses	6

49	Harlow's studies with monkeys around contact with the infants	https://www.psychologicalscience.org/publications/observer/obsonline/harlows-classic-studies-revealed-the-importance-of-maternal-contact.html	6
50	The Beast marked 666 in 'Revelations', the last book of the Bible	Https://en.wikipedia.org/wiki/The_Beast_ (Revelation	6
51	'Debutante' movie by ex JW Kamilia Dydyna, wins the Audience Award at CIFF and it was nominated for an IFTA	https://www.KamilaDydyna.com	6
52	Executive Producers Scott M. Homan, Chris Stuckmann and four others win award for 'Debutante'	https://ChicagoIrishFilmFestival.com	6
53	XJWDoc movie producer Scott M. Homan's award winning docu 'Witness Underground'	https://www.WitnessUnderground.com	6
54	Did Mary Boleyn have an affair with French King Francis 1? - The Anne Boleyn Files	https://www.theanneboleynfiles.com/mary-boleyn-was-she-really-the-mistress-of-francis-i/	6
55	Did Mary Boleyn feel her family might hope that Francois 1 would marry her?	http://under-these-restless-skies.blogspot.com/2013/09/mary-boleyn.html	6
56	English History discusses Mary being shunned by the Boleyn family.	https://englishhistory.net/tudor/citizens/mary-boleyn	6
57	The Tudor Trail on how Mary Boleyn met William Stafford	https://onthetudortrail.com/Blog/2021/03/14/part-1-the-trip-of-king-henry-viii-anne-boleyn-to-calais-by-olivia-longueville/	6
58	Richard Clements the courtier	https://en.wikipedia.org/wiki/Richard_Clement_ (courtier	6
59	Treaty of Perpetual Peace	https://en.wikipedia.org/wiki/Treaty_of_Perpetual_Peace	6
60	National Trust about Sir Richard Clement	https://www.nationaltrust.org.uk/ightham-mote/features/richard-clement---ightham-motes-royal-courtier	6
61	The significance of 32 in Numerology & cabalistic paths of wisdom, by Sarah Scoop	https://sarahscoop.com/the-meaning-and-symbolism-of-the-number-32-in-numerology/	6
62	A description of Anne Boleyn – Wikipedia	https://en.wikipedia.org/wiki/Anne_Boleyn	7
63	Elizabeth Boleyn's three children, Anne, Mary and George - Wikipedia	https://en.wikipedia.org/wiki/Elizabeth_Boleyn,_Countess_of_Wiltshire	7
64	Anne Boleyn's speech at her execution – English History	https://englishhistory.net/tudor/anne-boleyn-speech-at-her-execution/	7

83	Thomas Cranmer, Archbishop of Canterbury, Wikipedia	https://en.wikipedia.org/wiki/Thomas_Cranmer	9
84	Pope Clement VII, Wikipedia	https://en.wikipedia.org/wiki/Pope_Clement_VII	9
85	Thomas Cranmer hosts coronation festivities in Canterbury – The Anne Boleyn Files	https://www.theanneboleynfiles.com/28-may-1533-archbishop-cranmer-proclaims-that-the-kings-marriage-to-anne-boleyn-is-valid/	9
86	Canterbury Cathedral: Power, Pomp and One Amazing Tudor Party! - The Tudor Travel Guide	https://thetudortravelguide.com/2022/06/10/canterbury-cathedral-power-pomp-and-one-amazing-tudor-party/	9
87	Thomas Cranmer's consecration as Archbishop – The Tudor Chronicles	https://thetudorchronicles.wordpress.com/2015/03/30/on-this-day-in-1533-thomas-cranmer-was-consecrated-as-archbishop/	9
88	Edward VI's 'Devise for the Succession' – Wikipedia	https://en.wikipedia.org/wiki/Edward_VI	9
89	Thomas Cranmer's marriage – Britannica.com	https://www.britannica.com/biography/Thomas-Cranmer-archbishop-of-Canterbury	9
90	The Dolphin Inn, Essex – Capturing Cambridge	https://capturingcambridge.org/centre/sidney-street/the-dolphin-inn/	9
91	Thomas Grey – Wikipedia	https://en.wikipedia.org/wiki/Thomas_Grey,_1st_Marquess_of_Dorset	9
92	Thomas Cranmer - Wikipedia	https://en.wikipedia.org/wiki/Thomas_Cranmer	9
93	Birth of Henry VI - The Anne Boleyn Files	https://www.theanneboleynfiles.com/28-january-1457-birth-henry-vii/	10
94	Meaning of number 28 – Sacred Scribes Angel Numbers	http://sacredscribesangelnumbers.blogspot.com/2011/06/angel-number-28.html	10
95	Lady Jane Grey, Wikipedia	https://en.wikipedia.org/wiki/Lady_Jane_Grey	10
96	Rose and Julia's FaceBook business page, @PeacefulMindsandSouls111	https://www.facebook.com/PeacefulMindsandSouls111	10
97	The Great Harlot, 666 and The Wild Beast of Revelation – Bible Gateway	https://www.biblegateway.com/passage/?search=Revelation%2017&version=MEV	11
98	Knole House - The National Trust	https://www.nationaltrust.org.uk/features/tudor-links-in-london-and-the-south-east	11
99	Otford Palace - The Tudor Travel Guide	https://thetudortravelguide.com/2021/08/14/otford-palace/	11
100	Tudor residences in Kent - The National Trust	https://www.nationaltrust.org.uk/features/tudor-links-in-london-and-the-south-east	11
101	Edward VI's disinheritance, Mary I – Wikipedia	https://en.wikipedia.org/wiki/Mary_I_of_England	11
102	Mary I's character – Wikipedia	https://en.wikipedia.org/wiki/Mary_I_of_England	11
103	The Kett Society	http://www.kettsociety.org.uk/	12

Printed in the United States
by Baker & Taylor Publisher Services